The Clean Daughter

The Clean

A CROSS-CONTINENTAL MEMOIR

Daughter

by JILL KANDEL

Jill Kandel

NDSU | NORTH DAKOTA STATE UNIVERSITY PRESS

Fargo, North Dakota

NDSU NORTH DAKOTA STATE
UNIVERSITY PRESS

Dept. 2360, P.O. Box 6050, Fargo, ND 58108-6050
www.ndsupress.org

The Clean Daughter: A Cross-Continental Memoir
By Jill Kandel

Copyright © 2022 Text by Jill Kandel
First Edition

Library of Congress Control Number: 2022932479
ISBN: 978-1-946163-30-1

Cover design by Jamie Trosen
Interior design by Deb Tanner

The publication of *The Clean Daughter: A Cross-Continental Memoir* is made possible by the generous support of the Muriel and Joseph Richardson Fund and donors to the NDSU Press Fund, the NDSU Press Endowed Fund, and other contributors to NDSU Press.

Events described in this memoir are based upon the memories of the author and formed over decades, continents, and multiple languages. Memories vary person to person, but all these stories are, to the best of the author's memory and knowledge, true.

David Bertolini, Director
Suzzanne Kelley, Publisher
Sarah W. Beck, Executive Administrative Assistant
Kyle Vanderburg, Acquisitions Assistant
Megan G. Brown, Editorial Intern
Oliver M. Sime, Graduate Assistant in Publishing
Kiri Scott and Kyle Vanderburg, Editorial Book Team

Printed in the United States of America

Publisher's Cataloging-In-Publication Data
(Prepared by The Donohue Group, Inc.)

Names: Kandel, Jill, author.
Title: The clean daughter : a cross-continental memoir / Jill Kandel.
Description: First edition. | Fargo, North Dakota : North Dakota State
    University Press, [2022]
Identifiers: ISBN 9781946163301
Subjects: LCSH: Kandel, Jill--Family. | Women--North Dakota--Biography. |
    Fathers-in-law--Death--Psychological aspects. | Euthanasia--
    Psychological aspects. | Americans--Foreign countries. | Netherlands--
    History--German occupation, 1940-1945. | LCGFT: Autobiographies. |
    BISAC: BIOGRAPHY & AUTOBIOGRAPHY / Personal Memoirs. | BIOGRAPHY &
    AUTOBIOGRAPHY / Women. | BIOGRAPHY & AUTOBIOGRAPHY / Cultural, Ethnic &
    Regional / General.
Classification: LCC F641.K36 A3 2022 | DDC 978.4034092--dc23

To Andrea.

My sister. My friend.

CONTENTS

Prologue: Intermarried 1

1. The Netherlands, 1980–1981 7

2. Zambia, 1982–1986 47

3. England, 1987–1988 77

4. Indonesia, 1989–1992 95

5. USA, 1993–2007 123

6. Moorhead, 2007–2011 157

7. Unspoken, 2012 183

8. My Story, 2015–2016 243

9. What Remains, 2017– 295

Epilogue: Hand in Hand 337

Acknowledgments
Discussion Questions for The Clean Daughter:
      A Cross-Continental Memoir
About the Author
About the Press

Have patience with everything that remains unsolved in your heart. Try to love the questions themselves, like locked rooms and like books written in a foreign language. . . . At present you need to live the question. Perhaps you will gradually, without even noticing it, find yourself experiencing the answer, some distant day.

—Rainer Maria Rilke, *Letters to a Young Poet*

Prologue: Intermarried

When I fall in love with and marry a man from the Netherlands—my blue-eyed boy—I get a new name and a new family. A Dutch family. I also become, for the first time in my life, a daughter-in-law—or as the Dutch say, *schoondochter*, a compound word that if taken apart and parsed literally would become *clean daughter*.

I marry in the Netherlands, in a ceremony presided over by my newly-acquired father-in-law, Izaak, wearing his long black pastoral robe. Father-in-law in Dutch, s*choonvader*, *clean father*. Mother-in-law, *schoonmoeder*, *clean mother*. We're all very clean and fresh and new to this joining, this cross-continental family we're creating.

This joining will permeate my existence for years to come as Johan and I work with subsistence farmers in remote areas around the globe, as my North Dakota prairie life—solid beneath my feet for as long as I can remember—shifts and tilts.

In the early 1980s, when Johan and I marry, the number of intermarried newlyweds—those with partners of differing ethnicity or race—makes up 5 percent of all marriages in the United States. But I'm not living in a progressive coastal city. My hometown—set in the middle of the United States and a few hours' drive away from the Canadian border—has a population of less than eight thousand. I don't have a single friend married to a person from another country.

Every marriage has its own challenges. A cross-cultural marriage even more so, but a cross-cultural marriage that seeks to live and work in a third culture might verge on being foolhardy.

Johan and I look homogenous. Light-colored skin, light blue and gray eyes, tall-ish, slender. You'd never guess from looking at us—walking hand in hand down any street—that we grew up in countries four thousand miles apart, separated by the stormy Atlantic. Our appearance a camouflage that hides our vast cultural differences. We grew up with different languages, music, literature, and traditions. We relished different foods, celebrated distinct holidays, followed divergent customs, and respected different laws and rules. Our reference points barely even coincided, although, we both grew up attending church—Lutheran and Dutch Reformed—and had our faith in common and our ideals. He wanted to feed the world; I wanted to help him accomplish his ambition.

If you'd have told me as a fifteen-year-old, riding my Appaloosa across the hills of North Dakota, that someday I'd honeymoon on the North Sea of the Netherlands, I'd have thought you were being ridiculous. If you'd said my mother-in-law and father-in-law would speak a different language than I did, I'd have thought you were joking. If you'd told me euthanasia laws enacted in another country would affect me personally, I would've laughed, incredulous.

I'm not laughing anymore.

Looking back, I can't believe how naïve I was. I didn't even think to ask relevant questions about marriage, let alone about the vast differences in our lifestyles and our pasts.

Where will we settle?

How often will I get to see my family and friends?

If we have children, what passport will they carry? What citizenship?

What language should we speak in our home?

If we mix our languages—his and mine and the various countries we reside in—how will I handle the endless misinterpretations, miscommunications, the never-ending struggle to speak a word when I can't find a word, the frustrations inherent in having different mother tongues?

When I speak Dutch, I'll always sound like an American. When Johan speaks English, his accent will forever give him away. His tone, the very cadence of his words marking him as other than a native English speaker.

One day, Johan says to me, "You're so small-hearted, Jill."

I'm offended. Then, he's offended that I'm offended.

We step back. We swallow. We each take a breath and ask for clarification.

Small-hearted is the Dutch way of saying big-hearted: your heart's so small that even the tiniest of things will move it. He's giving me a compliment and it takes a minor blowup before I can hear it. By the time I do, the compliment's been lost.

Word after word. Day after day. Year after year. Even after I think I've learned it all, we're still wading through a no-man's-land of linguistic perils.

It's not just my husband, there's my in-laws, too.

Continental divides exist between us—how smug those Europeans can come across, how childish those Americans. How can I build a relationship with them when there are so many barriers? And what about the war that shaped their childhoods? The Nazi-occupied Netherlands imprinted into my father-in-law's personality. I'm barely even conversant about WWII. I've got no idea the minefield I'm stepping into, the fear, the control, how sour a relationship can grow, how Izaak's decision to die will affect my entire family for decades.

Over thirty years ago, I said three words.

"Yes, I do."

A fairytale in the making.

A soft-spoken trinity that changed everything.

I stated these three words with simple open clarity, twenty-six years old and kneeling in a thin white dress on the ancient floor of an old Dutch church, my father-in-law's hand heavy upon my head.

Part 1: THE NETHERLANDS, 1980–1981

Jill and Johan Kandel on their wedding day, standing in front of a windmill in Hardenberg, the Netherlands. November 1981.

Izaak Kandel, preaching as a new pastor. The Netherlands.

Johan, 1980

I can't stop looking at his eyes, the perfect likeness of a prairie sky. A mix of azure and cornflower and steel. When I look into them, I see the distant horizons I have gazed upon my entire life. I've never seen such eyes. I am lost in them. I am at home.

When we meet, I'm twenty-five years old—a North Dakota prairie girl grown hungry for the sea—and primed for adventure. Johan's an international graduate student. His charming accent draws me in with its soft throaty *g*. His *th* comes out sounding like *d*. *The* becomes *de*, *wheat* becomes *weed*. People constantly ask where he's from.

"The Netherlands," he says patiently. Again, and again.

"Oh. You're from Holland," the frequent response.

"No, actually, I'm from the Netherlands," Johan says. "Holland is like saying Dakota. It's not a country. There's a North Holland and a South Holland—kind of like a North Dakota and a South Dakota—that are provinces. Like states more or less. So really. *Ja.* I'm from the Netherlands."

Sometimes when Johan says he's from the Netherlands, people say, "Oh! You're from Amsterdam!" This response elicits a smug European shrug.

"No," he says with an unwavering stare. "Amsterdam's a city. I have not lived in Amsterdam."

Johan and I spend more and more time together. I'm attracted to his kindness. There's something good about him. He's solid and stable, but also exotic. Someone I don't quite understand. I'm intrigued by him.

The Netherlands becomes my new pet project. I pat her on the head. I pretend to know her. Or perhaps, it's not pretense, but desire. I need to understand this country that Johan hails from, but I've never set foot upon her shore. I don't speak her language. I don't know her food. I don't begin to understand her cultural eccentricities. Her politics are a mystery. Of her seventeen million citizens, I've met only one, and I don't even know his middle name.

Son of a Clean Land, 1981

Johan graduates in May and returns home. I spend the summer nursing in northern Zambia, then fly to the Netherlands to be with Johan once more. How close we stand to each other. How we smile and cannot look away. How warm our hands, held tightly together as we walk out of the airport into the gray and damp fall weather.

Johan's parents, Jopie and Izaak, live on a street of brick row houses in the town of Hardenberg. It's an amazement to me. The terra-cotta tile roofs peak and rise down the long street, the houses identical in color, size, and shape. The front gardens are teeny and pruned to perfection. Each flower, each tree placed intentionally. There's hardly any grass.

Brick row houses don't exist in North Dakota. Houses in my hometown are large and square. Front yards, spacious, mowed and green. Houses in Valley City come in an inordinate variety of sizes, shapes, colors, and sidings. The house I grew up in had a flat roof, covered in rolled black tar paper.

During the next weeks—while I act more buoyant than rational, more moon-eyed than realistic—I fall in love with the land of Johan's birth. We go for endless walks. Each one a miracle. Each one full and new and filled with conversation.

White lace curtains hang in many of the oversized picture windows. White feather comforters drape out of top windows, airing in the breeze. The windows shine, even in the overcast weather.

"It must be 'hang out your laundry day!'" I say to Johan as we walk around the block.

"A lot of people throw their duvets out each morning," he replies. "Freshens them up."

In my entire life, I've never thrown a blanket over my windowsill to freshen it up.

"My mother was very particular," Izaak says that evening. "On wash day, she hung all of her wash out, from light to dark."

"What do you mean?" I ask.

"Each woman in the village washed and hung her white clothes out first, then the lighter color clothing comes, and last all of the dark clothings," he says. "The old women, they walk around the town to look and see if it was done correct. Ja. A woman who hung her laundry and it was not in the right order, she was not a good wife."

"You're kidding," I say.

"*Nee*. Cleanliness and order were very important to my mother. She got down on her hands and knees, every morning, and scrubbed the stoop of her door and after this, she washed the windows. When she took the laundry off from the line, she folded the sheets correct. The end used by the feet must never accidentally be turned and used for the head! Ja. Women back then they understood household duty; it was as a moral responsibility."

So, there it is. I know that if Johan and I marry, I'll flunk at being the good wife.

"Beside these daily and weekly cleanings," Izaak continues, as if those jobs are not enough, "there was always the *Grote Schoonmaak*: the big cleaning. Before Easter, the whole house had to be cleaned. It took weeks. Sometimes we slept on only the mattress on the floor because the bed stand was being put outside to be polished. Every closet emptied. All furniture out. Before it was done, the walls might get new paint, or at least the ceiling would be redone to a brilliant white. Women would not dare *not* to clean."

As I listen to Izaak, I think of my great-grandmother Dorthea, who hung her wash up on the North Dakota prairie. Miles from the nearest neighbor. The only ones who saw that swaying laundry would have been her boys, her drunkard-of-a-husband, and whatever livestock survived the previous winter blizzards. I'm pretty sure she was just grateful if the blue jeans and bib overalls didn't blow away.

I meet more of Johan's family. His sister, Andrea. His brother, Bert. I don't know what Izaak and Jopie think of me. I don't really pay attention. I'm happy, happy, happy. I love the sound of the Dutch language floating by my ears like a symphony I can't quite grasp. I love the old-fashioned white lace curtains, the gleaming picture windows, the uneven cobbled streets. And I love Johan, son of this clean and orderly land.

Engaging, 1981

A few weeks later, Johan and I take a day trip to Rotterdam, heading to Delfshaven, one of the few old parts of the city that remained standing after WWII. We walk through the harbor of the Maritime Museum and nibble fresh *stroofwafels* from a market.

Late in the afternoon, we stop for a rest, sitting on some cement steps. Johan turns to me and looks me directly in the eye. "Let's get married!" he says. "Right here in the Netherlands." Then he gets down on one knee and says, "Marry me?"

I'm surprised by the abruptness, but not the question. I've been waiting for and dreaming about these words. Waiting to answer. Yes. Yes. Yes.

"Yes."

We walk down the street hand in hand, stop at a jeweler, and pick out rings. We choose simple and plain: glossy gold bands, not too wide, not too narrow. The jeweler needs to size them.

A week later we go back to pick them up. We've set the date for our wedding and ask to have it engraved on the inside of the rings.

"11-06-81," I say to the jeweler.

"No, Jill. You mean 06-11-81," Johan says. "It's six November."

"But that's backwards," I say.

We stare at each other, even the days on our Dutch versus American calendars are spoken and written differently.

The Dutch say the day, then the month, then the year.

In Johan's thinking, 11-06-81 is the 11th of June.

Americans say the month, then day, then year.

In my mind, 11-06-81 is November 6.

In the end we compromise. His ring says *Jill. Nov. 6. 81.* Mine says *Johan. Nov. 6. 81.*

On the train traveling back to Johan's house, I see wedding rings everywhere. I can't stop looking at the hands of the women who sit beside me or walk by.

Confused by what I notice, I ask Johan, "Are there a lot of Dutch widows?"

"What do you mean?" he asks.

"Well, a lot of Dutch women wear their wedding ring on their right hand," I say. "In America, women often switch their ring to their right hand when they're widowed."

"That's funny," Johan says. "In the Netherlands, wearing a ring on her right hand means a woman is Protestant."

"Protestant?" I ask.

"Sure. Protestant women tend to wear their wedding ring on their right hand. Catholic women tend to wear it on their left. You see it especially with older women."

Living in the Netherlands, if I wear my wedding band on my left hand—which is what I've seen all my life—I'll be thought of as Catholic. If I choose my right hand, I'll be seen as a Protestant and feel like a widow.

On my wedding day, whichever hand I choose will give the wrong information. Maybe I should buy two rings, one for each hand. Then I'd be a Protestant, Catholic, Widow. For heaven's sake, what am I getting into? Where do I want to keep my own culture and traditions, and where do I want to embrace Johan's?

We arrive back at Johan's parents' home. I'm staying in a guest-room on their second floor. I'll stay until our wedding.

Later, Johan tells his brother, "I asked Jill to marry me while we were sitting under the Euromast."

"Euromast?" I ask, not sure what he's referring to.

"The Euromast," he says, as if I should know.

I look at him blankly.

"Sometimes it's called the Eiffel Tower of the Netherlands."

"I've never heard of it," I reply, feeling stupid and uninformed about my own engagement. There were so many things we both assumed.

The Clean Daughter, 1981

When I marry, I'll change my name from Jill Jensen to Jill Kandel. I'll gain a father-in-law, a mother-in-law, a sister-in-law, and a brother-in-law. We'll be family. We'll be new people, with new relationships.

I'm new to the Dutch language and ask if Kandel is a common surname.

"Not at all," Johan replies. "My mother's maiden name, ten Hoope, is fairly common. Lots of last names begin with ten, van, or van der. Those words just mean something like *from* or *from the*. They aren't capitalized. If you wanted to look my mom's maiden name up, you'd look under H for Hoope and not t for ten."

"Really?" I ask a bit incredulous.

"Yes," Johan says. "Take the name Vanderberg. In America it's all one word with a capitalized V. In the Netherlands, it's three words and only the last word is capitalized, van der Berg, meaning from the mountain."

I'm trying to learn a few Dutch words. *Schoon* is the Dutch word for clean. *Vader* is the Dutch word for father. With my limited knowledge of Dutch, I take the word *schoonvader* and transpose it in my mind to *clean father*. I find it slightly disconcerting. As if my own father were somehow not clean. To distinguish between these two men, will my father now be the *dirty father*, in the old-fashioned sense of *dirty*, as involved in my conception? If so, then Izaak is the clean father. A father, albeit, without the intimacy of procreation. Or perhaps it is *clean* as in *new*. He's the new father, the starting-over father, the one who offers us both a new beginning.

I continue this same line of thought, transposing daughter-in-law, *schoondochter*, to clean daughter. I think it's funny in and of itself. I'm not exactly known to be fastidious.

Years later, when I'm studying the Dutch language, I read that the word *schoon* not only means clean, it also means beautiful. Dutch is the only language in the world where *clean* and *beautiful* are the exact same word. It makes perfect sense that those overly cleanly and artistic Dutch would make this linguistic connection. Perhaps, I'm not the clean daughter, but the beautiful daughter.

And then, even later still, after decades of marriage, I say something offhandedly to Johan about being a clean daughter.

"What are you talking about?" he asks me.

"Clean daughter," I say. "Daughter-in-law. You know. Schoondochter."

Johan gets the strangest look on his face. He's trying to understand. Then slowly it dawns on him.

"That's really funny, Jill!" he replies.

"Funny?"

"No Dutch person would put it together like that. We'd never think of it. It's just daughter-in-law."

I'm incredulous, but his sister has the same reaction when I talk with her. She laughs and says, "That's kind of cute."

I've thought of myself as a clean daughter for over twenty years and am being told the image is of my own making, a figment of my imagination. I think about this for weeks, baffled at first, and then a strange thing happens. A friend gets new cupboards.

"Cool," I say, and ask what color and what kind of wood. I don't think of the words separately. I don't think of cup. I don't think of board. I only think of a cupboard, an entity in and of itself. Compound words are common in the English language. Honeymoon. Sweetheart. Thunderstorm. Lifetime. Bedroom.

As I think about them, I begin to understand, in a new way, that I'm not a clean daughter. I never was. Nor am I a beautiful daughter. And yet, I built a part of my identity upon these figments. What else in this, my cross-cultural and international life and marriage, have I built upon misconception when even the common words I use are so fraught with misunderstanding?

Blits Photography, 1928

In comparison to American homes, Dutch homes shine in a sparse, minimalistic manner. Izaak's home has a few pieces of Jopie's handwork and a cross-stitch picture in monotones hanging on the walls. There's one old photo on a cabinet that intrigues me, a black-and-white picture of Izaak's family.

In the family photo a young Izaak—seven years old—wears a sailor-style shirt, shorts, and long socks. He's a grade-school boy.

"My big sister, Jo, is sitting beside me," Izaak says. "You can't see it in the photo, but she had polio as a youngster, and her right arm and hand were quite lame. Her right arm was about half the size of the other one, but despite her deformity, she trained to be a seamstress. She used her left hand and wore long sleeves. Ja. She never let it hinder what she could or couldn't do!"

Big brother Piet, Mother, and Father all sit in the photo with their hands folded on their laps. They stare straight ahead. "Piet became a metalworker," Izaak adds, "and when he got older, he painted houses."

I bend closer to look at the photo and see a picture on the mantel of a young sailor in full uniform. A picture within a picture.

Izaak sees me looking. "That's a picture of Wes," he says. "My oldest brother."

Wes, a dashing sailor, stares straight back at me, eyes twinkling. He's the happiest-looking one of the bunch. Wes, when he first enlisted. Wes, who would re-enlist and become a newlywed before finally shipping off to war.

"We look so serious in that photo," Izaak comments. "It was taken with what we call *blits licht* and produced a sharp magnesium flare. We were all afraid of the light flash."

As he tells me this, I think he says *blitz* not *blits* and my mind wanders to the blitz and to blitzkrieg and to WWII in the Netherlands. I look at this family. 1930. In ten years, their world will fall apart.

Starting to Rain, 1981

A few days later, two of my fun-loving friends from Bismarck and our Mary College school days come through the Netherlands. They're backpacking their way across Europe. Johan invites them over to Izaak and Jopie's home.

I see them coming from a block away. Bryce throws open his arms. "Hey, Jill!"

"It's fantastic to see you!" I say giving him a big bear hug.

Johan shakes Bryce's hand, claps him on the back, and says hi to Terry, his traveling buddy. They throw their weathered backpacks, sleeping bags, and gear down in the hallway, and I offer to make tea.

Izaak's in the study, and I call out to him. "Bryce and Terry are here."

Izaak comes in, greets the boys.

"I'll go make some tea," I say. "Would you like some, Izaak?"

"Nee," he answers. "*Het* is not yet 4:00."

I'm slightly confused. I haven't asked for the time.

"Pa takes his tea at 4:00, Jill," Johan informs me. "At teatime."

"I didn't know tea had a time," I say grinning.

Johan doesn't grin in return. In fact, he looks a little grim, and I'm reminded of how much he and his father look alike.

"Should we wait?" I ask Johan, after Izaak leaves.

"Yes, that will be best. It's his house, after all," Johan replies.

We wait and chat and catch up with each other. At 4:00, Jopie makes black tea for us. She serves the tea in china cups with one cookie placed neatly on each saucer.

The brisk October day fills with raucous laughter, shared stories, and college memories. Izaak invites Bryce and Terry for supper, and I help him set out the dishes while Jopie cooks. She serves a simple Dutch meal: a piece of chicken, a potato, some peas.

Izaak sits at the head of the table and Jopie serves the food. He doesn't dig in. He waits for Jopie to come and seat herself, then lifts his chin, looks up to the sky, sighs loudly, looks down at his plate, and folds his hands. He waits till silence covers the table.

"*Hemelse Vader,*" he begins. Heavenly Father.

After the prayer, he looks up and surveys the table, nods his head, unfolds his hands. Jopie rises to get something from the kitchen. He waits for her return, then they look at each other and say together, "Eet smakelijk."

Jopie picks up her fork and knife. It's not until she takes her first bite that Izaak begins to eat. It's polite, in traditional Dutch homes, to wait for the woman serving the meal to begin eating before you start. It's a sign of respect. It all feels rather affectatious to me, but I smile, wait for Jopie, then mimic her with an *eet smakelijk* and dig in.

Bryce and Terry raise their eyebrows at me.

"Eet smakelijk is the Dutch version of bon appétit," I say smiling.

It's a relief to speak English, to tell jokes, to slap someone's arm and hoot over a shared memory. Being boisterous, being American, in this rather austere Dutch home rejuvenates me.

After supper Izaak excuses himself and goes back to his study.

Bryce says, "I was wondering if we can stay here overnight. We've got our bags and can just throw them anywhere. We're not fussy. Tomorrow we're off to Copenhagen."

"Sure," I blurt out. "That would be great!"

Johan's face tightens. "Let me ask my father," he says, throwing me a look I don't understand as he leaves the room. *Why's he being so grumpy?*

He comes back saying, "My father says it will not work for you to stay here." He tells us this information matter-of-factly, leaving no room for conversation.

"What?" I stammer. I pull Johan into the adjoining room. "What do you mean? That's just stupid. All they need is some space on a floor."

"Pa said that he cannot provide the right amount of comfort. He does not have beds. He will not have anyone sleeping on his floor."

"They have to stay somewhere," I whisper. "It's starting to rain. What do you want them to do?"

"There is a youth hostel near here. I will call and reserve a place for them."

I hope this is a joke. A *ha, ha, aren't I funny. Of course, they can stay* kind of joke. But Johan's not smiling.

"A hostel?" I ask. "Are you kidding me? You've got to ask your dad again. Tell him they're happy to sleep on the floor."

Johan goes back and speaks with Izaak again, but he doesn't change his mind.

I'm appalled and ashamed, hurt that Johan isn't sticking up for his friends. I'm also confused and don't understand Izaak and his declaration. *What's the matter with that man?*

I wonder if this is a Dutch thing. *Don't Dutch people like company?*

Or is it something specific to the Kandel family. Maybe it's just something *Izaak.*

I really can't tell.

I look at the floor, cheeks red, as Johan tells Bryce they can't stay.

"I'm so sorry, Bryce," I say, tears in my eyes.

"Not a problem," Bryce says in that nonchalant, midwestern way that I'd grown up with. That way of North Dakota Nice I'd been so thoroughly steeped in, I assumed it was universal.

I watch my friends pack up their bags, throw them over their shoulders, and walk to the door. They have an address and their bunks are booked. I feel like an emotional wreck. Frustrated, angry, and sad.

Izaak steps out of his study and wishes the boys well. He thanks them for the visit. As he comes back inside, I hug Bryce and Terry goodbye. I watch as they walk out into the rain and meld into the dark night.

Izaak closes the door behind them, then comes up to us smiling broadly.

I look at him quizzically. Look at him as if for the first time.
Curly wild hair covers the back of his balding head, giving him
the appearance of an aging Bozo the Clown. He's shorter than
Johan and has a paunch belly.

His cleft chin juts out at me, and he gives an uncomfortable
forced laugh all the while doing an odd jig-like dance step. It's so
strangely out of place. Not a goose-step, not a waltz, but a pecu-
liar mixture of both moves. He parades past me, a stiffly dancing
man with a grin upon his face.

"Come," he says. "It is 8:00. It is the coffee time."

Problems, 1981

I lie in the dark of my tiny room thinking about the day. The
language, the customs, the rationale. Living in another culture is
often the greatest thing on earth. But, sometimes, it's the worst.
I'm often perplexed. I don't know if any particular behavior is
really Dutch, or if it's just Kandel. I can't separate the two, and it's
frustratingly confusing.

Johan listens to his father with attention. With deference. He
tells me, "It's my father's home, not mine."

We speak about our upcoming wedding plans, and he tells
me to remember that his father is a pastor and the church we will
marry in is his father's church.

Yesterday, Johan asked to borrow Izaak's car.

"Nee," he replied curtly. "Nee. *Je mag niet.*" It is not your car.

I was dumbfounded. My parents offered me things before I
even asked.

"Jill, you're off to Fargo today? Do you need anything? If you'd
prefer, feel free to borrow one of our cars." We shared our lives.
Our needs. Our wants. We just shared stuff. I took it for granted.

As the days pass, Izaak's behavior and words begin to annoy
me. He tells me to shower faster. *Hot water's expensive.*

I'd love to, but it takes me five minutes just to figure out how to get the water hot. Is there some trick I don't know about? Or maybe he showers in cold water?

Don't use the fan unless you need it. Electricity is expensive.

Don't run the water while you're doing dishes. Such wastefulness.

I try to pay attention, to see how Jopie washes dishes. She doesn't rinse them, just sets them soapy into the dish rack.

"Why don't you rinse the dishes, Jopie?" I ask. She smiles kindly and begins to speak, but Izaak jumps in to answer. "The soap will drip off," he says. "There is no need to rinse."

I stop rinsing the dishes.

One day he chastises me for walking on the grass.

"*Yill*, can't you see the sign?" he exclaims.

I want to yell back at him, to defend myself.

I can't read the sign! Don't you realize how everything is new? Do you have any idea?

There are a million things that I do wrong, and I'm frustrated by all of them. I can't even iron my own shirt! I burn a brown hole in my favorite white one, not realizing how scorching hot the iron's set. I feel so stupid.

I journal, writing about the things I don't understand in the Netherlands, about Johan's family. Johan must get his gentle kindness from his mom. Izaak's a mystery, sometimes seeming sympathetic, other times a tyrant. I feel like Izaak wants me to admire him or look up to him or something. But he makes me feel like I'm one of his parishioners. There's something pompous and unyielding in his attitude. I can't put my finger on it, but I don't quite trust Izaak. Like his life's a line drawn in the sand; he's not used to people crossing him.

Usually, I'm pretty good at reading people, but he doesn't want me to read him. He offers me nothing of himself. I feel the distance. I don't want to be the foolish American, the rude daughter-in-law. I don't want to start off on the wrong foot. I keep quiet and hold my peace.

Sometimes, I rant at him, but just in my thoughts.

It's just a car. He's your son!

It's my wedding, not yours.

What is your problem? I could have gotten married in America. I came here because your son wanted this. Because your son wanted you!

Sometimes I wonder who the bigger problem is, Izaak or me. We're both doing a pretty good job of filling that bill.

Eye on the Bull, 1965

When I was little, the big event in Valley City was held in the dreary, cold, transitional month of March, in that season which couldn't make up its mind if it were winter or spring. Ice, sleet, mud, or rain, the Winter Show opened its doors. We attended no matter if the weather dipped to five below zero or if it topped forty degrees and felt balmy on our winterized skin. Held under a domed tin roof, the Winter Show ran for ten days and hosted a variety of shows: 4-H events, crop and animal competitions, tractor pulls. The highlight event was the PRCA: the Professional Rodeo Cowboys Association's rodeo.

Normally, clowns scared me. I didn't trust or like them. Such creepy smiles. But it was different at the rodeo. Here, clowns weren't just hungry for applause; they had a job to do. And even though they wore suspenders, too-big pants, and hats that spouted daisies, we all took them seriously. When a rider fell off a bull, the clowns skipped in to divert and challenge. Every cowboy knew the clowns were his best protection if he got thrown from a bull.

I remember one clown in black-and-white-checkered pants who got down on his hands and knees in front of an angry bull. The clown pawed the ground, dramatically throwing dirt up into the air behind him. On his knees, dirt flying, he faced that bull. The bull put his thick head down, and I was afraid he would charge. But instead, he began to paw the ground, too.

The clown and the bull locked onto each other's eyes for a moment, as I held my breath remembering the year before when my daddy was called into the ER to care for a clown who'd been gored. I needn't have worried. The clown stopped pawing dirt, threw back his head, and laughed. The bull startled and backed up slowly. Another clown ran past, and the bull turned and snorted at him. And the clown down on his knees rose, picked a daisy out of his hat, and dropped it down the baggy seat of his checkered pants while he sauntered away.

But even as he walked away, that clown never took his eye off the bull.

Opa Schuller, 1935

Izaak owns the largest Bible I've ever seen. It's black and looks like it's a hundred years old. It must weigh several pounds.

Izaak sees me looking at it and says, "That was my Opa Schuller's Bible." He hands it to me and I open it to the inside cover page.

> *Bijbel, Dat is de Gansche Heilige Schrift, bevattende Alle De Kanonieke Boeken des Ouden en Nieuwen Testaments. Op last van de hoog-mogende heren staten-general der Vereenigde Nederlanden en volgens het besluit van de Nationale Synode gehouden te Dordrecht in de Jaren MDCXVIII en MDCXIX.*

I can't read a word of what it says, my lack of Dutch painfully obvious. "Could you translate it for me?" I ask Johan. And he does.

> Bible: The Entire Bible containing all the Canonical Books of the Old and New Testament. By order of the Mighty Men of the States-General of the United Netherlands, and according to the decision of the National Synod held at Dordrecht in the years 1618 and 1619.

"Opa Schuller moved in with our family in 1935," Izaak continues. "His full name was Pieter Leendert Schuller. He was my mother's father."

Opa Schuller was the last of Izaak's grandparents to die—his other three grandparents already dead. I listen to him recite the names, loving the sounds of them: Gijsbertha Poldervaart, Wessel Kandel, and Johanna Jacoba Duebel-Schuller.

"We shared a bedroom," Izaak says. "He was eighty-four years old, and he never went to bed before kneeling down and praying for a long, long time. My father was anti-church, and even though my mother would have loved to attend church, Father did not allow her to attend. It was out of the question. So, this prayer time was something new to me.

"Before each meal, Opa bowed his head and prayed. Father allowed this silent moment out of respect for the aging man, not out of any shared convictions."

Izaak puts the Bible up on the shelf and continues speaking about Opa Schuller.

"His eyes were not very good, and he could barely read by himself, so after the meal, Mother would sit beside Opa Schuller and read a chapter from the Bible out loud to him.

"There was something peaceful and friendly about Opa Schuller," Izaak said. "Something I could feel even as a child. He only lived with us one year. He died from complications of a fall and pneumonia, but that one year was exceptional. Opa Schuller was one of the great influences of my life."

I wonder if Johan and I will ever have children. If we do, how will Izaak and Jopie influence their lives? I wonder about family, lineage, and ancestors I've never met. Strange to me, how intertwined the dance of life.

Vacation Days, 1981

The shape of the Netherlands resembles a right hand. The thumb is a peninsula of land that juts into the North Sea. Three weeks before our wedding, Johan and I take a bus part way up the inside of the thumb to Volendam. We pass by mile after mile of winding dikes. Johan says there are over 1,400 miles of dikes throughout the Netherlands. The ingenious Dutch haven't just stopped the watery invasion of the North Sea, they've audaciously taken land from the seabed.

"Polders—properties pumped dry and reclaimed from the sea—make up nearly twenty percent of the land mass of the Netherlands," Johan says. "Look over there, see! That used to be underwater."

In a country that charts approximately 160 miles by 200 miles, polders are a vastly ingenious and highly prized addition to the landmass of the Netherlands. The Dutch Delta Works and Zuiderzee Works have been declared one of the Seven Wonders of the Modern World. All this in a pint-sized country. All this. And today I'm seeing some of it.

"There's a common Dutch phrase," Johan says as we walk along the inland lake, "*God schiep de aarde, de Hollanders schiepen the Netherlands. It means, 'God made the earth; the Dutch made the Netherlands.'"

I try to repeat the Dutch words, which is a joke. The Dutch *ie* is way beyond my tongue's ability to reproduce. Johan laughs at my pronunciations, but he also encourages me.

"Schiep," he repeats patiently. "It means *made*. It's the same word that's used in the first part of Genesis: *In den beginne, schiep God den hemel en de aarde.* In the beginning, made God the heavens and the earth."

"That's a little much," I say. And go back to practicing schiep. Made.

Johan smiles and squeezes my hand.

"And what will you call me after we're married?" I ask playfully.

"*Schatje*," he says. "I will always call you schatje." It's his pet word for me and it means *treasure*. I am his treasure.

Over supper, we tell Izaak and Jopie about our day.

"Back in 1930, I took a trip with my parents to the seaside village of Scheveningen. My father only had three days of vacation each year. Not like people these days," Izaak says. "My mother rented a one-person beach chair with a little reed house around it for privacy and modesty. Father and I walked on the beach while she sat."

Izaak smiles as he remembers.

"My father, as he always did, wore a three-piece dark suit, a white shirt, and a tie. He had a silver watch chain draped across his vest and wore a modern-style straw hat. I would have been seven. I wore a one-piece swimsuit. Father and I walked hand in hand for a while, down the beach, close to the water's edge, and he took his dress jacket off and threw it over his arm. And then he surprised me completely. He took off his shoes and rolled up his pants a little so they wouldn't get wet. He walked barefoot on the sand!"

I try not to laugh as Izaak talks, as I imagine his father, a stiff and formal gentleman with glaring white ankles.

"As we walked toward the pier a beach policeman called out, 'Sir, you cannot walk on this part of the beach with your clothes on! You must have a swimming suit to walk here.' The policeman pointed us to a different section of the beach. 'You can go over there, to walk with your feet in the water, *meneer*.'

"We turned around," Izaak says, "and went back to where Mother sat. And then we headed home."

When Izaak finishes his story, I laugh out loud. It's simply astonishing, the law, the rigidity, the compliance. I'm so surprised by this law-abiding mentality of the Dutch and all I can say is, "Really?"

"Ja," Izaak says without a blink. "*Zo was dat.*"

And that was that.

"We follow, of course, the rules."

History Decided by Geography, 1920s

In the years ahead, I'll spend an enormous amount of time thinking about Izaak's childhood in the Netherlands. Wondering what memories he stored away, what memories he couldn't or wouldn't talk about. I'll come to believe that the ways in which WWII played out in the Netherlands had a vast impact on his life. More than he even realized. Or at least, more than he acknowledged.

I've stood on the northern and western shores of the Netherlands, stepped into the cold waters of the North Sea. I've traveled to her eastern border, touched Germany with my hand. This geography, this joint border with Germany, set in motion much of the backdrop of Izaak's young life. History decided by geography.

In the late 1920s, when Izaak was a baby, Germany panted breathlessly next door. By the time Izaak turned ten, the Nazi party was the second largest political party in Germany. In August of 1934, Hitler united the chancellorship and presidency of Germany under the new title, Führer. A month before Izaak turned eleven.

In 1936, Izaak turned thirteen. On July 12, Sachsenhausen concentration camp opened without fanfare, just north of Berlin, receiving its first fifty prisoners. Two weeks later, the 1936 Olympics were opened by Adolf Hitler to a stadium packed with one hundred thousand onlookers.

Maybe Izaak rooted for Jesse Owens. Maybe he listened to the radio, fascinated as Dutch athletes won gold. Seventeen-year-old Rie (Hendrika Wilhelmina) Mastenbroek—second only to Jesse Owens in terms of medals won—captured gold in the women's 100-meter freestyle, the 400-meter freestyle, and the 4 x 100 free relay. She grabbed silver in the 100-meter backstroke. The press called her the Empress of Berlin.

Izaak continued in school as the year passed to 1937; he was fourteen now. Getting taller and thinner, all knees and elbows. Maybe he sprouted a chin hair or two. By now, he certainly wore long pants. No longer a little boy. Across the border, German Criminal Police began to round up persons deemed asocial, criminal, or Gypsy, and Buchenwald concentration camp opened its arms.

In 1938, when Germany invaded Austria, Izaak was fifteen, old enough to understand. Kristallnacht. All the fragile glass broken. And then, 1939. Nazi Germany took over Czechoslovakia and invaded Poland. Britain and France declared war on Germany. And Izaak's big brother, his favorite brother, his storytelling exuberant brother, Wes, went to sea once more. A sailor shipping out with the Dutch navy. This time, not just going to sea. Going to war.

Izaak turned seventeen, eighteen, nineteen within the confines of this escalating war, as if it were normal. And for him, it was normal. His bones grew long and strong in the steady uncertainties of war. That war—the coming-war, the Hitler-war, the can't-be-contained-or-changed-or-altered-war—had been in the news for as long as he could remember. War was the air filling Izaak's young lungs. His breath of life. And WWII would come to define and divide his life story.

How little I knew of the war back then. How little I cared.

Once, while driving me home from a grocery store, Izaak said to me, "Look, Yill," pointing to the distant side of the highway.

"What do you see?" he asked.

I scanned the road, seeing a windmill in the distance. I saw a dike, cows grazing on the lower side, road signs I couldn't read, a busy bike path.

"I don't know," I said, seeing so many things. Seeing nothing.

"That large cement box," he said. "It's from the Second World War."

And then, I saw it. Hundreds of tons of cement, sitting tilted on the edge of a field full of contented cows. I hadn't even noticed. So much to look at. So many new things in my vision that I missed the one glaring item. That bunker.

"Huh," I said to myself, thinking. *World War II. It really happened. It happened here.*

The moment passed. And we drove on. A bunker in my peripheral vision. It would take decades before I really saw it.

A New and Holy Trinity, 1981

Two weeks before our wedding, Johan and I walk over to Izaak's church—Hervormde Kerk te Heemse—for the big plan-the-wedding-day meeting. As we walk, I think about the things that won't be a part of my wedding. Things I grew up imagining, even expecting. There won't be a bachelorette party or bridesmaids. No cutting of a multi-tiered wedding cake, no tossing of a bridal bouquet. I'm giving these things up so that Johan's father can officiate our wedding.

My mother and father are the only people attending from my family. This wedding takes place over four thousand miles away from my home. I'm giving up friends, family, and traditions without a second thought, because Johan loves his father and wants him to perform our ceremony, and because I love Johan.

Izaak welcomes us into the church like guests. He's clearly delighted to show us his church. We follow him down the hall and into the vestry: the pastor's room where he changes in and out of his black clerical robes. He shows us a closet with several differing vestments: black Geneva gowns with large bell-sleeves, long white scarves called preaching bands, cotton clergy collars, a brush to remove any lint. A black biretta hat with a silk pom-pom adornment hangs on one hook and reminds me of old pictures I've seen of Martin Luther.

Izaak, clearly in his element surrounded by pastoral collars and clergy cassocks, smiles self-importantly as he points out the various aspects of his attire. He's every inch in charge. With a swoop of his hand he opens a door and ushers us into the main sanctuary.

"This is where the ceremony will be held," he says.

An overhead pulpit looms high in the large dim room. A wooden canopy, the *abat-voix*, above the pulpit both impresses and intimidates me. I can imagine Izaak standing up there, over his congregation, dressed in black, reading the Holy Scriptures.

We traipse behind Izaak through the church and into a reception area.

"Here. We will sit here to talk about your marriage ceremony. You will of course first be married legally, by the state, in the gemeentehuis in Hardenberg," he states. "That will occur at 11:00."

"The courthouse signing is before the church service?" I ask.

"Always," he says. "When you come to the church, it is considered a formality. You do not have to be married in a church. Many young people today do not ask for a church blessing on their marriage."

"In America, we sign the legal papers in the church," I say. "After the ceremony."

"Yes, well. We are in Nederland," he states.

Izaak wants to know which scriptures to read, in what order, and which formal prayers to offer. It feels like a template and all we have to do is fill in the blanks.

> *Orde van Dienst*: Order of the Service
>
> *Gebed*: Prayer
>
> *Schriftlezing*: Hear now from the gospel
>
> *Prediking*: Preaching
>
> *Uniecollecte*: Collection, to be used to help the poor in other lands
>
> *Huwelijksformulier*: Formal Announcement and Wedding Vows
>
> *Gebed*: Prayer
>
> *The Father of all mercies, who of His grace has called you to this holy state of marriage . . .*

He's the pastor with a protocol to follow. I'm merely the bride. He's got a formula. I want a celebration. After listening with growing impatience, I interrupt his dissertation.

"I'd love to include the 'Wedding March,'" I say. "Do you know that song? Sometimes it's called the 'Bridal Chorus.'"

Izaak looks at me aghast. I see the muscles of his jaw clamp tight. "No! *Absoluut niet.* That song will not be sung in my church."

I look at Johan. We've talked about our wedding, what we want the day to look like and be. I wish he'd say something, but the more forceful Izaak becomes, the less Johan says anything at all. He's gone still and silent.

I stare at Izaak not knowing what to say. I'm flabbergasted by his statements, his absolutes. Every wedding I've attended played the "Wedding March." I don't understand his objection.

"Do you not know what opera that song comes from?" Izaak asks me pointedly.

I have no idea where the song comes from. I feel like a dunce.

Years later, I find out the "Wedding March" comes from Wagner's *Lohengrin* opera and that the Dutch Reformed Church had held a long-standing dispute with Wagner and his pagan ideas. I don't know it at the time. I only know that Izaak makes me feel small and ignorant. I'm trying to plan my wedding in a foreign culture, with limited Dutch, and with an opinionated father-in-law-to-be who refers to this building as *his* church.

I'm relieved when the organist arrives. Izaak introduces him and beams as he turns toward the magnificent organ and begins to tell me about its history. I've never really liked organ music. It feels so old-school, pompous, and holy. I really hoped for guitar.

"I've brought along some sheet music for a song I like," I tell the organist, as I pull out the music. "'This Is the Day,' by Scott Wesley Brown. Do you know it?"

The organist takes the sheet music from my hand and skims over it.

"Ja. *Natuurlijk.* Of course. I can play this. I can play it on the organ," he says kindly.

I don't think Izaak approves of the music. He's scowling at me. I've interrupted him. He stares at me and I stare back. I'm unprepared for my father-in-law, for his numerous opinions, and for the obstinate way he holds them.

"Perhaps you can play the song when my father walks me down the aisle," I suggest to the organist.

"And what do you mean, your father walking you down an aisle?" Izaak demands. "This is a church service. We do not parade in a church service. This is not a carnival."

I wish I would've said, "This isn't just a Dutch wedding. It's an American wedding, too." If I could go back, I'd say that to Izaak. I'd look him in the eye and hold my ground. He wasn't the only father involved in the wedding. I had a father, too.

In the future, I'll look back at my wedding day and pretend. I see myself waiting at the back of the church, standing in a white wedding dress of my own choosing, standing beside my dad. We smile at each other and he takes my hand in his, squeezes it, and gives me a kiss. The "Bridal Chorus" plays. People stand. I watch myself walking arm in arm with my dad. We walk slowly down the aisle. His right hand lies gently upon my own.

But I don't say anything to Izaak. I just look over at Johan who's quiet and caught between the animosity of two people he loves.

I don't want to hurt Johan, so I bow to Dutch convention, to Izaak's desires.

I bend to this, our new and holy trinity.

The father, the son, and the daughter-in-law.

God help me if I don't believe.

The Dutch Door

There's a particular style of door in the Netherlands, known as a *boerendeur*, or farmer's, door. Divided horizontally so the bottom half can stay shut when you open the top half. When the Dutch settled in the New World, they brought their door design along with them. In the United States they became known as Dutch doors. The British call them stable doors. They're also called half doors or double-hung.

Back in the day, before barbwire and screen doors, a Dutch door allowed air into the rooms of a house while keeping animals on the farm outside and children inside. A Dutch door also added security. You could open the top to speak to a stranger, without allowing him access to come into your home.

When I look back on my life, the image of the Dutch door helps me visualize my relationship with Izaak. Half open. Half closed. Neither one nor the other. Come this far and no farther. I will open the door to speak with you, but not let you in.

Izaak made me feel both accepted and rejected, simultaneously. At the time, I didn't have the maturity or the understanding to know how to respond. He saw the door open. I saw the door closed. Neither of us was wrong. Neither of us was right.

Fourteen, 1937

That night Izaak says, "The first time I ever stepped into a church, I was fourteen years old. I didn't go for any particular reason. Just walked in and listened. Pastor ten Kate was preaching, and I was intrigued."

"You didn't grow up in church?" I ask astonished.

I thought he'd been churched since birth. He seems so pious, so *Christian*.

"Not at all, Yill," he says. "My father was socialist. A strict man who did not allow us to go to church. He was very anti-church and said, 'No! You do not go to church.' So, we did not."

What Izaak remembers most about that service was the collection. He had only a half-cent coin in his pocket, so when the velvet bag passed down the row, he put it in. Later in the service, when the traditional second collection was taken, he had to let it pass by, embarrassed. He didn't have a single coin left in his pocket.

When he went back the next week, he brought two coins, one for each collection.

Since he's in a talking mood, I ask him about how he and Jopie met.

"We were both fourteen," he says, looking over at Jopie and smiling.

"I became a member of the CJMV—Christian Young Men's Association—which later became a part of the YMCA. The organization had various clubs: music, drama, sport, scouting, and gymnastics."

Izaak joined Jubal: a drum, fife, and brass corps with 150 members. He practiced on Saturdays after school, wanting to be a drummer. On Sundays, even though his father was anti-church and disapproved, Izaak gathered along with hundreds of other boys and girls for Sunday School or Bible Study Club. Izaak and Jopie first met at a CJMV Children's Choir meeting.

Izaak doesn't say what attracted them to each other, but years later when he writes a small history of his life he writes, "Jopie noticed me because I often participated in one of the lead roles at performances."

In that history of his life, Izaak talks about what Jopie noticed in *him*, *his* lead, *his* performance. It's curious what he doesn't write about. He doesn't write about how *he* first noticed *her*. He doesn't write anything about what he saw in her.

Izaak's family history is extensive. He writes about the street he grew up on, including his neighbors' names and the details of their occupations. He writes about how the shoemaker who lived next door could talk to him while holding a mouthful of nails. He writes about the intricacies of the lamplighter's business, the milkman's deliveries, the vegetable man's wares, the man and horse who collected reeking tubs of bodily waste. He talks about soccer, about his band, about the plays he acted in. His jobs, his successes, his business deals, his secretaries, his bosses. Yet, in all of these pages and pages about his life, Izaak doesn't write once about young Jopie, the girl he fell in love with.

What was she like at fourteen? What did she wear? What songs did she love?

I wonder if she wore a ribbon in her hair. If she wore lipstick. I wonder if she wore heels. I wonder what she was like, when she was fourteen and young, when she was both a little sister and a big sister, fitting snugly in the middle of a large and happy family.

I wish I'd asked Jopie about her view of their first meeting. What she thought. Always so quiet, she just let Izaak talk on and on. Coming from a happy-go-lucky family with seven children— Gerrit, Herman, Cor, Wilhelmina, Arij, Jopie, then Nell—maybe Jopie saw a playful boy, a confident boy who sang and drummed with the best of them. Maybe she saw a friend. Maybe she fell for the color of his eyes.

Arriving in Style, 1981

My mother purchases a wedding dress for me and sends it to the Netherlands by mail. Until the day she died, she insisted I asked her to buy my wedding dress. I don't remember asking. The dress—a white Gunne Sax typical of the 1980s with its laced and filmy material—arrives in a large box, via the post with dozens of stamps on it.

I stand in front of a mirror and try it on. I don't like it. It's too large. The neck is square. It has ruffles on the bottom.

Jopie finds a seamstress, and I stand in the kitchen wearing the dress while the seamstress tucks and hems. I don't want to wear this dress on my wedding day, and I don't want to hurt my mother's feelings. I know all too well how that'll go. I've endured her breakdowns, the guilt she slings, her self-centered words— *you don't love me*—much of my life. I sigh.

I'll wear the dress. I'll tell her it's lovely. I'll stifle my feelings and thoughts, settle for peace between us. When my mom wins— when there's peace—she's a radiant human being.

My mom also sends me a silk nightgown. It's a soft pink satin on the outside with a cozy flannel interior. Her note says, "It will look so lovely on your honeymoon."

Mom and Dad arrive at Schiphol Airport five days before the wedding. Mom's planned this trip down to the bobby pins. Dad gets off the plane wearing a brown polo shirt, tan-and-brown plaid pants, and a matching plaid hat.

Mom's wearing what she calls her "signature glasses." She always chooses large white frames. Her new ones are round. And huge. You can see her eyes, her eyebrows, and half of her cheeks through the lenses. They're excessive, even in the 1980s large-glasses craze. My mother enjoys excesses.

They arrive, every inch 1980s, every inch American, but that is what they are. My mother seriously loves fashion, and with fashion, she arrives. She loves her silk blouses, silk scarves, tans, browns, and oranges. Padded shoulders are a plus. She's packed several wigs: a curly short, a straight pixie-cut brunette, a wavy one with exceptionally blonde highlights.

The Kandels and the Jensens, 1981

Johan and I take my parents on day trips around the Netherlands. We tour the quaint old fishing village of Marken. We go to Amsterdam, take a typical tourist canal ride, and then window-shop down the famous Pieter Cornelisz Hooftstraat, Amsterdam's high-end shopping street. My mother's in her glory, pointing, commenting, talking nonstop throughout the day.

We stroll through colorful flower stalls at the Bloemenmarkt on the Singel canal. We end the day with a walk through De Negen Straatjes—The Nine Little Streets—an area full of quirky boutiques and eateries.

My mother epitomizes an American tourist: bright makeup, tennis shoes, loud voice, exuberant. She talks to anyone within twelve feet of her. Asking personal questions. Telling them about herself. I look at her and wonder how much I act and look the same. Will I ever fit in? Will I ever be able to blend and meld into Dutch society?

One of the things on my mother's wish list is to visit a store that sells Delft Blue—Delfts Blauw—pottery. Kitsch blue Delft is everywhere: windmills, wooden shoes, and tulips all painted with the traditional blue and white flourishes and florals. Mom loves the mixed shades of blue—cobalt, royal, azure, powder, and sky—all painted on white glaze, but she wants the *real* stuff. We plan a trip to the city of Delft, where artists have been making the famous blue and white pottery since 1653.

Royal Delft is both a store and a museum. We walk through their collection enjoying the iconic blue and white pieces—some of them four hundred years old—hand-stamped with a date, the Royal Delft insignia, and autographed by the individual artists who painted them. The collection includes contemporary pieces in blue and white as well as something called polychrome, which incorporates more earth-tone colors.

After a wonderful exploration of historical and modern pieces, we amble through the store. I'm attracted to the candleholders. The old-fashioned one I like best has a small square plate that holds a candle in the middle. It has a loop-style ring to slip my finger through.

I buy the beautiful piece, thinking if Johan gets the job he's hoping for, we'll be moving to Zambia. He's applied for a job working with subsistence farmers. Who knows if we'd have electricity or not? The candlestick holder is both beautiful and pragmatic. It will also be a sweet reminder of this fun day out, with my folks, in Delft.

I expect that we'll hang out with Izaak and Jopie until the wedding. Go shopping. See a movie? Sit in their garden. I don't know. I just expect the six of us to be inseparable. My parents won't be flying across the ocean again anytime soon to see the Kandels.

Our days fly by, fabulous and full, but Izaak and Jopie don't invite us over. Maybe they're busy. Maybe they don't want to interfere. I'm so surprised. I'm used to North Dakota Nice—hospitality and stopping in for a cup of coffee, anytime, no need to call ahead. Just when I've decided it's another cultural anomaly and something I'll never understand, Izaak extends a formal invitation to supper. Johan and I and my parents go over. I coach Mom how to pronounce Jopie's and Izaak's names. She concentrates and practices on the way, saying "Ee–zock" and "Yooh-Pea" over and over.

Izaak greets us at the door, takes our coats, and introduces Jopie. She smiles sweetly and kisses my parents on each cheek in typical Dutch greeting.

My mother says, "Hello, Yooh-Pea," a little too loudly. A little too slowly. "I'm Betty Lou, and this is Doctor Warren." She pronounces everything carefully.

Jopie is short like my mother. She wears a gray skirt, a white shirt, and a sleeveless gray sweater. Her gray-brown hair is cut in a rounded bob. Her wire-rim glasses are almost as large as my mother's, but not quite.

Izaak wears a suit and tie. He and Jopie are both dressed in gray and white. My dad wears a suit and tie, also, but his shirt is pink and his tie maroon. My mother's dress is a matching pink.

Jopie welcomes my parents with a shy, happy smile. She's gone to a lot of work for tonight, having prepared a formal, sit-down meal with candles, linen, and a beautifully set table. Everything is, as the Dutch say, *gezellig*. It's a strange word that I'm beginning to hear over and over again. We don't have a comparable English word. It means cozy and pleasant but carries a hint of being pampered or content, much like the Danish *hyggelig*. The Dutch are very proud of making a house gezellig, a room, an event, an evening. I guess, it also means to make comfortable. I'm sure my mother approves of all Jopie's preparations.

Izaak shows us where to sit and glances down the table before he takes a deep breath, bows his head, and prays. Izaak raises his head slowly, benevolently, and says, "Eet smakelijk. Bon appétit."

To begin the meal, Jopie serves shrimp cocktail over ice. Izaak interprets for Jopie. I find small talk, in and of itself, awful. But small talk that must be translated into another language, while you wait and your smile wanes, becomes a slow torture.

We smile a lot.

We smile, nodding and being convivial. We smile trying not to crunch our food too noisily. We smile complimenting the soup, the chicken, and the sauce.

My cheeks hurt from smiling, as we offer praise to Jopie, as we eat our way through four courses. Mostly Izaak talks. He talks about his parish, his parishioners, and his church. He instructs my parents about the protocol for the courthouse wedding ceremony. He tutors us in the order of the Reformed Church wedding rituals. He smiles grandly, explaining customs and details and the various protocols. Jopie barely says a word. She serves dishes and removes them. She smiles shyly. She notices everything.

We drink coffee. Followed by juice. All in all, it's a rather painful evening, stilted and pretentious. A little over-performed. But also, very 1980s, very European.

I didn't have the maturity to understand that marriage begins at birth. Johan and I had been in training since the day we were born. Schooled in how husbands treat wives, how wives treat husbands. How we respond. How we hide. How we demand. How we acquiesce. We both had master's degrees in interpersonal communication and didn't know it.

Looking back, I realize that even then I was picking up clues, hints about my father-in-law that would come back and make sense to me years later. But I did not see them at the time. I only had eyes for Johan.

Honey, 1981

We're surprisingly nonchalant about planning our own honeymoon. When one of Izaak's wealthy parishioners offers to let us stay in a cabin they own, he accepts their offer. The cabin is near the North Sea, in an area covered with dunes. It's wild and windy there. A bit isolated. Sounds fine to both of us.

That evening Izaak takes us aside and says, "You must take good care of this cabin. It is very great of him to let you use it. It must be clean when you leave. You will be very careful for this kind gesture."

He tells us the address and explains how to find the key. He's specifically concerned about the heater. How to turn it on. To be sure to turn it off. Not to use it overly much.

"I must not be embarrassed by you breaking anything," he says. "I am taking a risk to accept his offer."

I don't pay too much attention. I'm sure everything will be just fine. Why all the fuss?

I write home to some of my college friends that I'll be honeymooning on the North Sea. It sounds so exotic. Me. Getting married in the Netherlands. In reality, Johan wants his dad to marry us, and since Izaak lives in the Netherlands, that's where we'll marry. I don't care. I just want to be with Johan. That's enough for me.

This is Our Day, 1981

The morning of our wedding, Johan and his family drive over to the cottage my parents are renting. I've been staying with them since they arrived.

Flowers adorn the hoods of each car. I've never seen cars decked out with flowers, and it looks silly to me. A big bouquet drooping over the hood, reminding me of a funeral, a casket draped in flowing gladiolas. Johan gets out of the car and presents my father with an arrangement of flowers. Dad's not quite sure what to do with them. We say good morning, take a few pictures then drive over to the gemeentehuis. Our slot is scheduled for 11:00 a.m.

Johan's sister, Andrea, and his brother, Bert, are at the gemeentehuis waiting for us. Jopie and Izaak, along with a few family members and several of Johan's friends, are there, too. The only people from my family and friends group are my mom and dad.

A woman dressed in a black robe, white shirt, and tie presides over the ceremony. She asks us the official questions, and we say yes, while our immediate family looks on.

Izaak and Jopie can't stop smiling, looking relaxed and at home. My parents hold hands, a little tightly. They look out of place, slightly uncomfortable and confused.

We sign official Dutch marriage papers, are pronounced man and wife, and give hugs and handshakes all around.

The church service is scheduled for noon, so we head right over.

Izaak goes to his dressing room to don his attire. Johan and I sit in the front pew, next to my parents. Kandel friends and family file in and sit down. The organist plays Bach's "Jesu, Joy of Man's Desiring," and the melody uplifts and fills me. It is the only blessing I need on this day.

The service is long and Dutch and formal.

Izaak calls us. We stand up, walk to the front of the church.

Legally, we've been man and wife for an hour. The papers already signed. But we stand here, in the sight of God and man, and do something I've never done before. I make a vow. In Greek, the word vow means *to pray*. In Sanskrit, *to sacrifice*. I give my life to this man. I do so with words coming out of my mouth in a foreign language that I hadn't even heard of twelve months ago.

Ik wil. I do.

I could say it a thousand times. *I do. I do. I do.*

There's not a question in my mind. Not a doubt or fear. I'm head over heels. All in. Completely besotted by the blue-eyed man who stands so tall and trim beside me.

Izaak gives us his blessing. The church's blessing. We sing another song. Pray. Sing again. Then, Johan and I walk arm in arm down the aisle of the church as the organist plays "This Is the Day."

They're playing our song, and this is our day.

We've asked Johan's brother to take our wedding photos. Izaak won't allow us to take any during the wedding ceremony. It's prohibited. Or at least he says it is. Maybe it's just his preference. I don't know. There are so many things I don't know. There are so many things I don't even ask.

Later, sometime after the service, we go back inside the sanctuary, and Bert arranges us for a few photos. We pretend we're getting married. Dominee Kandel wears his black vestments and white collar and tie. He smiles down at us from his high-above-us pulpit. Later, he descends into the room. Johan and I kneel before him, staring down at the floor. Izaak stands above us, bows his head, and blesses our union, his hands laid upon our heads.

When Bert finishes taking the sanctuary pictures, we go outside, and he takes pictures of us in front of the old brick church and in front of a nearby windmill. It's a cold November day with a bright blue sky. Johan wears a black wool suit. I have a crocheted white shawl wrapped around my shoulders, covering my light-weight dress. In the pictures, the wind blows my dress, revealing small white slippers.

Johan holds the official white wedding Bible that his father has given him. I carry a bouquet of baby's breath and freesia, laid across my arm, hugged into the crook of my elbow.

By today's standards, we were not very coordinated. My hair is pinned up in a bun, and I'm wearing a hairband of white baby's breath with a red flower to one side. There's a lavender orchid pinned on my dress and a pink ribbon hanging from my bouquet. Johan wears a red flower on his lapel. His shirt is gray, his striped tie gray and maroon. We're a little thrown together. And we can't stop smiling.

After photos, Johan and I and our two families head over to a restaurant at an expensive hotel. Shining copper pots hang from the rafters, an open fire blazes in a stone hearth, and our two families sit down to eat together. Three Americans. Seven Dutch. Making small talk between two families who don't know each other exhausts the hardiest of people. Add to that a loud restaurant, a long day, and two separate languages. I think we're all relieved when the meal finally finishes. Everyone says their goodbyes.

I take Johan's hand. He is mine. And I am his.

We've done something that defies the norm. In pledging our life together, we not only have joined two people and two families, we've also joined two languages and two nations.

We have no idea.

Looking back, I sometimes wonder about the details of that day. I've never listened to the cassette tape we so painstakingly asked a friend to make. I wore my wedding dress one other time, on our first anniversary. After that, I moved it to the back of my closet and eventually threw it out. Most of the things we did, or didn't do, made very little difference in the long run of our marriage. Our flowers wilted. The white Bible got put in some closet somewhere, faded, then cracked. The photos filled an album we seldom open.

And that pink satin nightgown?

Late in the evening after our wedding supper, when we checked into the honeymoon suite, after I shower, I put that pink satin gown on. I stand in the small bathroom of our hotel room, look at myself in the mirror, shake my head no, and promptly take it off.

My mother won't be a part of my honeymoon. She's invaded so many parts of my life, so often, but not here, not now. This evening is for me alone. For me and Johan as we fall into the wonder of our shared love, into the marvel of this new life together.

The next day, we take a bus that drops us off near the cabin belonging to Izaak's parishioner. We unpack and walk uptown to buy groceries and rent a bike. Johan bikes while I sit behind him on the fender. I goad him to go faster, holding onto his waist, and tickling him.

We cook our first meals together, sit by a heater in the chilly evenings, and wrap ourselves in the cozy blanket of our love. The cold North Sea wind and rain no deterrent to our joy, our laughter. We hold hands and run down the dunes, laughing at the cold spray of the sea. Laughing at the sheer joy of life and of being together.

Three days after our wedding, Johan and I sit down to seriously discuss a job offer that he got a couple weeks ago. It's from the Dutch Volunteer Organization. They're asking Johan to work as an agricultural adviser in Zambia, Africa. They want him to teach wheat and rice production to Lozi farmers in the village of Kalabo, on the western side of the country. Johan gets out the job contract and reads it again.

"Are we going to sign it, Schatje?"

Carole King might as well have been singing her old song on the radio—the one I'd sung along to throughout my senior high and college years—"Where You Lead, I Will Follow."

I nod yes, find a pen, and hand it to Johan. We impulsively put the camera up on a tripod and set it to take a photo. I sit on Johan's lap. He signs the paper. The camera clicks.

And so it is, on November 9, 1981, we sign away the next three years of our life.

We're moving to Zambia.

Johan spent nearly three years in Zambia with the Dutch Volunteers before we met. He's returning to a land and job he knows and loves. For me, it's all new. A new marriage, a new language, a new job, and now another new country: Zambia.

The Dutch Volunteer contract is long and written in lawyerly Dutch. I don't understand most of it. I listen as Johan translates the specifics. The Dutch Government will provide our living stipend. The Zambian Government will provide our house. They'll give Johan a month for preparation study in the Netherlands. He'll study the land, agriculture, and farming methods of the Lozi people.

Nobody gives any thought to the fact that I'm going, too. There's no training or preparation or language study for me. There aren't any classes, discussions, or cultural hints. We're given a hotel room near the university where Johan will study. We stay there for the month. Each morning Johan goes off to his studies while I wait and whittle away the time.

Looking back, I'm appalled at my placid acceptance, my lack of preparation, the fact that he studied and I wasn't asked to join in. The fact he didn't consider including me. But what bothers me, even more so, is that *I* didn't ask. At the time, I don't give it any thought or consideration because Johan kisses me each morning before he goes out the door, because we're in this together, because I can't imagine anything other than joy in our future.

Falling, 1982

We leave the Netherlands on a cold, bright day in January. Standing at Schiphol Airport, we say our goodbyes to Johan's family. I remember saying goodbye to my mom and dad just a month ago. My eyes well with tears as Jopie kisses Johan farewell. She'll miss her son terribly. We most likely won't see them for the next three years.

Izaak kisses me goodbye in typical Dutch style—left, right, left, pecks on my cheeks—as I bob like a chicken trying to avoid clanking eyeglasses. I don't dislike Izaak. Neither do I like him. He simply exists as Johan's father. At most, I find him irritating. A piece of sand in my shoe, rubbing me the wrong way.

Johan walks beside me and holds my hand as we board our Africa-bound airplane. Nothing but excitement. Nothing but hope. Youth is so oblivious. So self-oriented.

Johan and I circle each other like two planets locked in orbit. The stars could fall. The moon fade. We only see each other. Bound together by a gravitational pull too strong to separate.

How we hold onto each other as we sling our way out to Africa, to Zambia, to Kalabo Village. A comet burning brightly, we hurl; we don't even notice that we are falling.

Part 2: ZAMBIA, 1982–1986

Jill and Johan Kandel standing near Kalabo, Zambia. 1982.

An African Honeymoon

During our twenty-hour bus ride west across Zambia, we're treated to four blown tires and a massive rainstorm. By the time two more tires blow, my knuckles are white from holding onto the seat in front of me. The bus lurches to a tilted stop on the side of the road. We're somewhere in the middle of Kafue Game Park. It's dusk and growing dark.

The driver says, "No more spares."

Everyone leaves the bus, wandering into the six-foot-tall grass to relieve themselves.

The driver says, "Not to worry. Another bus, she will pick us."

The night settles around us as we wait for another bus—any bus—to come along this remote stretch of road. The bus that finally stops is already full. We climb on board even though there's no space to sit, barely enough room to stand, the bus squished to twice its legal capacity. I stand on one foot the last two hours of our trip—my other foot leaning gingerly against a basket of tomatoes wedged beside me on the floor—as my calf cramps and my head nods. When we finally arrive in Mongu in the early dark morning hours, I limp down the bus steps, a tomato stuck to the bottom of my shoe.

The next day, Johan and I board a dilapidated canoe-style boat—a *banana boat*. It sports a 35-horsepower engine. Besides the coxswain, we are the only passengers. I sit down on the rough wooden plank, the soles of my flip flops wet from the water seeping through the cracks on the side of the boat.

We putter out of the harbor and meander into an ancient world with no electrical lines and no billboards. We pass an occasional canoe. The world slows into silence, broken by the plaintive call of a fish eagle or a heron. I crane my head to watch the herds of long-horned cattle standing knee deep in the water and grass of this floodplain. Hours later a bloat of hippos bellows at us, baring their large, stained teeth, shaking their water-shined skin.

Women, naked from the waist up, bend over to wash clothes near the banks of the river, their breasts swaying. Little children point at us and wave timidly as we pass. I wave back at them and wonder how it is that I'm here. I'm a long, long way from home.

I daydream as we travel. After eight long weeks of hotel life, I'm on my way to our first home. My thoughts are as fluid as the river beneath me. What will our house be like? How many rooms will it have? I dream of what colors to paint the walls, what materials to sew curtains, how I'll arrange the kitchen, the living room, our first bedroom.

I sit on the plank and watch the amazing birdlife that soars and flashes, hides and dives around me. I dip my fingers into the river and pull at a pale pink water lily. The back of my t-shirt is wet from sweat. I watch mesmerized with the world floating by, the new landscape, the colors, the sounds. My North Dakota winter pale skin burns to pink and then red. Hour after hour I sit, my butt sore, my back stiff, my bladder full, as we're swallowed up into this land as vast and flat as the prairies I grew up on.

As the afternoon fades, the coxswain pulls our canoe over to a sandy cove. He stops the engine and points up an equally sandy road. "Here it is, Bwana," he states. "Kalabo."

I squeeze Johan's hand as we walk up the path. We spend our first night in the Kalabo Rest House, a rundown sort of hostel. The next morning, Johan's up early and off to meet the agricultural staff. He comes home after dark, exhilarated, talking nonstop about agriculture in Kalabo District, the numbers of extension workers, the size of the farms, the types of crops. He has been assigned a translator and team guide, Mr. Chitaqua. Johan's job primarily includes teaching district extension workers and helping organize several local women's projects. The possibilities are endless. His excitement palpable.

I don't know it yet, but Johan has lost his heart to Africa. She allures and pulls; she pleases and teases. A geographical mistress of immense proportions and exotic offerings. Though I try, I'll never be able to compete. Her needs will always be greater than mine.

When Johan pauses from talking about his work. I ask, "And what about our house?"

"Um," he says. "Ja, the house. Well, there's a problem."

"Problem?"

"Ja. Well. It seems a policeman in town liked the house. And, um. He moved into it."

There's nowhere to turn when a policeman takes your home. All we can do is wait. Maybe he'll be transferred. Maybe he'll find another house he likes better. Maybe not.

I'm so disappointed. I want a home of my own. Some privacy. A place to fix up and pamper. I'm tired of living in hotels and hostels and in other people's spaces. We're told that we can have two rooms in the Rest House while we wait for our home. One will be our bedroom. One will be everything else.

The next day, when Johan goes to work, I unpack our suitcases. We have two each. In the bottom of mine, wrapped carefully inside layers of socks and t-shirts, I find my Delft Blue candlestick holder. It made the trip in one piece. The blue and white floral design looks so clean and festive sitting beside our bed. I put a candle in it. Tonight, when the electricity goes out, as it most likely will, at least I'll have some light to make my way down the long narrow hall to the bathroom.

Johan goes off to work each morning, and I'm alone. I don't speak the language. I don't have an interpreter. What I have is a one-plate electrical burner set up in the hallway of the Rest House on a rickety table. This is my kitchen.

I begin each day the same: boiling water. We've been strictly advised not to drink the tap water; it's full of germs and pathogens. I arrange to buy milk from a local farmer. Three times a week, a young boy delivers it and I pour it— filthy with cow hair and dirt floating on top—from his pitted plastic jug into my own.

The presence of TB in the milk makes it unsafe to drink raw. I strain the milk through a t-shirt and then boil it slowly for half an hour, watching so it doesn't scorch or boil over, tapping my finger on the table, bored, but unable to walk away. Burnt milk today will mean no milk to drink tomorrow. Milk that doesn't simmer hot enough and long enough, will mean that the TB is alive in the next cup we drink.

There's a small outdoor market near main street, under a large tree. After finishing my milk and water chores, I slip on plastic flip-flops and walk to the market. My feet sink into the hot sand as I walk. Four or five elderly women sell vegetables, and I can usually find tomatoes and cabbage, sometimes onions or pumpkin leaves. Whatever I find is what we will eat. There is no grocery store, no frozen meat aisle, no shelves bulging with choice. There is only this market and one other store. The one with the nearly empty shelves.

I point at what I want, and the women smile and hold up their fingers indicating the price. We cannot talk to each other in words that are mutually understandable. I become adept at pointing to tomatoes or cabbages. I become adept at digging out the correct number of copper coins. I become adept at not speaking.

One afternoon, I buy a few extra vegetables, cook a larger than normal batch of tomato sauce, and am happy at the end of the meal to set aside enough leftovers for tomorrow. For one day, I won't need to walk to the market or cook! Huzzah!

I don't have a refrigerator, so I set the leftovers on the table when we go to bed. When I open the Tupperware late the next afternoon, the food has grown worms or maggots or something wiggly and squiggly enough to make me nauseous.

We stop doing leftovers.

My daily life's so odd and draining. I cook and boil and walk and cook some more. I carry the dirty dishes to the toilet room with its little sink at the far end of the hall and wash them. I carry them back. I wash Johan's filthy, mud-encrusted blue jeans and wool socks. I wash them out by hand, in the same cold-water sink down the hall, then throw them over a bush to dry. Day upon endless day I do the work of keeping Johan and me clean, fed, watered, and alive.

Up until I married, my life had been full of electrical household help that I'd never paid attention to, hardly even noticed. I miss having a washing machine. I miss the refrigerator, the freezer, the air conditioner, the food processor, the crockpot. I even miss the vacuum. I miss the radio and the television and the telephone.

I miss my life.

I've lost twenty-five pounds.

When Johan comes home, we eat and then sit under the starry night, beneath the sparkling Southern Cross, hold hands, and sip African red tea. It is hot and sweet.

On weekends, Johan and I hold hands and walk through Kalabo; we smile at everyone. Then, on one of our walks, a woman looks at me askance. She points at me and shakes her head.

I start to notice the same response from other women.

I ask one of the nurses at the local hospital what is going on. I've met her before, and her English is good. She won't look me in the eye, but speaks softly, looking at the ground. "You must stop," she says.

"Stop what?" I ask.

"You. You cannot hold hands in public," she says, leaving me confused.

"Hold hands? With Johan? But why not?" I ask, then add, "We're married," as if that will make it better.

"Only a *bad* woman holds hands with a man in public," she states.

I'm so startled by her statement; I don't even know how to respond. I don't understand her logic or her train of thought. People in Kalabo commonly live in polygamist marriages. Married men openly have one or two or three girlfriends on the side.

But married men and women are not allowed to hold hands in public?

I'm confused and baffled and so much of my time is spent alone. I try to ask my questions to Johan, but he's spent three years of his life in Zambia already. He's acclimatized and happy. He feels at home. It only makes me feel more alienated to see how well he's fitting in and getting on.

A few months ago, I was a Jensen. Now I'm a Kandel.

I was a nurse. Now I'm referred to as a wife, an entity I don't begin to understand.

I was a daughter, a sister, a friend, a student, an employee, a fiancée.

Who am I now?

A newlywed with a husband seduced by Africa.

A newlywed with no home to call my own.

A newlywed unable to hold my husband's hand in public.

And so, I toil and boil and hike my days away through the sands of Kalabo. Washing, cleaning, scraping, clinging, reeling as I fall into bed and wake up hungry, as my husband leaves, and the sun blazes, and the water and the milk need boiling again. I do this day after day after day, hell-bent on survival, until I don't know who I am anymore.

I do. I do. I do. Till death do us part.

The thin-cheeked woman I stare at in the cracked mirror is a stranger to me.

Sometimes, when we walk through the village, people ask Johan how he likes Kalabo, and he laughs and says the same thing over and over again.

"Kalabo? It's fantastic. We're having an African honeymoon!"

The Empty Letter Man, 1982

It's difficult to explain the loneliness I feel. The walk to the post office can make or break my day. I long for friends, a night out at the movies, hours of delicious browsing in a bookstore. I long for the hum of the refrigerator, the smell of a library, a hug from my sister or brother. I long to sit over a cup of coffee, the radio singing in the background, my mother busy about the kitchen. But I don't have any of these things.

I have letters.

Letters are my only connection to the outside world. Our much-awaited mail arrives randomly. We go months without any letters, then a bonanza with a dozen arriving at the Kalabo Post Office on the same day.

I love getting mail from my mom. Her letters are full of news from home and the goings on in Valley City, both gossipy and funny. Reading her letters is like reacquainting myself with a past life that I have almost forgotten exists.

Mom's letters arrive in a myriad of shapes and sizes, often with a Hallmark greeting card included. Her envelopes are as large and as colorful as her personality and often contain pieces of gum. She sends a lot of photos. She sends me cheer. She sends me hope. She's wishing for my happiness, but I know her well enough to know she's covering her own worries by indulgently shopping for me, wrapping things up, mailing them my way, keeping busy. She hides her concerns and sends me macaroni and cheese.

I have to hand it to my mother—her daughter marrying foreign and off living in a remote Zambian village—if I were her, I would've killed me.

Mom mails boxes crammed full of good old American processed and packaged food. Sometimes I think her packages are half the reason we're still alive: dried chicken soup, dried fruits and vegetables, strawberry licorice, spaghetti, cereal, Jell-O of every flavor and color.

I thank her over and over for all the things she sends. She says not to worry, quipping, "I'm single-handedly keeping the USPS afloat."

Mom's packages arrive in all sorts of conditions, but definitely not pristine. They have traveled airways, buses, and banana boats.

They have crossed continents and oceans, forded the Zambezi River, and crossed the Zambezi Flood Plain to find us.

The packages arrive with heat stroke, wilted cardboard that has seen better days and now smells like diesel or mold. They arrive battered or torn, re-taped or open. Sometimes the contents have been nibbled on by who knows what rodents. Sometimes the spaghetti noodles or cereal come with a bonus addition of weevils or accompanied by little black bugs I don't know the name of. I've become proficient with my strainer. The only thing she sent that I had to throw away, sadly, was a box soaked inside and out with diesel. I tried; I just couldn't eat that cereal.

I know that I'm spoiled by my mother's letters and packages. How could I not be? I grew up with her wild exuberances. I'm comforted by them. My mother's packages are Christmas and Easter and birthdays all wrapped up in crinkled, colored paper.

Letters from Izaak arrive typed on blue prepaid aerograms that fold over and become their own envelope. They're difficult to open. Sometimes, I slit them the wrong way, cutting the letter in half. Though the actual arrival of Izaak's letters is unpredictable, he writes them faithfully, punctually and precisely, one every week. I don't believe he ever sent us a package. Not in all those years. Not that I remember.

I bumble my way through reading his letters—my Dutch improving from the CD language course I brought with me to Zambia—but the effort of reading Izaak's words, combined with so much information that I have no reference to, wears me out. He drones on about meetings, lectures attended, and symphonies heard. He writes of trivia and timetables. He covers his agenda of the past week. I feel like a secretary reading a memo. Eventually, I lose interest and stop reading.

I wish Jopie would write, but she doesn't; she's ceded her words to Izaak.

When Johan comes home, we eat supper and then sit side by side while he reads Izaak's letters out loud and translates them where necessary.

Izaak's one of the most important people in Johan's life, and I feel like I don't know him at all. He lives thousands of miles away. We don't talk on the phone. We don't drop in on each other for coffee. Letters are the only link we have, our one connection.

At first, I try hard to concentrate when Johan reads the letters to me. I try to care. But more and more the letters irritate me. It's like listening to Izaak lecture. I can't comment back. I'm silent and mute before him. His words bounce through our cement house, echo, and reverberate. This isn't a conversation. Our *relationship* is not a two-way street.

Izaak signs his letters with greetings from Jopie; he speaks for them both. Johan finishes reading the letter and smiles.

"Nice to hear from Pa, again," he says.

I nod, but don't agree. I wish that Jopie would write. I'd like to know her better. I wonder what she's doing these days.

I begin to resent the letters, Izaak's voice, his intrusions into my life, the tiresome self-righteous view he holds of the world. How he circles and circles around himself. I try to think of nice things about him, but end up remembering Bryce's trip, or the day we planned our wedding. I hear Izaak telling me not to walk on the grass, not to rinse the dishes. The truth is, I don't have that many memories of him, and the ones I have aren't all that pleasant. So, maybe it's more than just the letters that are irritating me.

I don't feel any closer to Izaak after listening to a letter than before. The distance between us not traversed, but slightly widened. I'm disappointed by his precise letters. No surprises inside or out. It's true, he writes intelligently and clearly, placing his words accurately, solidly, on the paper. Just the way he wants them. Black on white. The problem I have with his letters is that below their cloudy sincerity, there isn't much depth, just the facts: times, dates, locations, activities, and events. They feel like another sermon. Something he's prepared to offer to the masses.

His letters are full of words and puffery.

His letters are empty.

Neverland, 1970

I think of my childhood often, trying to make sense of my new world. Trying to paste the two worlds together as if they were paper, as if glue would be enough. Sometimes, as a form of escapism, I think about my teen years. I need to exist, if only for a few moments, if only in my own mind, in a land and a culture that feels familiar. That feels like home. That feels like love.

My first love was a horse named Mi Amor. I called her Mia. She was only a horse. And I was only a girl. But what would I be without her?

I used to feed her, hop up onto her back, and fall asleep to the rhythmic crunching of her oats. On a twenty-below, clear winter day, in an unheated barn, she was the warmth beneath my coat. My Appaloosa mare. Her white-speckled, copper-penny coat thick with winter growth.

I remember the feel of her muzzle, warm and cupped in my young hands. Pink and white in places, mottled tans and black in others, with sparse wiry whiskers. She'd nicker softly while I stroked her velvet nose.

In the cool of an early spring morning, I'd find her asleep in the pasture, stretched full out on her side, the bright morning stars still shining in the black sky and I'd lay my head down upon her neck, my body curling between her shoulder and foreleg. An hour later, I'd wake to her rising, as she pulled her pillow-neck away, and I'd look up stiff with cold to see her underside, her hoofs straddling my head. She was my comfort. My safe place.

She only hurt me once.

I walked into her narrow stall, sidled up beside her, and poured a coffee can full of oats into her bucket. As I turned to leave, she laid her ears back flat. Beware! I took one step, and she turned and bit me on my back. Lips flared, teeth bared, she drew my blood. I walloped her nose so hard, I think it startled both of us. She hung her head as I wept, blood soaking my shirt behind my left shoulder blade.

She must've been in quite the mood. But then, I had my days, too. Thirteen, fourteen, fifteen, sixteen. My horse saw me through those turbulent, teenaged years.

I remember the feel of summer-hot blue jeans. Riding bareback, she'd sweat beneath my legs. And when I jumped down, my pants would stick wet to the inside of my thighs. I'd tug them free, the damp material clinging. And I'd look over at her and see a perfect shadow of my legs and bottom etched onto her white-speckled back, in a dark sweat pattern.

I remember how she quivered, her skin rippling quickly, when a black fly settled on her shoulder. I wondered how she could move her skin just so and tried to imitate her, but never could.

I remember the wind in my face when we raced flat out across the prairie. How a few strands of my long dark hair always found a way into my mouth. I'd chew on those strands and urge her on. In all those years, she never fell. When I was on her back, I didn't touch the world. She was my barrier, my carrier through an adolescent storm.

We rode together, oblivious to the world. This is what Mia gave me: this gift of detached time. When everything else vanished, and there was nothing but us.

I remember the pleasure of kicking off my boots and riding her bareback, my toes dangling and catching tallgrass seed between them. We roamed our world together under a domed and endless sky. When I remember her, a prairie breeze blows strong across a sun-soaked sky; I'm young again, sixteen years old, and life's as soft and sure as she is.

I am Peter Pan. She is my Neverland. My never, ever land. A time and place I'll bring along with me, no matter how far I roam.

Sixteen, May 1940

It never occurred to me when I lived in Zambia to wonder about Izaak's life when he'd been young. My sixteen-year-old life full of horses. His full of war.

Years later, after he'd died and forced the breath right out of me, when I needed information like I needed air, I went back to his story. Went back to the small family history he'd written and those empty letters that Johan so diligently saved. Only then did I begin to read between the lines and listen.

Izaak wrote about the day the war began, that day when he was just sixteen years old.

On the morning of Friday May 10, Izaak and his brother Piet woke up early—4:30 a.m.—to a strange sound they couldn't place. It sounded like explosions. Looking out the window, they saw dozens of people on the street. Just like the boys they were, they sprinted down the steps and joined the group of curious neighbors.

They all stared up at the early morning sky dotted with hundreds of airplanes. Dark, with clearly visible black and white crosses painted underneath.

He wrote, "All of a sudden we saw large packages drop from the planes right above us. We did not know what they were until the packages opened and we saw a large number of parachutists. We stood with our mouths open in surprise, not understanding that it was dangerous."

The boys and their friends ran to the end of the street to watch as German soldiers landed in a large open field. Hundreds upon hundreds. They stood gawking as a straggle of men from one branch of the Dutch army arrived. They were *pontonniers,* soldiers specialized in building pontoons, not infantry men trained to face elite German forces. Two more waves of German planes flew overhead. More parachutes dropped from the sky. When the shooting began, the stunned boys ran for cover.

That night, the Kandel family sat in front of their radio listening to news of the various battles raging through their tiny land. The day they hoped would never come had arrived in force. Arrived with 16,000 German airborne troops parachuted into their homeland and 2,500 dedicated German support and transport aircraft, dropping soldiers, dropping bombs.

Izaak included an old newspaper clipping with his story. A black-and-white photo taken that day shows seventeen white parachutes floating serenely in the air. Spread wide and rippled. The picture is both captivating and deceptive. It appears so peaceful, a sky dotted with nothing but billowy clouds, but actually they're parachutes. Beneath each chute, a small doll-like man hangs floating in the air. Floating towards the ground. There's no indication of what those men will do. Rereading Izaak's story, looking at this photo, I realize that Izaak's sixteen-year-old life couldn't have been more different than my own. I rode the prairie lands and daydreamed of being a senior in high school, going to college, choosing a profession. He watched his country overturned, his life barricaded, the future a thing he could only pray for.

Easier to Stay, 1984

After six months of living in the Kalabo Rest House, the policeman who lives as a squatter in our home receives a transfer. The house is ours! We spend a week getting it ready to move into. We patch the few screens that hang crooked over the broken windows, and then, finding no glass available, board them over. We scrub the blackened kitchen. A firepit, dug in the middle of the floor, explains the ever-present soot. The sagging ceiling boards and sound of a bat colony in the attic explain the dripping muck running down the walls: guano. To say our home is a fixer-upper isn't quite right, as we have little in the way of tools or supplies to fix anything. But I'm happy with what soap and water and a whole lot of elbow grease accomplishes.

I hire a man, Mr. Albert, to help me with the household chores, and I no longer have to walk to market every day. Mr. Albert buys veggies and comes back smiling and full of village small talk. I teach him bread baking; he teaches me the seasons. I teach him to make pie. He tells me the names of birds, explains customs and habits, and occasionally brings me a flower from his walk into town.

Mr. Albert works two days a week, then three. Eventually, after a couple of months, he comes Monday through Friday. I enjoy his presence and deeply appreciate having someone to help with all the work, someone to talk to, someone to help me understand this new and confusing life that threatens to consume me.

One morning I wake up feeling more tired than normal. A deep bone-weary fatigue I've never felt before. I drag myself through the day, thinking it will pass. But it hangs on. Day after day, the weary weeks melding together. I begin not sleeping well, then throwing up.

I'm pregnant.

Johan and I talk about me going back to North Dakota for the delivery and find out the airlines won't let me fly after the seventh month of pregnancy. Johan can't take two months off work. I'd have to go alone. The idea of traveling overwhelms me, the canoe ride out, the long road trip, finding a place to stay in Lusaka, the various flights, and connections. Would I really want to live with my parents for two months?

Somedays I wake up and think, "I'll go home!" Other days I wake up thinking, "It'll be fine. I'll stay." The days slide by and my belly grows and I'm too tired to make a decision. In the end, it's just plain easier to stay.

Opa and Oma, 1984

On a sweaty-hot morning in March of 1984, I lumber down the hallway to the maternity department of the Kalabo Hospital. Pieces of tile are missing from the ceiling; a faded curtain hangs crooked over a cracked window. I lie on an old bed, with a peeling metal frame, the pillowcase stamped G.R.Z. The Government Republic of Zambia. The doctor is Dutch; the midwife is Zambian. And there, after twelve sweaty hours of labor, I give birth to a little girl. She's one month early and weights exactly six pounds. I hold her in my arms and stroke her face; she's bald and pink and tiny and perfect. Her gray-blue eyes blink as she looks up into my face. I've never seen anything so beautiful. We name her Kristina.

I stay in the hospital for one hour after her birth, then ride home and crawl into bed. I'm thankful for a mosquito net and clean sheets. I'm thankful the electricity's working and that we own a fan! I'm amazed at this new life that mews beside me, stretching and blinking her way into my heart. I feel like I've known her all my life. Each freckle already memorized.

My little girl, so small and new, and already so international. She has three choices for citizenship: her mother's, her father's, or her place of birth. She can be American, Dutch, or Zambian. The world an open book. I fall asleep, a smile on my face, Kristina in my arms, wondering about her life to come.

Kristina is Izaak and Jopie's first grandchild, and her birth gives them new names, *Opa* and *Oma,* the Dutch words for Grandfather and Grandmother. Izaak no longer signs his letters *Pa.* He begins to sign them all *Opa.* Johan stops calling his parents Pa and Ma. Overnight they simply become Opa and Oma.

My parents, Betty Lou and Warren, become—improbably— grandparents twice on that same day. My sister, Jan, gives birth to her little Anna, in North Dakota, just a few hours before Kristina enters the world in Kalabo. We call them the Twin Cousins.

On that remarkable day in March—with their two little granddaughters thousands of miles apart—my parents decide they want to be called Opa and Oma. I don't really know why.

Mom says, "It's easy to say."

Perhaps, in their own fashion, they're trying to embrace their foreign son-in-law.

Personally, I think it makes her feel European and posh. But for whatever reasons, from then on, my parents will be known as Opa and Oma.

Opa and Oma Kandel. Opa and Oma Jensen.

As Kristina grows, I read to her each evening. She has a favorite book of animals. She loves the sounds they make.

I read to her, "Moo, moo, says the cow."

Johan walks by and bends down to Kristina. "What does the cow say?" he asks her, then answers, "Boo. Boo. The cow says boo."

I look at him quizzically. "Boo?" I ask.

"Of course," he says.

The conversation grows and soon Kristina is making animal sounds in two languages. Dutch pigs say *knor-knor*, not oink-oink. Roosters in the Netherlands wake up saying *kukeleku-kukeleku*, not cock-a-doodle-do. Chickens peck the ground proclaiming tok-tok-tok, while strangely enough ducks and frogs say almost the same thing: *kwak-kwak* and *kwaak-kwaak*.

All four of the grandparents are anxious to meet Kristina, but Johan's so busy. His job has really taken off. And in truth, we don't have enough vacation time built up, and we haven't saved enough money to purchase tickets. We'll wait.

My mother says she's sending me a baby care package. She writes, "Actually, it didn't fit in one package. It's coming in two separate packages." She hasn't told me what it is. She only writes, "I can't imagine having a baby without one."

I wait anxiously, curious about what the two-package gift will be.

Three months later, a large box arrives, battered and worn. I tear into it and find the legs, back, and rockers of a rocking chair. My mother mailed me a rocking chair! Well, half of one anyway. I wonder what I will do if the other half doesn't come, but a couple of weeks later, another large package arrives containing the seat and arms. That night, I rock Kristina to sleep in our very own rocking chair. In years to come, I'll rock Kristina a thousand times, as we sway back and forth in the heat and heart of Zambia.

Ifs and Maybes, 1984

After three years in Zambia, Johan's original job with the Dutch Volunteers has grown so much that it's been taken over by the Dutch embassy. He's signed a three-year contract with the Dutch Ministry of Development. This contract includes a half-a-million-dollar budget. There's money to hire helpers, build infrastructure, and expand agricultural extension services across Kalabo District. He's completely pumped about it all.

It's been three long years for me. I seriously want to get away from Kalabo. Kristina's seven months old, I'm more than ready for some vacation time. I think a visit to South Africa would be fantastic. I'd love to do a safari. I want to shop in Johannesburg, swim in the ocean, and hike in the cool breezes up on the veld.

"I hear South Africa's gorgeous," I say to Johan one evening.

"Yes, but we need to go home," Johan answers.

"To the Netherlands?" I ask.

"I'm worried about my dad's health," he replies. "Ever since he had that heart attack, I just don't know how long he'll be with us."

"He had that heart attack ten years ago!" I say incredulous.

"You never know," Johan says.

I'm let down and frustrated with the *ifs* and *maybes* that surround his relationship with his father. We're here in this amazing part of the world, and he wants to use our vacation to go back home. To see his father.

"Opa and Oma will want to see Kristina," he says. And that seals the deal. I let go of my dreams and say yes. Since we're going to see his parents, I talk about traveling to the United States to see mine, too. We decide to use all of our vacation time, empty our savings. We'll stop in the Netherlands, then fly back to Zambia via North Dakota, giving all of the grandparents their fair share of Kristina time.

In One Corner, Hardenberg, 1984

We fly out of Lusaka on November 13, 1984.

"We're going to go see Opa and Oma!" I tell Kristina.

Izaak, Jopie, and Andrea meet us at the Schiphol Airport. We see them standing behind the big glass window when we get through Customs.

"Look, Kristina! There's Oma. There's Opa. And that's Andrea with them!"

Johan gets our suitcases and we walk through the sliding glass doors.

"*Dag,* Yill!" Izaak says, kissing me on one cheek and then the other and back again. He greets Johan the same, peck, peck, peck. Right, left, right. Kristina, a jetlagged toddler, puts up with these new people for a few minutes, wiggles in their arms, then wants me back. I hoist her from hip to hip while she vacillates between smiling and tearing up.

We head out to the car and drive to Izaak and Jopie's home in Hardenberg. The cool fresh weather invigorates me. I love it so much more than the sluggish heat of Zambia. We drive by bushes and trees with a few colorful leaves still hanging on. It feels so odd to be coming back. The last time I saw this house was right after Johan and I got married. And now here we are, three years later, with our daughter.

As we walk into the house, Izaak says, "Jopie has decorated for you!"

A large Dutch flag and a large American flag hang over the coat closet. Both are red, white, and blue. At least the two countries involved in this marriage don't have clashing colors.

Jopie knit Kristina a pale-yellow cabled sweater and hat. She sewed her a white jacket. Several pieces of play clothing, t-shirts, pants, and dresses lie on the dining room table. Jopie, festively dressed in a bright red blouse and gray skirt, can't stop smiling at her granddaughter. Kristina grins back shyly.

Lieve Kristina is what both Izaak and Jopie call her. *Beloved Kristina.* They're both so happy to see her; I'm ashamed I hadn't wanted to come. There's carpet on the floor and curtains in the windows. The coffee's fresh and hot. Izaak serves celebratory apple tart. Everything inside the house is spotless and feels wonderfully gezellig. Everything outside peaceful and fresh.

I open a package my mother has sent. It contains a pale pink snowsuit for Kristina. It's November and cold compared to Zambia. We put the suit on Kristina and go for a walk. She's a bundle of fleecy material. The pink snowsuit hood peeks above her pale-yellow hat, making her look like a miniature, pastel, fluffy gnome.

I notice the quietness most. There aren't any roosters crowing, no barking dogs running feral in the streets. No herds of long-horned cattle bellowing in the distance.

I'm happy beyond reason. The chill wind on my skin feels like home. Each day we bike around the area or go for a long walk in the forest. Kristina loves being outside. She sits happy in her backpack, peeking out over Johan's shoulder as we sightsee and then return to Izaak and Jopie's home.

I spend a lot of time and effort trying to get Kristina to warm up to her opa. She's taken to Jopie's sweet and gentle overtures but avoids Opa. She won't look at him. After four or five days, I'm desperate. I call Izaak aside and whisper, "Why don't you get her a little doll or a teddy bear? Nothing big. Just a little something, you know." I need some bonding to be going on here and I'm not above stooping to bribes.

"No, Yill. I will not do this," he says. "I wish her to like me for who I am, not for the things I will give to her. No. I will wait. You will see."

I'm startled by his words and confused. How can a man be so inflexible? If I'd have asked my mom to get Kristina a doll, she would have rushed out and come back with five. One of them would have been life-sized. The others would have walked, talked, wet their pants, and blinked their eyes.

The days tick off, one by one, gone. Never to be recovered. Kristina in one corner. Izaak in the other.

Kristina loves the new foods, especially the Dutch breakfasts with their creamy, sweet *vla*, a cross between vanilla pudding and yogurt. She likes the late fall chrysanthemums, growing in bright yellows and oranges, pointing to them as we pedal by. She adores throwing pieces of bread at the ducks swimming in the pond. But she doesn't warm up to her opa.

After a week of mostly stare-downs, Kristina crawls over to Opa one afternoon. She looks up at him, and he picks her up. She sits primly on his lap for a few seconds, then scrambles away.

Izaak sits triumphantly drinking his tea, vindicated by his ten-second time-slot. He looks over and flashes me a look recognizable in any language: *I told you so.*

Requirements

There are so many things that you require, Izaak. Quietness, predictability, organization. Respect and deference. Clear and verifiable facts, cleanliness, order. Conventional questions. Conventional answers.

I can't keep up with these things, these precious necessities you hold dear and close and sacred. I don't even want to. I want to be loud and unpredictable and haphazard. I want to cut to the chase, throw my laundry on the floor, thumb my nose at convention.

You're as white and crisp as a straitjacket. Every time I enter your life, your home, you hold that jacket out to me. You offer it so graciously. Impervious to the fact that I might want to choose otherwise. I think you don't even comprehend that there's another choice that might be made.

You whisper into my ear. *Here it is. Put it on.*

When your daughter visits, she puts the straitjacket on. Conform. Obey. Do not ask questions. Your son willingly pulls it over his head and ties the cords. They walk stiff and straight as they enter your world, synchronize their watches. And isn't this the way you raised them?

And here I am, *the clean daughter.* The clean daughter. Isn't that a funny one? I'm the one who likes to finger-paint, eat a burger without a knife and fork. I love the smell of horses. You just don't know what to do with me. I'm not conventional and compliant. Not what you wanted. I won't take the straitjacket from your hand.

Sometimes, most sacrilegious of all, I even laugh at these, your assumptions. I don't laugh to do you harm. I don't mean it to be nasty. It's just that sometimes it strikes me all as so funny. So truly ludicrous. This mountain of things that you so desperately require. This mountain that I'm disinclined to hike.

Peppermints, 1984

On Sunday, we go to Izaak's church. Kristina sits quietly; she's the only child I see in this elderly congregation. The large sanctuary's more than three-fourths empty and echoes eerily. After a prayer and a Psalm, a red velvet bag with a wooden handle is handed down the aisle. People drop coins into the bag and pass it on.

Dominee Izaak mounts the steps going up to the pulpit. He stands above us, looking down from his perch and begins the sermon, the *preek*. At the moment he begins, I hear a loud crinkly noise. Looking around, I see people in the congregation wrinkling open rolls of what look like candy. The woman sitting at the end of our row passes a roll our way—each person taking a piece and passing it on. The roll, wrapped in white, has navy and red print on it: King Pepermunt. Inside, a stack of hard, white peppermints waits. The elderly parishioners all around us pass pepermunt.

Johan takes a mint and hands one to Kristina. I take one, too. *When in Rome.* I pass it on to Jopie, who takes a candy, puts it in her mouth, and passes the roll to the person sitting beside her on the hard pew. It astonishes me to watch this group of grown adults simultaneously dig in their pockets and purses for candy and then pass the sweets around to one another without a second glance. We listen to Izaak drone on, his voice sonorous. We suck on peppermints.

Over the years, I've heard this Dutch custom referred to as "beginning of the preaching mints," or "mid-service mints." Sermons are sometimes referred to as "one-mint sermons" or "two-mint sermons" depending on their length.

I want to burst out in laughter as I watch these solid Dutch believers enjoying their sweeties. My shoulders shake with the laughter that burbles up inside me; I clamp my mouth tight. I squeeze my eyes shut. Laughing would totally put me in the doghouse.

"What the heck was that?" I ask Johan after the service.

"What was what?" he asks.

"The peppermints!" I say. "What is that all about?"

"I don't know," he says. "It's what we always do."

Customs are the oddest of things. Unexpected. Difficult to explain. Obscure. But this is one of the oddest. I shake my head again as I think of Izaak's black cassock, his stern face peering down from above, the conformity of the parishioners' actions, my mouth sweetened against all those sober words earnestly filling the mostly empty room.

Later, still curious, I ask Izaak.

"Afschuwelijk. Een raar gegruik!" he says, then adds to make his point, "Awful. A terrible habit!"

He says it's very difficult to concentrate on his preaching when he's listening to his parishioners peeling paper rolls open. Watching them pass the candies down the pews. He doesn't like it. People aren't paying good attention to him.

The following week, I buy a dozen rolls of peppermints. They'll make great gifts to take to the States. They'll make a great story.

We're leaving the Netherlands in two days and will miss the Dutch celebration of Sinterklaas by one day. It's a new tradition for me; the closest thing we have to St. Nik is Santa Claus. But Sinterklaas is celebrated with presents on December 5 and has no association with Christmas. In the Netherlands, Sinterklaas and the celebration of the birth of Christ are two very separate holidays. Gifts are given on December 5. It's not common to give Christmas gifts.

When we go over for tea, Oma comes in holding a package. She hands the small box to Kristina, lets her open it, and then helps her take the present out. It's a large piece of chocolate shaped like the letter K. A traditional Sinterklaas gift called a Sinterklaasletter.

Kristina squeals happily and nibbles one leg of the big chocolate K.

As Kristina bites off another piece, Izaak chides Jopie, "Why do you give her this? It is not yet Sinterklaas."

Oma doesn't pay attention to his words. She beams at Kristina and croons, "*K voor* Kristina. *Ook voor* Kandel."

Kristina smiles and licks the chocolate.

Who wouldn't love an Oma like this?

We fly out to the United States, where the time sprints by faster than imaginable. We meet my brother's wife and their daughter. We meet my sister's daughter. We laugh and play, sit in front of a cozy fire, play board games, and go to the donut shop. My mother presents us with gift after gift after gift. And then, it's over; the suitcases bulging, the plane waiting. Dad hugs me to himself, warm and strong. Mom cries. Johan has that *back to Africa* twinkle in his eye, nothing but excitement. And me? I'm caught in it all, torn in half, breaking my heart again.

Telegram, 1985

Nine months later, on a hot day in September, after a long hard labor, our second child is born in Kalabo village. After the birth, Johan walks over to one of the council members' homes to ask if he can use their telephone. He calls both sets of grandparents and tells them, "You have a grandson!" Our little boy, Joren, is the first grandson on either side of the family. The next generation to carry the Kandel name.

The next day, the postman comes to our door. He's delivering telegrams.

From Opa and Oma Kandel:

DANKBAAR MET JULLIE ZEGEN EN BESTE WENSEN. MAPA KANDEL. Thankful with you, blessing and best wishes.

And another from Johan's sister Andrea:

GEFELICITEERD. Congratulations.

I'm used to letters that are six weeks old when they arrive. How odd. To give information and the next day receive information back. How tight time feels. How geography shrinks. What would it be like to live in the same country, to call, to bike over, to live in the present moment so fully?

My life's divided by continents and time zones and miles and miles of sand.

We send pictures and letters back and forth, six weeks old by the time they arrive. Opa puts all the photos into a small photo album that is thick and square. As the albums fill, he buys new ones. They sit in the living room, a stash of photos his closest contact with his grandchildren.

Pictures are a time-warped mirage. Opa and Oma open our letters and see a newborn. In real time, in real life Joren's already in his second month of life.

I hold the telegrams and think about time and life and living here in Zambia.

We live with the reality of sinuous and extensive rivers, vast and roadless expanses of sand, messy potholed highways, and long-distance airplane trips. We live with these multiple physical barriers separating us from our previous life. They barricade us into this *present,* this *moment* in time.

In some ways, the telegrams feel like an intrusion. I think about the geographical barriers that hem us in and restrict us, and also keep things out. The balance of it all isn't lost on me.

Putten, October 1986

In May of 1986, just before Joren turns one, Izaak retires. He and Jopie can't remain in their house since it's a parsonage, owned by the church. They decide to move, away from Hardenberg, away from the home they've lived in ever since I met them.

They choose to move to Putten, a town about sixty miles to the southwest. It's slightly smaller than Hardenberg and known for its proximity to the largest national park in the Netherlands, Hoge Veluwe. Putten's known for its famous Vanenburg Castle, too. But primarily, the town of Putten's practically synonymous with WWII.

Putten: *The Village of Widows and Orphans.*

Near the end of September 1944, a Dutch resistance group opened fire on a vehicle carrying members of the German Wehrmacht. One German officer captured, one dead, two wounded. The captured officer was released as a gesture of goodwill. The Nazis were not interested in goodwill.

At 6:30, on the morning of October 1, German troops surrounded the city of Putten and rounded up all of the residents, locking them up. Boys over the age of fifteen were kept with the men. That evening, the Germans released the women and children and burned over one hundred homes to the ground.

The next day, sixty men—all over the age of sixty—were allowed to leave. The remaining 601 men and boys were loaded onto trains and transportation vehicles and sent to a concentration camp in Amersfoort. They were then moved to concentration camps in Nazi Germany. Thirteen escaped en route.

The wives, the children, the little brothers, and sisters received no information. None. They waited. The months passed. The war escalated and ebbed and flowed. The war ended. Still, they waited, hoping beyond hope that their husbands and sons had survived somehow. Hoping each morning that they would wake up and hear that familiar voice again. Going to bed each evening, falling asleep with a prayer upon their lips.

It wasn't until seven months after the war ended that a few men began to trickle back. Only forty-eight returned, five of whom died shortly after reaching home. Dutch citizens, 533 men and boys, from the town of Putten perished in concentration camps that bore the names Buchenwald, Dachau, and Bergen-Belsen. They died of disease and malnutrition and beatings. And sadly, they also died from wounds sustained as the Allies bombed their way to victory, bombing raids that hit and missed targets, that made the terrors of war all the more terrible.

Every year, Putten holds a memorial service, a moment of silence to remember and honor the victims from October 1944.

Once every year, Izaak was reminded deeply, intensely, and thoroughly of the war, the past ever-present in his life. The past lived, not just in the Putten Memorial Service, but in the lives and memories of people who lived down the street and across the road. A small community of people, many of whom remained in place after the war.

Izaak would have already resided in Putten for six years, when in 1992, the Memorial Room had its grand opening. This building, a large charcoal-colored cube, is known by the date written in huge white letters on its exterior wall: OKTOBER 44.

Inside the memorial, the story of the raid is written and drawn and pictured. The names of each man who died listed. History remembered. Putten is a farming community. And among the lost, perhaps none suffered more than the Bakker family: six sons, two sons-in-law, two grandsons. How do you survive such a loss?

A monument called De Vrouw van Putten stands testament to the atrocity. Variously transcribed into English as The Lady of Putten, The Little Woman of Putten, or The Woman of Putten, the monument, revealed on October 1, 1949, by Queen Juliana, consists of a memorial park and a sandstone sculpture of a woman in folk dress with a handkerchief in her hand. Her eyes focus on the distant Oude Kerk, Old Church, where long ago those men and women and children were forcibly separated from each other.

A memorial stone on Oude Kerk depicts a simple cross with these words written above it in capitalized letters.

VAN HIER WERDEN ZIJ WEGGEVOERD
FROM HERE THEY WERE TAKEN.

Piccadilly Circus, 1986

In early 1987, the Dutch Ministry of Foreign Affairs wants to extend Johan's work contract. They want us to stay an additional three years. I know that I can't survive more of this. Six years in Kalabo Village is enough. More than enough. I'm weary and worn and at my end. I'm done with Zambia.

I tell Johan no. No more. I'm finished.

Johan would love to stay another three years, but he listens. We start making other plans and he applies to graduate school in Reading, England. A few months later, we get an acceptance letter! Johan will be doing his master's degree in tropical agricultural extension. We pack our bags. For better or for worse, we're leaving Zambia.

We fly to the Netherlands and spend some time in Putten with Opa and Oma Kandel, then fly to the US for a month, and then return to the Netherlands to gather our bags and suitcases. It's back to school for Johan.

Johan and I, along with our children, take the Koningin Beatrix Ferry from Hoek van Holland to England, traveling with everything we need for the next year. The boat takes us to Harwich, where we catch a train to Liverpool Station in London.

It's my first time in England, and I think we're a little crazy. Two kids, a stroller, four suitcases, backpacks, an overflowing diaper bag, and us. We trot up and down the station stairs to different platforms. Johan grabs two suitcases and runs them up the stairs while I stand with the kids and the other two suitcases down below. Then he runs down the stairs and grabs the last two suitcases while I manage the backpack, the stroller, and the diaper bag.

We finally locate the underground to Paddington Station and try to board. A few people help us, holding the doors of the train open for an extra moment while we shove in our suitcases. Some shake their heads at us. Some are angry: *you shouldn't be traveling on the underground with so much luggage. You're holding everyone up.* A few smile sadly at us. Maybe they think we're homeless.

When we arrive at Paddington Station, we go up and down long staircases to find the train platform to Reading. By the time we arrive, we're exhausted and it's late and dark. Johan hails a taxi and we go to a hotel for the night.

The next morning, we move into our rental property, 3 Porch-field Close, Reading, England. While Johan works on his university degree, I intend to make the most of England. Reading's one hour north of London. It's out of Africa and into Piccadilly Circus for me!

Part 3: ENGLAND, 1987–1988

Official Royal Dutch Navy photo of Wes Kandel, Izaak's oldest brother. Taken in the Netherlands before WWII.

Mummy, 1987

At nearly four years old, Kristina's a jumble of curiosity and energy. At two and a half, Joren's a follower. Anything his big sister Kristina wants, he does with gusto. My children, village-bred and born, have been surrounded by nature most of their young lives. Living in a remote village in Zambia was pretty extreme in some ways—the heat, the isolation, the lack of modern amenities, snakes, bats, and mice galore—but from a kid's vantage point, it was an idyllic home.

I used to say, "Kristina, my little bug, what are you fussing about? You've got the largest sandbox in the world just outside your door." Then I'd tickle her under the chin. If she didn't laugh, I'd run my thumb along her wrist. "I'm a little green gecko," I'd say, and my thumb gecko would crawl slowly higher and higher toward her ticklish armpit.

Both kids loved the tiny geckos, which fell off the slippery damp bathroom walls and into the tub at bath time. Sometimes, the geckos hung on the walls of the dining room and stared at us while we ate. Kristina would scream with laughter, "Gecko! Go 'way, gecko!" and she'd jump down and run into the back-yard where our yellow Labrador, Lasso, would hear her and come running over to join in whatever fun was at hand. Joren tagged behind. Everywhere Kristina went, he was sure to follow.

The two children lived and joyed in our village life. They played with our neighbors, the Snapper kids, and their menagerie of chickens and dogs. No television marred my children's imaginations. Cattle roamed the sandy hills, and a star-filled sky covered their home each night where they slept sweetly, under the twinkling approval of the Southern Cross. For their entire lives, my children woke up to mornings of bright and African sunshine, their blonde hair bleached white. Their lives a storybook. *Little House on the Zambezi.*

I'm not sure how the kids will react to the bustle and noise of England, but they're curious and playful and take it all in stride.

Kristina begins greeting our new neighbors on Porchfield Close
with a mimicked *cheerio*. Within a few weeks, she starts calling
me *Mum*.

"Mum!" she calls. "Mum! Mummy! Tell Joren stop!"

While Johan studies, Kristina and Joren and I take taxis and
double-decker buses and trains. We go to Blenheim Palace, Wind-
sor Castle, and the Royal Victoria and Albert Museum. We skip
along the Thames, throwing bread upon the water and watching
as the ducks gobble it up. We visit the Shire Horse Farm and take
long walks through the hills. We get to know our neighbors.

I learn some British nursery rhymes, and the Zambian gecko
morphs into a tiny brown teddy bear. My fingers circle Kristina's palm, then walk up her forearm heading toward her armpit.
*'Round and 'round the garden went the teddy bear. One step. Two
step. Tickle under there.*

I wonder if Kristina and Joren will remember England when
they are older. What things do children retain? How will their
growing-up years affect their lives? How old must they be to begin having their own memories? I wonder about growing up in
Zambia and England. What things are going on, imprinting on
their little minds, changing their lives forever? Will having a father from a different culture be an enhancement, a widening? Or
will it become a division? Will their cross-cultural childhoods be
a blessing or a curse?

Never Give Up, 1971

My childhood was the furthest thing from cross-cultural, living in
the same midwestern town from the age of three till when I went
to college. My fondest memories were of gymnastics, girlfriends,
4-H, and horses.

When I was sixteen, time was a prairie breeze. My horse
and I played at life. We galloped up steep hills, forded flooded
streams, entered parades and horse shows; she never flinched.
One of those calm and easygoing mares. She stepped over obsta-

cle courses without a blink or shake of her mane: hay bales, tires, bridges made from plywood.

She was the best of ponies, until the day we came across a sheet of black plastic stretched out on the ground. A big, old garbage bag, just lying there. She shook her head. Her ears went back. The skin on her withers trembled. A redhead with freckles. She acted as if the plastic was her darkest fear, a black witch of a thing wilted on the ground, a spook rising in the wind.

I turned her around and we trotted away, then trotted back. Mia stopped a foot away, throwing her head in the air, eyes wide and white with fear. When I prodded too hard, she reared and nearly took us over. The fact that she weighed a ton and I weighed in at one hundred and ten pounds didn't matter. I was sixteen and fearless.

Mia began to rear more wildly. I sat alert in the saddle. I knew every twitch of her ear, every nod of her head. She snorted at each flap in the wind and pawed the ground. She threw a hissy fit and stomped her hoofs like a two-year-old in a tantrum, her whole body jerking.

A horse can be a stubborn thing, but that's nothing compared to the tenacity of a teenager who believed that she was right. I wouldn't stop trying until she'd walk across it.

This became our contest of wills. Day after day. My friends said it didn't matter. Move on. Teach her something else. But the more Mia refused, the more I clung to my demand.

Finally, one afternoon, after two hours of skittering around that plastic, I felt her skin grow taut beneath my legs. She gave one fearful quiver, hunched her hind legs underneath herself, and gave a mighty leap. We were on the other side before I even had time to think.

I praised her mightily. She shook her head, threw her nose in the air, and snorted her relief. I leaned over her neck and whispered in her ear, "I knew you could. You old goat! Good job, girl!" And then, I turned around and made her cross over again.

Her leap, quicker. Smoother.

The next time, she set a tentative hoof down on the plastic before giving a half-hearted jump. And finally, she just plain walked across the thing, as if it was nothing new, as if I hadn't just spent weeks cajoling her. As if it had been her idea all along. Perhaps it was.

She was the teacher. I was the student.

Face your fears.

Never give up.

Don't quit.

I incorporated these ethics without realizing it, embracing them in the form of a copper-speckled Appaloosa mare who held me to a standard.

That night, I fed her oats by the handful, and she leaned her head down and nuzzled my palm like a puppy. I still feel those oats lying in my hand, held out to her: the soft fuzz of her muzzle, the warm damp in the exhale of her breath, the way her thick lips parted and searched my hand gently for more. Time stands still. Retreats. Silences itself. And the prairie wind picks it up and blows it softly away.

Your Invisible Calendar

Opa and Oma Kandel want to come over to visit us in England. It's not a surprise. The Netherlands isn't far away. This is the closest we've ever lived to each other.

I know Johan's hands are more than full with classes, research work, studies, and writing, let alone with finding time for his parents. I want to give Kristina and Joren time with their grandparents, but I'm not looking forward to seeing Izaak. How he ruffles my feathers.

I know that when he comes, he'll greet me with the same information that he always does: The date when we were last together.

The last time I saw you, it was 9 April . . . It was 25 October . . . It was . . .

Sometimes he counts it out.

It has been two years, five months, and ten days since you were last here.

From the moment he opens his mouth to remind me of those verifiable facts, I begin to sag. His memory precise.

"Do you not remember, Yill?"

"Not really, Opa."

"How can you not remember this?"

I'm abysmal at remembering dates. I still need to look up my mother's birthday. It's Johan who remembers our anniversary, not me.

Izaak's a master of the dates; dates that I don't have much concern for. I happily traverse my life without a general use for them. Instead, I remember the seasons and the happenings that surround my life events.

That happened just before Kristina was born.

That was the week after the big storm came through.

That was just after the puppies were born!

I remember the story. He remembers the date and time. He carries an invisible calendar in his mind. His brain organized like a pocketbook day planner. He's nothing if not efficient.

Perfect Four-Year-Old, 1988

Opa and Oma Kandel arrive bringing sacks of *dropjes*—salty black Dutch licorice—a Dutch tradition. The sacks are clear plastic, cone-shaped, and filled with a wide assortment of colorful drop: black licorice strings, thin and swirled into a disk; black logs filled with creamy, light-brown licorice; black licorice pipes; and double-salt coins so strong they make your tongue tingle. Kristina and Joren each get their own sack, tied with a ribbon. I'm thrilled. It's one of the Dutch candies that I've come to love. There's nothing quite like them.

I do my best. Oma mostly sits and smiles. Sometimes she seems puzzled by her environment. She isn't used to England or the English language, but still, she seems a little more lost than what I expected.

Being in the same house with Izaak, even for one day, reminds me how opposite our personalities are. I live outside the proverbial box, while he, on the other hand, lives so deeply inside the box that he doesn't even know he's in it. He can't imagine eating lunch half an hour early or half an hour late. He can't imagine that I might want to stay up till midnight or sleep in. His life's a timetable. As reliable as a Dutch train.

While Johan studies and goes to class, and Oma fills in crossword puzzles, I try to get Opa to play games with squirming Joren and curious Kristina.

I've just purchased a new game. Match-a-Balloon, "A first colour matching game," illustrated by Dick Bruna. It's simple, like a color-coordinated game of bingo. Throw a colored dice, then place a matching colored balloon on the card in front of you. The cards depict rabbits, or children, or a balloon seller, each holding a bouquet of multi-colored balloons. First person to fill the card wins.

Kristina throws the dice and places her color. Followed by Opa, then Joren. So far so good. They continue playing till the cards are nearly full. When Joren throws a color he already has, he rerolls the dice.

"You must only roll once," Opa says.

Joren looks up at him with big eyes.

Opa shakes his head. "No. Your turn is over."

Joren's eyes fill with tears.

"You have already rolled," Opa states.

Joren begins to cry. Kristina's eyes open wide and her chin trembles.

"It's okay, Opa," I say. "He can roll again."

"No," Opa says. "The rules say only one roll."

This is the way he lives his life. Read the rules. Follow the rules. No excuses, no exceptions. The game ends in frustration and tears. And honestly, I'm pretty close to tears myself.

After tea, Opa grabs his big black umbrella and thrusts it overhead.

"*Kom!* Follow me!" he calls to the children. He's the leader of the parade. He struts around the living room, head held high. The children imitate him, grabbing a brush and a comb to hold overhead.

He swaggers. They follow.

The sound of his *traa-laa-laa* echoes through the house as he leads his imaginary big brass band through the hall and out into the kitchen.

Sometimes I see this tiny, tender core. This Izaak that houses a happy man. His grandchildren bring it out. It's like watching a circus, the clown putting on an act in the limelight of the crowd. He puts his cheerfulness on and takes it off like a suit. The problem is, I never know which Izaak I'll find. The clown dancing in the front room or the man who wags his finger.

By the time Johan gets home from school, I'm frustrated to the point of anger.

Johan takes over. He sits and talks with his parents. He plays with Kristina and Joren. I make coffee and serve it with one cookie, just the way Opa likes, at 8:00 p.m. sharp.

They talk for an hour. I clean up and hear Opa state, "Time to go to bed, Jopie." As if her bedtime is based on his decision. As if her bedtime is based upon a clock.

Later, when Johan crawls into bed, he whispers, "Thanks, Jill. I know it's hard."

"I'm doing it for Kristina and Joren," I say. "And for you."

And it's true. I put up with Opa Kandel for them. They adore him. I try to accommodate his quirks and fancies. I pretend I like him. It's exasperating. I chafe against his restrictive rules. I bristle at his ability to make me feel like everything I do is subpar, not quite good enough, lacking in some way or another. My tea isn't brewed properly. The coffee isn't hot. Supper's served late. Or too cold. Everything is too . . . something.

I love that he adores my children. I want them to love him, too. I don't even know where this need comes from. Why is the role of grandfather so important to me?

Johan adores his father. I don't pretend to know what he sees in him.

Each morning that week, I wake up to Kristina and Joren's eager enthusiasm.

"Opa and Oma still here?" They eagerly ask. "We play Opa and Oma!"

Kristina speaks perfect *four-year-old*. She can say something completely intelligible to me, and Opa and Oma don't understand her. Opa's English isn't bad. But Kristina's accent at this point resembles American-British with a Zambian flair. I spend a lot of time simply translating what she says.

Then I hit upon a game that works. It's an old favorite of mine: Button, Button, Who's Got the Button? You can play without words, and there aren't too many rules and regulations. Just three things: button, hide, find.

Opa hides the button in one of the pockets of his suit jacket, while Kristina and Joren cover their eyes.

"You can look!" I say. "Find the button!"

They search my pockets and shoes.

They search Oma's hand and flounce her skirt to see if it is underneath a fold of the fabric. She shakes her head and laughs. Kristina looks around the room and sing-songs, "Button, button. Who's got the button?" She and Joren descend on Opa and search his pockets. They squeal and pull the big red button out of his coat. And the game continues.

It works for a while. But we all wear out. Plain and simple.

All afternoon, Opa tells Joren to put his shoes on. Joren has other plans for those two small items. He pulls them off and fills them with Legos. Or abandons them completely.

Opa says, "Where are your shoes, Joren?"

Joren looks quizzically at Opa, and goes to find his shoes, laughs and points at them, thinking it's a great new game: Hide and Seek the Shoe. He's spent most of his life without shoes, walking in the Kalahari sand, stomping barefooted on cockroaches and ants. I didn't mind.

I worry the shoe game will turn sour. Opa has that look on his face. I try distraction.

"Would you like some tea, Opa?"

I should've known better.

He looks at his watch and shakes his head, "I will have my tea at 4:00. It is not yet 4:00."

Johan comes home each evening to three adults tired of smiling at each other and two toddlers who need to blow off some steam, run and play, dig a hole, or throw some sand up into the air.

When I put the kids to bed each night, Opa and Oma come up and kiss them good night and Kristina says her nighttime prayer.

Now I lay me down to sleep.

I pray the Lord my soul to keep.

And if I die before I wake.

I pray the Lord my soul to take.

I think Opa approves. He lays his hand on her head, as if in blessing, and whispers, "*Welterusten, lieve Kristina.*"

Good night, beloved Kristina.

Black Snow, May 10–14, 1940

Izaak talks one day about something called The Black Snow. It sticks in my mind, and I think of North Dakota and the dirty snow locally called snirt. Or sometimes snoil. I have even heard of sneet and snirty. But never black snow. We do have black ice: that thin invisible ice, coating highways and sending trucks and cars spinning into ditches. But black snow's new to me. I've never heard of it.

I don't remember what brought the topic up. I don't remember many of the details of the conversation. But it had something to do with a recent visit to Rotterdam. Is that what brought the topic up? There are so many things I wish I could remember.

Izaak will later write, "After the early morning invasion of the Netherlands, my family waited in our home in Dort. We waited by the radio to hear some news."

Hitler and his commanders projected that the invasion and total occupation of the Netherlands would take just one day— such a flat country, such a small amount of terrain to cross. Drop in on Friday, May 10. It should all be over by the end of the day.

But the Dutch resistance fighters had other ideas. The assault continued.

On the third day after invasion, fed up with the slow speed of progress, the German Reich threatened to bomb Dutch cities. Knowing what a catastrophic loss of life would occur, the Dutch began negotiations for a ceasefire, but their negotiations didn't come in time.

On May 14, ninety Heinkel bombers flew in tight formation towards the city of Rotterdam. When they arrived, hatches opened. Thousands of bombs dropped on the second largest city in the Netherlands. A completely senseless killing of nearly one thousand ordinary, extraordinary people.

One square mile of the Rotterdam, more or less flattened. Destroyed buildings included 25,000 homes; 62 schools; 24 churches; 2,350 shops; 2,000 factories.

The fires started immediately. Oil tankers on the river burst into flames. People ran. The fires spread. Ashes, pushed up by the heat and carried miles on the wind, fell like snow.

That night eighty-thousand Dutch people slept in Rotterdam under a sky red with fire and no roof over their heads. The city burned for weeks and the ash continued to fall, dark and gritty as sand. Years afterward, when people spoke of the time Rotterdam burned, of the week when the ash fell dirty and black in a sixty-mile radius around the city, they called it the time of The Black Snow.

Dordrecht, where Izaak lived as a child, was only fifteen miles away from Rotterdam. Izaak had most likely walked in various parks in Rotterdam, seen the great old post office, been inside a few of the ancient churches. And within a few hours, whole blocks were simply . . . gone. His classmates, friends, and neighbors lost aunts, uncles, cousins, sons, and daughters.

I think those ashes followed him the rest of his life. Irritated his eyes, blurred his vision, and skewed his sight.

Cracked Lips, 1988

In July, we return briefly to the Netherlands via ferry boat. We walk the deck, and the kids wave at the whitecaps rolling behind the ferry. We play in the Kiddy Korner and in the evening, go to our room. A set of bunkbeds lines each wall, with a small walking space in-between.

I give Kristina and Joren each a small Gouda cheese snack. Kristina pulls off the red waxy wrapper, shapes it into a pyramid, and sticks it onto her nose.

"Look, Mum! I'm a clown!"

Joren follows suit, "Cown!"

As we disembark, Kristina sees a young boy with his hair tied up in a ponytail.

"Mum!" she calls out loudly, "Mum! Look. There's a boy, and he's got a ponytail!"

The people around us turn to look, the boy turns red-faced at the attention, and I tell her, "Yes, honey. I see. Ponytails aren't for girls only."

I enjoy seeing the world through her eyes. Her wonder and surprise.

Izaak has purchased *gebakjes*—small handmade tarts purchased at a local bakery—to celebrate our arrival. The adults have almond-filled creams or apple-topped strudels. Kristina and Joren get tarts decorated with clowns—made with big round bubble gums—on top. The clowns wear polka-dotted triangular hats;

their faces painted with red smiley grins. Late into the afternoon, long after the cupcakes have been eaten, the kids are still chewing their bubble gum clowns.

We've come home to celebrate Jopie's sixty-fifth birthday. Her sisters Cor, Miep, and Nell have all come to the party, too. We gather around a long table at their home. Jopie wears a blue floral dress and a string of white pearls. Her hair, white and cut in a short bob, looks lovely.

Nell has come from the longest distance. She and her husband, Martin, emigrated to New Zealand after the war when the Dutch economy tanked. At that time, many Dutch citizens moved abroad hoping to improve their future prospects. After the war, Jopie saw Nell only two, possibly three, times.

One of those times was when Jopie took a "trip of a lifetime" and traveled by herself to see Nell. No Izaak. Just Jopie visiting her sister. After the visit, while Jopie sat on the long flight home, Izaak—back in the Netherlands—suffered a heart attack. When Jopie arrived, suntanned and full of stories and joy, her children met her at the airport with long faces and grim news. All the discussions about Izaak, about the heart attack, the treatment, the medications, the prognosis.

Izaak recovered just fine, but he'd stolen her show. Her one big, happy show.

And now, after all those years, Nell has returned home to see Jopie and celebrate her birthday with the entire family. Nell has four children, but the children don't know their Dutch aunts and uncles and cousins. Families separated by years and miles and decisions made back in the 1940s.

It's odd that now, in the 1980s, it's all pretty much evened out. Both the Netherlands and New Zealand being on somewhat equal footing economically. In the end, Nell's prospects, whether in New Zealand or in the Netherlands, wouldn't have been that much different. But she and her husband didn't know that. They made their choice, and it affected the entire family.

Today is such a special day for Jopie. Her family sitting together. I see the joy in her eyes as she visits with Nell. I imagine them talking about and remembering her big trip to New Zealand years ago. As I watch them, I also notice that Jopie's eyes dart off to the side, occasionally, as if searching the room, as if imploring, as if she's a little lost.

Even though the day appears smooth and lovely and sweet, underneath it all the questions have begun. The kids and Izaak discuss it quietly whenever Jopie goes upstairs or out into the garden.

"I'm worried about her," Andrea says. "I wonder if it's allergies."

Jopie's lips remain cracked and dry. Her skin grows blotchier. Her thinking foggy. We are baffled as to what's actually taking place. The weeks pass into months. Jopie's skin becomes increasingly problematic, and the fogginess of her memory increases into a constant forgetfulness. Her memory problems become routine, till they are the norm. Saddest of all, her personality begins to change. And this woman, whom I have only known as sweet and kind, starts to raise her voice, starts to yell, and mock those around her with searing scorn.

Dream Job, 1988

Johan finishes up his studies at the University of Reading and graduates with a master's degree in tropical agriculture. The next six months are some of the most discouraging and bizarre in our married life. Job hunting leads us to Germany, where we attend a four-week investigative bootcamp. A German organization called Christoffel-Blindenmission, works with blind farmers all over the world, and Johan loves the sound of it. At the end of the four weeks, we're enthralled. Johan signs the contract. His assignment will be teaching blind farmers in Burkina Faso. The mission purchases our airline tickets, and then, I'm sent in for a routine medical check. The organization had forgotten this step in their procedure.

"It's nothing," they say. "Just routine. Sorry we forgot to do it earlier."

It's not routine for me.

When we go in for results the next day, the doctor says there are problems.

He says my liver is permanently damaged.

He says I have hepatitis C.

He says we'll never be able to live in the tropics again.

I can hardly take in all this information. It's so unexpected. So surreal. What is he talking about?

As we stand up to leave, he adds, "You know, you'll never be able to have any more children."

I leave his office gasping.

We had a job. We were going back to the tropics. I was hopeful for more kids. And now? Now, we're jobless and without a clue.

Johan has a newly-minted degree in tropical agriculture, and we can never work in the tropics again.

We leave Germany, travel back to the Netherlands, and find an old trailer to rent.

I'm a busy mother of a three- and a four-year-old, living in the Netherlands, riding my bike to the grocery store, the market, the bakery. Pedaling the shopping home, cooking, cleaning, doing laundry. I'm run ragged, tired, and sick. But it's not just my body that hurts. I'm heartsick over not being able to have more children. Those lovely newborn days never to come again, the cuddling, the hugs, the bonding. I'll never feel another baby stretching inside my body. Never nurse. It's a dream I'm not ready to give up, and yet I must.

Oma and Opa Kandel come to visit off and on. I serve them tea or coffee according to the time of day. We take walks in the forest sometimes. We sit. We small talk. We smile.

In November, celebrating our eighth wedding anniversary, we travel to Hardenberg, to the church where we were married. The kids stand in front of a historic windmill, marked with a large

1533 date on its side, and pose for pictures. Eight years ago, it was just Johan and me. And now we are four.

November turns into December, and we celebrate Sinterklaas with wooden shoes filled with chocolates and Sinterklaas letters, and then we go to a parade down the main street of Putten. The cold sets in, the months go by. The pipes in the trailer freeze. There are no jobs for us, and we don't have a clue what to do next or where to go. Each day feels heavy and long. We exist in a darkness. Each day as clear as mud.

Johan and I decide our best choice is to move to the United States. We do mountains of paperwork, filing a petition for Johan to obtain an immigrant visa and become a Legal Permanent Resident, the legal term for someone who holds a *green card*. Once the paperwork is all on file, the embassy sets the date for Johan to come in and have an interview. If all goes well, and he's granted residency, we'll have six weeks to arrive in the States. If we don't arrive within that window of time, my understanding is that his application will be cancelled, and we won't be given a second chance.

As we wait for Johan's interview, I don't feel well and go into a hospital for tests. I wonder about the hepatis C diagnosis. Wonder if I have other tropical diseases. It turns out I don't have hepatitis C as the German doctor pronounced. I have a combination of bilharzia and giardia, both picked up in Zambia. These parasites are treated easily enough once they're discovered. I take a few handfuls of pills for a few weeks and banish Zambia from my body.

In the weeks after I finish the medications, my new heathy self begins emerging. Two days before we are scheduled to go to the US Embassy interview, Johan gets a phone call. And then, in one of those quirks of providence, those sweet kisses of fate, he's offered—unexpectedly, unimaginably, out of the blue, blue, blue—an agricultural extension teaching job in Indonesia. It's as if providence has thrown a Hail Mary and landed it right in our arms, when we weren't even looking.

Indonesia!

After months of confusion and despair, we're dazed. We take it as a gift from the universe, a sign from God, and say, "Yes! Yes, we're very interested!"

Johan and I go for the job interview together. He says I have to like the sound of the location and job. He says, "We're in this together. You'll be living there, too. If you aren't happy there, I won't be either."

The job, working with low income coffee farmers in the highlands of Sumatra, sounds dreamy. The location looks like a cinch after Zambia. We're both ecstatic. We say yes, sign the papers, and then call up the U. S. Embassy to postpone our appointment.

It's all happened so fast. So unexpectedly. So perfectly timed. We're astonished and delighted. Indonesia, long a part of the Kandel lore, is about to become a part of our story, too.

Part 4: INDONESIA, 1989–1992

Kristina and Joren Kandel, followed by Jill carrying Benjamin, walking out on a plank to visit fishermen. Takengon, Indonesia. 1990.

Lore

This is what I know about Indonesia.

In 1919, a few years before Izaak was born, his parents, brothers Wes and Piet, and sister, Jo, moved to Indonesia, then known as the Dutch East Indies. The city of Surabaya had a natural harbor and the largest naval base in the Dutch colony. Izaak's father worked there, supervising and overseeing the crew in charge of building the new Surabaya Harbor Project.

Izaak showed us pictures of Father Kandel looking every inch the colonial: a tanned, mustached man wearing a white suit jacket adorned with a pocket watch. He sported white pants, a straw hat, and held a cigarette in hand. The Kandel family lived there, in their island paradise, as part of the Dutch colonial elite for four years.

Izaak was conceived in Indonesia.

When the heat became too much for his mother's health, she and the children returned to the Netherlands. Izaak was born in 1923, a few months after their return home.

Izaak's family looked back on those four years with a homesickness and enthusiasm that he wasn't part of. At bedtime when Izaak's father said goodnight to his children, he used the Dutch word, *welterusten*: rest well. He followed with the Indonesian words: *Selamat tidur*: sleep well. To Izaak's young Dutch ears, *sela-mat-ti-dur* sounded like the Dutch words *sla met die deur*, which translates as *slam the door*. As a child, Izaak knew slamming doors was prohibited in his home and made his father unhappy. Whatever could these words mean?

Each evening, Izaak's brothers and sister smiled and repeated the words back to Father Kandel. "Welterusten. Selamat tidur, Pa." Indonesian and Dutch words mixed together at bedtime like dreams from another land.

Years later, Izaak's oldest brother, Wes, returned to Indonesia. As a sailor in the Royal Dutch Marines, he sailed the waters of the Java Sea during WWII. Those turquoise waves, the last thing he set his eyes upon as his ship, hit by a torpedo, floundered beneath the sea.

I don't know much else about the story. I've seen Wes's photo. I know he died in the war. This is also a part of the Kandel family lore of Indonesia.

And now, in one of those oddities, those quirks of fate and history, Johan and I are headed to Indonesia. We'll eat the same foods, learn the same language, play in the same waters. In years to come, I'll send my children off to bed with the words that Iza-ak's father used over ninety years ago.

"Welterusten, Kristina and Joren. Selamat tidur." Goodnight. Sleep well.

And Johan will chime in with a grin, "Night, night. Slam the door."

Eden, 1989

On February 18, 1989, Johan, Kristina, Joren, and I board Singapore Airlines and fly out of the Netherlands on our way to Yogyakarta, Indonesia. We live with an Indonesian family at a local homestay and take six weeks of Indonesian language classes at the University of Yogyakarta. In all of the pictures, the kids' bangs are plastered to their foreheads, wet with sweat from the heat and humidity. The change from February in the Netherlands to February in Indonesia is acute.

We have classes four or five hours a day and practice our new Bahasa Indonesia words as we eat with our hosts and as they take us to visit local sights. My favorite is our tour of a local batik factory. We watch women hand-painting hot wax onto cotton and silk cloth. After waxing, the cloth is dyed, then rewaxed, and redyed multiple times. It's a long and artful process that produces swirls and florals distinctively Indonesian.

I expected Indonesia to be more like Zambia, and I am blown away by the healthy babies, the quantities of food, vegetables of every variety and sort. Fruits displayed in bamboo baskets, on batik cloth, and in large colorful plastic pails overflow and spill out of the stalls in vibrant abundance.

There are dozens of fruits I've never seen before and can't name. I walk through market stalls heaped with brown-colored pears covered in lizard-like scaly skin, red fruits with the texture of rubber that sport black, waxy hair spiking out in all directions. I see piles of tan oblong fruit—the size of soccer balls—thorns decorating their thick skin. The most beautiful fruit is hot pink with lime green wings. I can't imagine what it must look like inside.

In the years to come, I'll grow to learn the names of these fruits—*salak, rambutan, mangosteen, sirsak*—and love eating them. I'll learn how to choose them, telling the unripe from the ripe from the overripe. I'll learn to skin them, open them, and juice them. We'll learn which fruits we like—almost all—and which ones we cannot stomach, decidedly and most especially *durian*. But for now, before this knowledge is born, these Indonesian fruits are mystery and expectation. Indonesia has begun to tutor me in the school of my senses. Something I pushed aside and hid from during the harsh years of living in Kalabo. I'm inundated with beautiful smells, colors, tastes, and textures.

I practice my Indonesian from dawn to dusk. At supper, I try to say, "I have a cold" (literally, I have a wind in me). I mix up two words *angin* and *anjing*. I've actually said, "I have a dog in me." Not what I meant!

Our host laughs and shakes her head. "*Baik. Baik,*" she encourages. Good, good.

"*Coba lagi.*" Try again.

After only six weeks, I'd gotten a solid start, more language than I ever acquired in Zambia. I open my heart and arms in the gentle warmth and abundant beauty around me. I feel my life start over, fresh and wild and free.

It feels as if I've moved to an ancient and mystical location, a place I dreamed of before I came into existence. A place called Eden.

Elephant Village, 1989

After Indonesian language school, we fly from the island of Java to the island of Sumatra. It's a four-hour drive, up a narrow logging road, from the airport to our new home. We drive the steep, muddy road, leaving the humid coast behind us, going higher into the cool volcanic mountain range. The village we live in, Pondok Gajah, translates to The Elephant Village. It lies high in the mountains, surrounded by coffee fields, among the Gayo people.

The project Johan works for provides us with a home. Large knobby brown trees, their bark splotched with white and tan, grow on each side of the lane leading to our new house. "This tree is *kayu manis*," our driver states. "Sweet wood. In English, it is called the cinnamon tree."

There's no six months' wait to move into our home like we had in Kalabo. The house is ready: clean with high ceilings, cool tile flooring, lovely bamboo furniture, and large picture windows. I step out onto the open veranda and overlook a backyard lush with banana, lime, and guava trees growing alongside hot pink bougainvillea and huge poinsettias. The front side of the house overlooks coffee fields, and further down the road I can see the coffee factory.

We settle in while Johan acclimates to his new work. He's teaching extension staff, visiting coffee farmers, traveling to remote villages, setting up coffee seedling cooperatives. He's promoting a new coffee variety, Catimor, which has the potential to increase coffee production for these small farms. He wants to help the farmers become certified organic.

The temperatures are perfect, in the high seventies and low eighties every day, all year long. I'm not sweating like I did so much of the time in Zambia. I'm not shivering like half of the year in North Dakota. How can such a perfect climate exist? I hardly ever need a sweater or a fan. My body was made to live here, unashamed, relaxed, at ease with the world around me.

We meet our neighbors, and in the afternoon the kids play in the red-berried and white-flowered coffee field across the road with their new friend, Mathijs. In no time at all, they're a three-some. They rollerskate down the wide black lane leading up to our home and when they're hungry, they stop and pull a piece of cinnamon bark off a tree and chew the sweet spicy wood. Mathijs teaches them to pluck the red coffee cherries, chewy, juicy, and sweet.

We swim in the cement pool next door, fed by a cold-water mountain spring. We collect wild orchids, wash our hair in the warm monsoon rain that pours off our roof, and buy a small golden puppy. Once a week we drive the narrow winding road to Takengon, through bustling small villages, passing chickens and goats and children playing beside piles of drying coffee beans. Heaps of coffee beans—tan and shriveled and thrown to sun-dry atop burlap sacks—line the road on both sides. Small stands dot the roadside, women selling the tiniest wild bananas I have ever seen. We stop and buy a bunch.

"These bananas have seeds!" Kristina says. She's right, perfectly round black seeds dot the insides. We're eating original stock of what I only knew as Chiquita. They're called *pisang ayam,* chicken bananas, since a bunch of them is similar in shape to a chicken's foot. I'm told there are hundreds of varieties in Indonesia alone, a thousand varieties around the world.

Pisang Ambon, Pisang Raja, Pisang Mas.

I never knew that so many types of bananas existed.

We go to the market and wander through exotic sights and sounds. Indonesian words flow off my tongue. I can talk to these women! I can haggle prices, answer questions, ask for information.

Apa kabar? How are you?

Namanya adalah Kristina. Her name is Kristina.

Dia empat tahun. He is four years old.

I feel like a real live human being. I can talk! It's far from perfect, but I don't care. I know how to laugh at myself. I know how to smile and start over when I get a word wrong. We fill our baskets full of fruit and veggies, snacks, cakes, and tea. I lack nothing. Simply going shopping becomes a delightful part of our week.

We begin to think about what schools Kristina and Joren might attend. They speak Dutch and Indonesian to our neighbors and English at home. We want them to have a real mother tongue, English. We don't want to send them abroad to a boarding school. Homeschool it is.

I order curriculum from Calvert School—commonly used by embassy employees—and a month later, two boxes arrive in the mail marked *Kristina Kandel* and *Joren Kandel*.

"You have mail!" I call out to the kids, and they come running.

Opening the boxes, they find books, paper, notebooks, crayons, markers, and yellow pencils with the name Calvert etched in golden letters on each one. Their school days are planned and organized. Art, history, alphabet, reading, math. They each have their own correspondence teacher who'll work via mail with them throughout the coming year.

As part of their English lessons, I ask Kristina and Joren to write or dictate a letter every week to Oma and Opa Kandel, and to Oma and Opa Jensen. In the years to come, this will be our major form of communication. No internet. No phone.

The letters are simple and sweet.

I saw a big blue bug!

We had a wild boar in our house!

I rode an elephant!

We climbed up a volcano!

The kids love their exclamation points. And all of life, indeed, seems to be one glorious exclamation point after another.

A Taste of Indonesia

My neighbor, Mai, wants to learn American cooking, and I want to learn Indonesian. We begin to cook together. Mai has sleek black hair, long and luxurious; she likes to pull it back in a low tail at the nape of her neck. She has perfectly arched eyebrows, honey-brown skin, and slender wrists. She's tall for an Indonesian; still, I'm taller than she is. Mai teaches me the words I need for cooking.

To steam food: *mengukus*. The aroma of food: *bau harum*. To fry: *goreng*.

I buy a cheap notebook and slowly fill it with recipes: curried chicken, steamed coconut cookies, rice cakes with palm sugar syrup, hot spicy shrimp. I write one side of the book in Indonesian, the facing page in English.

As Mai teaches me, we mix our English and Indonesian. We find our own multi-lingual cooking language.

Kepulaga, cardamom. *Cengkeh*, cloves. Kayu Manis, cinnamon.

I've never heard of many things used in Indonesian cooking and sometimes we get stuck. How can I ever translate *lopis*? What English word exists? Sticky rice, flavored with coconut and brown sugar, wrapped in a *pandan* leaf, to make a triangular packet that is steamed. Mai teaches me things that don't translate but become a part of my life. I'll never forget the feel of her cookies shaping beneath my hands, the aroma of them as they bake. Their taste still lingers on my tongue.

Mai was my first and dearest Indonesian friend. She welcomed me into her home and heart. We cried together when she miscarried. We laughed in shared joy when, years later, her son was born. And years after we left Indonesia, when Mai's home in Banda Aceh was inundated by the terrible 2004 tsunami, when she and her husband and their son all lost their lives, a part of me perished, too. But this one thing remains. From an Indonesia saturated with happy memories and loveliness, this is my sweetest memory of all: I had a friend.

Envelopes, 1990

Johan and I purchase a computer. We can't go online, but the kids use it to learn typing skills. They write weekly letters containing a few sentences and a couple of very large photos. Enough to fill one page. They print out two identical letters, one for each set of grandparents, then decorate and sign them before we mail them off.

Unlike Zambia, the mail service is regular. Letters arrive from sisters, brothers, friends, and always a letter from Opa Kandel each week. As regular as clockwork.

One day we get a letter addressed to Johan that looks unusual. It's square and white, and charcoal gray lines of various widths border the envelope, all the way around. I wonder if it's a kind of honor or prize.

"Hey, Johan," I call out, "Look at this. It's kind of pretty, has a decorated envelope."

He comes, and I hand him the letter.

"Don't you know what this is?" he asks me. "In the Netherlands, envelopes with black or gray borders contain death announcements."

"You're kidding."

"I suppose it's sort of like a warning," he says. "So you know before you open it that it's not good news."

I feel so stupid. I thought it was some sort of special award. *Surprise! You've been awarded . . . death.* Not at all what I'd expected.

Johan sits down to read his mail. He takes the envelope of dying, slits it open with his knife edge, and reads.

"It's an old friend," he says. "Someone I used to know in Zambia. You wouldn't know him."

Odd, those Dutch people, that treat death like a holiday. Send it out like a birth announcement. The black-inked envelope for all the world to see, like a frame around a picture. Finished. Ready to hang upon the wall.

How the mind flits from celebration to finality before the eye can blink, and the tiniest drop of knowing can change a thing completely. How just when I think I've gotten this cross-cultural game figured out; I'm reminded again that there's always some new misunderstanding on the horizon. Always.

Decades later, a similar envelope—solemn and gray bordered—will arrive at our home in the United States. Inside, the name of the deceased written in italic: *Izaäk Kandel.* Reading it, I'm surprised at the umlaut above the a, uncommon in Dutch, more something you see in German or Hungarian names.

When I ask Andrea, she says, "I don't really know. Sometimes he'd write his name that way, on official papers. It was kind of like his legal name."

Izaäk Kandel.

I didn't even know how to spell his name correctly, not until after he had died, not until his formal death announcement came, all black and white and framed in gray.

The Dream, January 11, 1942

We send letters back and forth, and I think about you, Izaak. I think about the story you often told us, set here in Indonesia, back in WWII, back in 1942. Your brother Wes had been in the naval service for a couple of years. No word from him, no news of anything. A sailor off at war; military secrets the norm.

And then one night your mother woke up screaming in her sleep, "Wes! Wes! My God! No! Wes!"

Your father woke up.

"I saw him!" she gasped, breathing fast, tears falling down her face. "Wes drowned. I saw the ship sink with all the crew. Wes drowned."

"It was only a dream," your father said.

"I saw him. He came to me."

No one could talk her out of it. Not the next day. Not the next month. Not the next year. In your mother's mind, Wes died, his ship sinking beneath the waves, and him coming to her in the dark of night, in her dream, to say goodbye.

The war lasted three more years. I wonder, during that time, Izaak, if you believed your mother's dream was true. You never said.

Your mother believed.

Your father didn't.

Time would tell which one of them was correct. Three more years, to be exact. Three more years until you hear about his ship, The *Prins van Oranje,* sailing in the Java Sea. Just off of Surabaya Harbor. Throughout those years, your mother's dream, her continual story remained the same. She told it to everyone who would listen.

"Wes drowned. I saw his ship go down. He came to me in a dream."

Over and over again she repeated her story.

Did you think she was delusional, Izaak? Did the story bother you? Did you get tired of hearing it and walk out of the room?

"Oh, Ma. Not that story again."

Although you told me the story of your mother's dream a dozen times, you never told me your own thoughts. Your own beliefs. It seemed you just needed to tell that story. I sometimes wonder why. Why the story of the dream was the one (of all the war stories) that you retold most often. Looking back, I see you hide behind your stories—like the great Oz behind his curtain—and I regret that I never pulled the cloth away to look at the real you.

Perhaps, you were afraid.

Perhaps, I was too.

Benjamin, 1990

I can feel it in my body. Two years of good food, a pleasant climate, and little stress. I'm healthy. I'm also—happily, exuberantly, unexpectedly—pregnant.

I visit the local women's clinic. The male Muslim doctor refuses to touch me, even to take my blood pressure, which he directs a nurse to do. I don't think a delivery here is my best option. I'll go home to Valley City, with Kristina and Joren, six weeks before I'm due.

In April of 1990, Kristina, Joren, and I board Malaysian Airlines and fly home to North Dakota. Each of the kids has their own small backpack filled with toys, books, and colored pencils. I pack a few surprises to hand out to them when they're crabby and worn out. They stroll through airports, board planes, color on fold-down trays, and talk to stewardesses who give them plastic gold pins shaped like airline wings. We arrive in Fargo thirty-six hours later. The kids are bedraggled, tired, and happy. They each have three sets of plastic airline wings pinned onto their zip-up sweatshirts.

Johan joins us the first week of May and is welcomed by an unexpected snowstorm. The kids build snowmen while I wait impatiently. The following week—seven days past his due date—our son is born. He weighs in at exactly seven pounds. My biggest baby so far. He's got long and lanky limbs and a head of black hair. He smiles at me, one eye closed, as if winking his way into the world. As if he has a joke to tell. We name him Benjamin.

While we're getting used to Benjamin, Johan makes a trip to North Dakota State University. He's looking into potential agricultural job openings around North Dakota. Opa and Oma Jensen are eager for us to return to the States. We've been living overseas for almost ten years. They really want their grandchildren to live nearby.

Johan comes back from NDSU with an interesting idea.

"The dean asked me if I'd like to come and pursue my PhD, and I met a professor who said he'd love to work with me. He asked me to think about coming to do the program."

I'm astonished. I've never considered Johan doing his doctorate, but it's not unreasonable. We put it on the back burner, something to think about in the years ahead.

Mi Amour, 1990

We stay three glorious weeks in North Dakota. The kids play swimsuit-clad in the cold-water creek at Little Yellowstone. We picnic at Chautauqua Park, fish in the Sheyenne River, swim at Bald Hill Dam. One afternoon, I get an unexpected phone call from the family who purchased my old Appaloosa mare, Mia. Would I like to come out and see her?

She must be twenty-some-years old now. I can hardly believe she's still alive. I take the kids out to the farm, stand by the fence line, and call her, "Mia! Mi Amour!" I don't know if she comes because she recognizes my voice or because I'm shaking an oat can. But she comes.

Joren and Kristina sit on her bareback while I lead them around. She's whiter, but still covered in tiny copper speckles. Her eyes are bright; her back a little swayed. I remember her pink-splotched muzzle. I remember her lazy bottom lip, hanging a little loose, and joggling when she shakes her head. She's lively and beautiful and I can't believe that I'm standing here, a mother of three children, stroking her soft ears once more. Feeling her warm breath against my hand. Tears fill my eyes and I lean over and place my head against her neck, breathing in the smell of her.

I'm thirty-five years old. I'm sixteen years old. How can I be both at the same time? There are parts of our lives that live within. That never leave. That are at home with us no matter where we live or how old we become. I'll always have that sixteen-year-old inside of my body, my memory, my mind. The feel of Mia's muzzle softly etched onto the skin of my palm.

Going, Going, Gone, 1990

We fly back to Indonesia via the Netherlands, spending a week with Opa and Oma in Putten. We rent a cabin at the Heihaas and go to Opa and Oma's house every day to visit. Tea or coffee. Sometimes lunch or supper. Bert visits with his two children, and it is fun to see Opa and Oma with all of their grandchildren together. Bert's daughter and son joining my three. The cousins get on just fine. Playground slides and climbing bars, fun enough for all.

Jopie's gained weight and has open raw sores on her nose. Most of the time she doesn't wear her glasses. They irritate her skin. Her face is red. Her eyes roam the room in confusion, then fall on Ben. She reaches out to hold him, takes him in her arms, and smiles so sweetly it makes me want to cry.

When she isn't holding Ben, Jopie sits in the corner with a newspaper or magazine on her lap. She scribbles at crossword puzzles. Trying to fill them in. Struggling over them. She hardly talks, lost in her own world.

When Ben cries, Jopie looks up from her magazine, searching the room for the location of his cry. She holds out her arms once again, takes him gently, and smiles down at his tiny face, the fluff of his black hair sticking out of a blue flannel blanket.

She's seeing doctors. Trying supplements. The family doesn't have a diagnosis. But words like dementia and Alzheimer's float just below the surface. I wonder where she goes in her mind. What is she remembering or thinking about as she loses her connections with the world? I don't know. I only see her retreating into herself, going silent. Going, going, gone.

Virtuoso, 1990

I sit in the Netherlands and watch you, Izaak. After we have tea, you often put some classical music on. How you love to sit in your wingback chair with your eyes closed, Bach or Mozart playing on your record player. Your hands outstretched, beating to the time of the music.

You hold an invisible baton and wave it up and down, side to side, like a conductor directing an orchestra, making the motions over and over, as we sit in the room, as we quietly watch you, sitting with your eyes shut, your arms moving.

I don't understand this family ritual, with you at its center and Jopie on the wings. There are parts of the Kandel family do-ings that baffle me. From my point of view, it feels like a presentation. A manufactured show.

What do you think about as you conduct? Up on your stage. Directing your show. In front of the pulpit. In front of your family. Are you lost in the love of music? Are you resting in the joy of the elegant sounds? Maybe it is here, in the middle of the melody, that you allow yourself to simply rest.

I dislike watching you. Your virtuoso on display. The way the family goes silent, sitting around the circle of the room, watching your movements, not wanting to interrupt or disturb. Your self-satisfied smile.

Perhaps you're just enjoying the moment. I don't know. It's one of those baffling family happenings accepted, normal, just the way it is. Something Johan grew up with and never thought about. Pa conducting the music. A one man show.

I turn away, gazing out the large picture window. I'm tired of these Kandel traditions that I neither understand nor enjoy. Tired of watching Izaak.

She Knew, 1946

There's a picture on the wall of Izaak's brother Wes. A large black-and-white of a handsome smiling sailor. Kristina loves the picture and asks for a copy of it. She asks about Wes, and Opa tells her the story of the dream, and of Wes's ship.

Mother Kandel's dream hung like an unsolved mystery over Izaak's home. A nightmare they couldn't wake up from, ongoing, even as the war ended. Even as 1945 turned into 1946. Still no official word on Wes. They would learn the fate of sister Cor long before they knew of Wes.

And then, in 1946, a shipmate turned up at the Kandel door, trembling and pale. He said he'd taken it upon himself to go to every family of every sailor on his ship. To tell them the story of what had happened to their sons, their husbands, their brothers.

He said a family deserved to know. Especially a mother. Especially a widow.

Wes's shipmate told the story of their ship, the *Prins van Oranje*, giving all the details.

I think you might have expected it, Izaak. A year since the war was over is a long time with no word. But still, hearing it, that's another thing. Your big brother Wes wasn't coming home. No more hope. The news was final.

After the sailor told his story, after all the words were out, your mother told him about her dream. Counting backwards, they determined that Wes died on the same night that your mother had that dream. Wes indeed had come to her to say goodbye.

Did you grieve that day, or was your grieving already done? Had you known along with your mom or scoffed at her sureness? Either way, you'll tell this story for the rest of your life. It will become the story of your mother's dream, even more than the story of Wes. You will say, "There is a special connection between a mother and her son that cannot be explained. There are bonds that defy understanding and communication that goes deeper than what we can see."

You'll refer to this dream repeatedly, tell it in sureness. Emphasizing faith: your mother *knew*. You'll tell it to the next generation and the next, you'll tell it to me, your daughter-in-law. Some of the facts you tell me about the ship prove wrong, the number of survivors, the number of sailors. But still. You'll throw this dream down like a gauntlet, cling to it like a religious relic.

I don't know what it is you're trying to say.

You tell me the story with triumph in your voice. *She knew!* That's always the ending. *Mother knew.* Not Wes. Not his death or burial at sea. Not the fact that you never saw your brother again.

Why of all the war stories that you could tell, is this the one you cling to?

And why is your mother the hero of the story, not Wes?

She knew.

Two Drops of Water

The whole Kandel clan goes for a walk in the forest today—a proverbial Dutch pastime that bores me to tears—and I glance at Johan. His facial gestures look so much like Izaak, that I have to look away. He is his father incarnate. Same hairline, Romanesque nose, sloping forehead, and slightly dimpled chin. They hold themselves with a similar posture. They walk with their hands clasped behind their backs. When he's happy, Johan does the same funny goose-step dance that his father does. It makes me cringe. Their profiles and synchronized expressions.

In the Netherlands, there's a common saying, *als twee druppels water,* which means, *like two drops of water.* A sea-faring nation's version of *two peas in a pod.* I've always liked the saying. And, in Johan and his father's case, it's beyond true.

I know exactly what Johan will look like when he is in his seventies. I've never wondered. Take a look at Izaak and you see his son. They could be twins.

As we spend time in the Netherlands, Johan begins to revert back to what I call his Kandel Behavior. It's nothing specific that I can put my finger on. It's just that everything becomes a little more black and white. He frowns quicker. He smiles less. His shoulders tense. Although Johan doesn't notice these subtle changes in his behaviors and stances, I do. He's easier to get along with when we're living in another country. When we find a neutral zone. No previous occupation.

I'm ready to leave. To make my own life, away from his frowning father. I'm exhausted by the furrows and frustrations of living within the strictures of Izaak's world. It embarrasses me that I feel no love for him. I'm mortified and shamed. He rubs me like a jinn. His own private genie in a lamp. Come out and obey. Come, agree with me. Come, do as I say.

I'm tired of the lamp. Tired of being rubbed the wrong way. Tired of the Netherlands.

I'm tired of myself.

Get-to-Know-the-Kandel-Family, 1990

Once we're back home in Indonesia, in an effort to be mag-nanimous—an attitude I seriously dislike but feel driven to—I begin to ask Johan questions about his family. After a couple of evenings of this get-to-know-the-Kandel-family exercise, he wonders what's up.

"Why all the questions?" he asks.

"It's for the kids," I say. I'm not really telling the truth. But I'm not really lying either. "I want them to know more about their Dutch heritage."

Johan, it turns out, isn't much of a resource. I've never met anyone who has so few family memories.

"What was your mom like?" I ask him.

"Oh, you know. She was mom. Nice. I don't know."

"Did you go on vacation as a family?"

"We went to Austria and hiked in the Alps. I loved it."

"Did your mom like it?"

"I don't know. She never said."

"Did she hike?"

"She hiked some, but mostly we went because Pa chose it. We traveled to the same town every year and we rented the exact same cabin. It was great!"

"Tell me something about her."

"I don't know. She always had a snack ready when we came home from school."

"But what did she like to do? Did she have close friends? Hobbies?"

"I don't know," Johan says clearly frustrated. "Ask my sister."

I try to pay more attention to the letters Opa sends us each week. I slog through Izaak's Dutch or wait for Johan to read them out loud in the evening, translating them for the kids. It's all I can do to stay awake. It's like reading a calendar of events. My mind wanders after a few sentences, bored to death.

I try a new tactic. I ask Kristina if she'd like to learn more about Opa. Maybe she could ask him a few questions about his childhood when she writes to him.

Kristina says that would be fun. In her next letter, she asks Opa about his childhood. Izaak replies that he'll write a small family history—the story of his life—for her. I'm delighted and hopeful.

The first installment comes to Kristina by mail. The envelope's much bigger than the normal aerograms he sends. There must be at least five pages included. We tear it open with anticipation and find several pages of typing on thin blue airmail paper. Izaak writes in Dutch.

Izaak's story begins with these words: *During the First World War (1914-1918), the Netherlands was able to remain neutral and therefore provided refuge to hundreds of thousands of Belgium citizens who fled because they were at war. After the war, the Dutch Government decided to strengthen their military capabilities in the East Indies (in contrast to the West Indies which was also a Dutch colony).*

Izaak's writing to his granddaughter. She's seven years old. He sounds like a textbook. Much of the information goes over Kristina's head. It's difficult to translate into English. I'm most likely butchering the words, but I get the gist of them. When Kristina's interest lags, I stop reading. Later in the evening, Johan reads the rest of the pages to us. I'm disappointed, but Kristina doesn't seem to be. With childish enthusiasm she picks out things to comment on and writes back asking Izaak a few questions.

Johan translates all of the pages into English while I type. The installments come, month by month and give me a grasp of the timeline running through Izaak's life, but his words feel lifeless. Johan continues to translate week after week; I type and print and file.

When we leave Indonesia, I'll pack all these papers and documents and stories and bring them to our new home, where I put them on a shelf in the back of the closet. In the busyness of life with children, I forget they even exist.

Decades later, when I'm tired of my anger, beaten down by Izaak's strangulating control, done in by his choices, I'll stumble across these papers and marvel that they exist. Later, these pages will become the scaffolding I need in my search to understand Izaak's complex personality and our surly relationship.

Missing, 1991

I'm trying, unsuccessfully, to teach Kristina how to write her birthdate, in both the Dutch and in the America tradition. A confusing cross-cultural hiccup I'm well aware of. I tell her the story of the day Johan and I bought our wedding rings and had them engraved. The compromise we made over the writing of the date. I repeat the information. Over and Over.

"In America, we say the month, then day, then year, For example, April 1, 1990. We write it out as 04/01/1990." She nods her head.

"The Dutch write the day first, then the month, followed by the year. For example, 1 April 1990. They write it 01/04/1990."

I think she's got it, but the next day she says, "I forget. Is this the Dutch or American way?" She's frustrated with it and wants to know why it matters. I try to explain, but I've never gotten used to writing Dutch dates. I make mistakes all the time. Even commas are used differently.

Ten thousand in English is 10,000. Ten thousand in Dutch is 10.000.

Living between two cultures: mistakes, misinterpretations, misinformation. Add in another culture. I'm trying to teach my American daughter about Dutch culture, customs, and language while living immersed in Indonesian culture. Most days it's all good. Most days it's a wondrous riot that I love partaking in, freeing and exhilarating. It's also exhausting. Sometimes, I'm just plain tired. Sometimes, it's all one big frustration after another and I feel like everything I do is culturally suspect. What am I going to get completely wrong? Who am I going to inadvertently insult or offend the next time I open my mouth?

Mispronounce. Misquote. Misread.

I miss hot dogs and ketchup and popcorn.

Misfire. Mystified. Misfit.

Miss, miss, miss.

Jam Karet, 1992

After three fantastic years in Indonesia, Johan decides to take NDSU up on their offer. He will pursue his doctorate. We reapply for Johan's visa, do the paperwork for his legal permanent resident status, and wait for his papers. We'll be moving to North Dakota's largest city: Fargo.

Because the airlines consider Benjamin an infant up until the age of two, we decide to finish up Johan's contract two months before Ben's birthday. We'll take an extended vacation in Malaysia before returning home.

We pack up our household and fly to Penang, Malaysia. Kristina celebrates her eighth birthday while we hike the Lambir Hills National Park, Ben in a backpack. We fly to the city of Kota Kinabalu and boat out to Manukan Island, the jewel in Malaysia's first Marine National Park. We spend a couple of days and nights there, on the edge of the deeply blue South China Sea; the kids hardly get out of their swimsuits. They eat noodle dishes easily with chopsticks, play in the fine soft sand, and find a spectacular lionfish tangled in the seaweed.

I've always wanted to see an orangutan in the wild, so on Johan's birthday, we fly to Sepilok Orangutan Sanctuary. It's only a short hop over, but the small plane brings us to a different world. My glasses fog as I step off the airplane. It must be near 100 degrees with a humidity pretty darn near 100 percent, too.

"Orangutan in the Malay language means *Person of the Forest*," our guide says. "Here at the sanctuary, we teach two things: survival skills and freedom. Our goal is to return these orangutans to the wild. Please do not touch the animals."

We watch baby orangutans learning to climb ropes and navigate a playground made of twines and trees. They swing and fall. The staff pick them up, placing the little orangutan hands on their jungle gym ropes, showing them how to hold on.

A young orangutan sidles its way up onto the boardwalk, saunters over, and grabs Joren's leg. Joren pats its head. The young orangutan's orange spikey hair sticks up into the air like a "Mohawk" haircut, accentuating its large, black eyes. It looks like an old man with wrinkled and weathered skin. The young orangutan stands there, hugging Joren's legs. I wonder if I should be nervous, or amused. Before I can decide, he lets go, ambles off the boardwalk, and disappears in the trees.

An hour later, hot and dripping with sweat, I set my water bottle down to adjust my camera. And just like that an adult orangutan grabs the bottle.

"Hey," I yell. "That's my water." As if yelling would do any good. The kids laugh at me and point to the orangutan. He scampers just out of reach, climbs a platform, and sits with my bottle in one of his hands. He grabs a stick and pushes it into the bottle, pushing it up and down. Taking it out and licking it.

I get out some crayons and paper, and the kids sit for a while and draw what they are seeing. They make birthday cards for their dad. By the end of the day we're drenched in sweat, tired and crabby. It's the best crabby I've ever been in my life. A day I'll never forget.

As we drive to the airport, I blow a kiss to Malaysia and to our wonderful three years in Indonesia. How good these years have been. I'm so grateful. I've seen and lived in the most wonderful of countries. I've learned a new language and a culture and lived with a people who will always be a part of my life. There are tears in my eyes as we board Malaysia Airlines, flying from Kuala Lumpur to Dubai. Dubai to Frankfurt. Frankfurt to Amsterdam.

ına and Joren board the plane with joy. They're world-
, kids who've navigated airports from Nairobi to Jakarta
ᵤ on with ease and curiosity. They settle in for the ride, the
food, the coloring books, the airline pins.

As the plane nears Schiphol Airport in the Netherlands, I remind the kids about how Dutch people think about time. "In the
Netherlands, the trains run on time," I say. "*On time.* If a train's
five seconds late, the people on the platform will be looking at
their watches and fussing about it."

"That's funny, Mom," Kristina says.

"Well, funny or not, your Opa's a stickler for time. If you can
remember that it'll help our visit with him be more enjoyable."

I think about the vast experiences my children have had. The
past three years they've lived with the Indonesian concept called
jam karet: elastic time.

In Indonesian we said, "I'll meet you at 4:00 jam karet,"
meaning anywhere between 3:00 and 6:00. People were seriously
relaxed about time. They put a great deal of emphasis on personal
relationships. If I walked past the market and saw Ibu Mai, I was
obligated to stop and acknowledge our friendship and engage in
conversation. It'd be rude in the extreme to say, "Sorry, it's 4:00,
I've to go now. I'm meeting someone else." Such disrespect was
unacceptable. No. You stood and talked and meandered and ram-
bled until each person was satisfied. Friendship solidified. And
then you moved on.

In many ways, our life for the last three years had been jam
karet, go with the flow, I'll come eventually. This lifestyle fit my
personality. And I liked it. I wonder about all the changes we're
about to face. For better or for worse, we're returning back home.
Back to my home anyway. Back to the USA.

As the plane touches down, I remind myself that Kristina and
Opa have been corresponding for about three years and I've been
working on my *I'll do better next time* mantra. I've gained some

background information on Opa's life. I hope and pray we'll do better this time. We're only there for a short while.

How hard can it be?

Warm Meals and Half-Before, 1992

We arrive in the Netherlands to the regular pecks and kisses. It's chilly March weather: gray, damp, and rainy. I miss Indonesia already.

We rent a cabin a few miles from Opa and Oma in Putten. "It'll give us some space," Johan says. "And I want to show you and the kids more of the Netherlands."

"Are you planning to make little Dutch kids out of them?" I ask playfully.

"Absolutely," he says. "The Dutch are brilliant, you know. They've created the Netherlands out of the sea!"

"If they're so brilliant, why did you have to go to America to find a wife?" I ask.

"I guess I just needed *you*," he says.

"Now, that's a great answer," I reply.

Today, we're going uptown to shop at the market and bring some groceries home. Then we're going over to Opa and Oma's for supper. Opa asked us to be there at 5:30.

That sounds simple enough. But life in different countries is often perplexing. Most often, it's the little things that trip you up.

If someone wants to meet at 9:30 in America, they say *nine-thirty* or *half-past nine*.

In the Netherlands, people don't say half-past nine. They say half-before ten. When this is said, without even thinking, my brain automatically fills in half-past, not half-before.

If I arrive at half-past, I'm an hour late.

"Your dad said to come at half-six," I say to Johan. "Is that half-before or half-after? 5:30 or 6:30? Good grief. I'm all mixed up again."

I've asked Johan so many times, that I've got him double guessing himself, too. He thinks about it a minute. "Half-six is half-before. That means 5:30." Johan replies, "Come on kids. We don't want to be late. We need to leave now in order to bike over to Opa's house and be on time."

"We're coming," they yell back, pulling on their rubber boots, putting on scarves and coats and gloves and all that cold weather clothing they've hardly ever needed before. All of this getting dressed to go outside proves new and awkward. And time consuming.

"I can't find my hat," Kristina says.

"On the chair," I yell over my shoulder, zipping up Ben's coat.

I hate having to shush and hurry the kids. "Time to go," I say, thinking fondly of Indonesia and *jam karet*. No elasticity here.

We march out the door underneath Johan's steady gaze. I can tell he's counting the minutes. We grab our bikes and pedal fast.

We arrive, and the strangest thing happens. Opa sets the table. He serves a typical supper meal of meat and potatoes and green beans. He's doing most of the cooking now. It's beyond Oma's ability. Izaak serves himself and Oma. Then, he gets out cold cheese sandwiches and sets them on the table for us.

He bows his head to pray and looks up smiling, "Eet smakelijk."

I look at Johan for cues. Is Izaak annoyed at us? Did we do something wrong? Why are we eating cold sandwiches and they are having a hot supper meal?

Johan carries on as if all is normal. I'm so confused. Did his dad treat him this way for punishment? Is it some form of passive-aggressive displeasure?

Later, as we bike back to our rental, I ask Johan, "What was going on over there?"

"What do you mean?" he asks.

"Why did we get sandwiches while your folks ate a full meal?"

"They were having their *warme maaltijd*, their warm meal," he answers. As if it should be as plain as day.

"I don't get it. Is he mad at us?" I ask.

"Jill, in the Netherlands, we only eat one warm meal a day. Pa knew we were out this morning and had warme maaltijd at a restaurant earlier for lunch, so he made us sandwiches."

I can't believe it! I can't imagine my mother serving different meals to different guests. And I'm not only offended; I'm hungry. Sitting with a cold cheese sandwich while people around me ate pork chops, potatoes, green beans, and applesauce just didn't do the trick for me.

It's late and the kids are crabby and tired. I tell them to get their pajamas on. Usually, they're asleep by this time. But I don't care. I go to the cupboard and get out some snacks.

The kids pad out to the kitchen in their sleepwear.

"Come on, kids," I say. "Let's eat. Hot chocolate and toast anyone?"

The Hunger Winter, 1944

Yesterday, while he was making supper, Opa started talking about stoves. "During the war," he said, "Blacksmiths made mini-sized cookers that we called MAJO stoves. They were basically a tin can, open on both ends with an inner metal tube. We put paper, kindling and wood slivers in the can to be burned. They required only a small amount of fuel. Once an item was cooked, we put it in a *hooikist,* a square box filled with hay or sometimes old garments for insulation. It kept the food warm while we were cooking a second item or boiling water."

Years later, I would learn that in the winter of 1944—one of the coldest winters on record—Izaak's family moved into the smallest room of their house, the kitchen. The occasional heat from their MAJO stove kept the room above freezing that winter. Most of the time.

While Izaak and his mother ate anything they could find, his father could barely swallow or stomach most of what they scrounged up. Nothing was considered too old or too moldy.

Nothing thrown away. His mother boiled field beets—grown for cattle food—and pounded the softened mixture into a pulp that tasted like mud. And then, they would look at each other, nod, and say, *Het is lekker.* It is good.

Desperate for food, they ate rotten black potatoes, peels and all. Izaak would never forget the smell of the rotting potatoes as they cooked, as he lifted his fork to his lips, put the blackened pulp into his mouth and swallowed. More than 22,000 Dutch people starved to death that winter. It became known as de Hongerwinter. The Hunger Winter.

Izaak doesn't tell Kristina these details. How could he? Would I even want him to? She likes the idea of the tiny stoves, cooking with barely any fuel.

"Did you eat the tulip bulbs, Opa?" she asks him.

"We would have liked to, but in our region, it was impossible to find *de tulpenbollen.*"

The story explained so much, yet I remained oblivious, considered it only a story told to a child. It registered in the back of my mind. That was all. Looking back, I wish I'd had an inkling of what Izaak's story really represented. I wish I could've internalized a bit of tenderness, and compassion. A touch of understanding. Five years at war. Winter. Hunger. Oppression. Hiding. Nazi control. Five years. How powerful and intertwined the stories we carry, tell, and hide.

This was Izaak's childhood, yet I only saw the man. I thought him judgmental and arrogant. And he was. But looking back, I see now, he wasn't the only one.

Part 5: USA, 1993–2007

Jopie Kandel, age 20.
The Netherlands. 1943.

Anneke Kandel sitting on top of Benjamin, who is kneeling on Kristina and Joren. Johan stands to the side of the children in their Fargo, North Dakota, home. 1995.

Miss INFJ, 1992–94

When NDSU sends Johan his acceptance letter for the PhD program in Fargo, I respond with a happy, "It's going to be great to be home again." Even as I say this, I realize that the vague term *home* applies only to me. Of the five of us returning to the United States, I'm the only one who grew up there. The only one who can truly call it home. My three children have spent their young lives in the tropics and we're moving to North Dakota. My husband grew up in the Netherlands and he's moving to my prairie country. I've been gone for ten years—living on three different continents—and wonder how much of my coding has changed. Maybe it won't be what I remember.

We have long discussions once we arrive in Fargo and decide to homeschool for a year. We want one thing to stay the same in the kids' lives, to give them a bit of continuity. It's a good decision for us. The kids love it, and so do I. We meet other homeschool families, settle in, and start our new routines.

Johan bikes up to NDSU every morning, spends the day, comes home for supper. We own one car. He says he'll bike year-'round. I tell him, "Maybe not. You're in North Dakota!"

He answers, "I biked in the Netherlands all winter long."

That winter, my mother buys him a turquoise and purple goose-down jacket with matching snow pants. He bikes to school through the snow or sleet or slush or ice. He bikes in his turquoise and purple coat looking like someone I've never met.

"It was on sale," my mother says. She always did love a good sale.

I begin to study the Myers-Briggs Sixteen Personalities and find that I'm an INFJ. These types are known for being imaginative, creative, and idealistic. They love getting to the heart of issues. They value authenticity, spontaneity, and sincerity.

An INFJ can be a closed book to others, but they speed-read the people who surround them. They chafe under rules, routine, and hierarchy. They don't give a hoot about prestige. INFJ's sometimes have a morbid sense of humor.

One day, on a whim, I pretend that I'm Izaak, and take the test again, through what I think of as his viewpoint. I try to be fair and thoughtful. Izaak comes out as an ESTJ: The Executive. It fits him to the letter.

Executives want to bring structure to their surroundings and represent tradition, law and order. They stick to their principles and have a large need to maintain their dignity. They can be harsh, inflexible, and stubborn. *Oh boy, oh boy! That's my man.*

An Executive by nature is self-confident, straightforward, and tactless. They loathe disorder and have forceful personalities. They're big on budget, time, and efficiency. As I read about the Executive, I feel like I'm invading something private. I also wonder how much of what I'm seeing reflects Izaak's European heritage. How much reflects the fact that he's a WWII survivor? And how much of it is just who he is?

Izaak (if indeed he is an ESTJ) and I are at the extreme ends of the personality pole, opposite sides of the teeter-totter, magnets that repel. He has a strong sense of facts, data, and memory recall. He prefers impersonal reasoning to solve problems. I'm energized by my own inner world, use hunches and speculations to build possibilities, and enjoy exploring the subjective. It's as if Izaak and I were built to misunderstand each other. The odds stacked against us before we even met.

Here I am, Miss INFJ, searching for the big picture, speculating, and associating and hunching my way through my complicated, messy, intercultural family. I'm both pushed and pulled toward an exploration of my relationship with Izaak. It's like wiggling a loose tooth, and I just can't stop. As if something inside of me knows that I won't survive without it.

The Woman Who Evaporated, 1994

Johan's busy with research, writing, and classes every day. He studies late into the evenings. He doesn't love school that much, but he's diligent and hardworking. He'll be glad once he's got the degree and can move on to using it in a job.

That March, Izaak calls on Johan's birthday. He calls every birthday. I don't think twice about it, just the normal felicitations, but it isn't. Jopie's not doing well. She's been in a nursing home with twenty-four-hour care, battling Alzheimer's disease for several years now. Izaak goes to visit her every day. His devotion has been unquestionable as she fades into her own world. But now, he says she's not expected to live much longer.

The next day, Izaak calls again. Jopie has passed away. The day of her death and the day of Johan's birth forever linked in our minds. Johan makes arrangements and flies to the Netherlands. He attends his mother's funeral, staying a week with his family. His sister is expecting her first baby. A baby who won't ever meet and know Jopie. After one week, Johan comes back, diving into classes and catching up on preparation for the research plots that his thesis will depend upon.

After Jopie dies, I realize how much time, effort, and thought I've put into understanding my relationship with Izaak. I begin to realize that Izaak's life isn't the entire equation. What about his "other half"? Where was Jopie in all of this? Who was she? I never really knew her, this woman Izaak chose to marry. This woman who's now gone.

In the early years, language separated us. I didn't speak much Dutch. She didn't speak much English. Geography a continual barrier. We weren't often on the same continent, let alone in the same country. By the time Kristina and Joren were born, and I could speak a little Dutch, Jopie was already disappearing into Alzheimer's. Looking back, I also see that long before her Alzheimer's began, she'd already started becoming a fog, a mist, a vapor.

"What was Jopie like?" I ask Johan after he comes back from the funeral. I've asked him so many times over the years. His answer the same, time after time.

"She was just Ma. She was always there when we got home from school. She'd have a snack ready for us. Some cookies. A glass of milk."

"I know," I say. "But isn't there something you can tell me about *her*."

"I don't know. She was mom."

I'm frustrated to tears with the lack of details.

I can tell you a thousand things too many about my mother. Her need for pheasant-feathered hats and purple suede shoes, her wacky sense of humor, her facelifts, her institutionalizations, her love of storytelling. I can tell you she was the North Dakota Republican Woman of the Year and attended Nixon's inaugural ball wearing an orange chiffon empress dress and long, white dancing gloves.

My mom's very best and life-long friend improbably grew up in Rotterdam in Nazi-occupied Netherlands and immigrated to the United States as an adult. We knew her as Johnna. She was the only vegetarian I'd ever met. She said meat was so scarce in her youth that she never learned to eat it.

I can tell you about my mother's fear of failure, the size shoe she wore, the names and colors of each of her poodles, and the name she most liked to go by: The Doctor's Wife. Ask me. I'm so full of stories about my mother, they bleed into my life.

I look at Johan and wonder, "How can you not remember?"

His gives his pat answer once again, "Ask my sister." But even she, the only other female in the household, has few and scattered memories of her mother.

Years later, while visiting the Netherlands, Johan, Andrea, and I sit down for supper with their cousin, the daughter of one of Jopie's brothers. They used to all vacation together.

"What was Jopie like?" I ask.

"She was the nicest woman!" the cousin replies, all cheer and delight. "Everybody loved Jopie!"

The cousin's husband nods his head. "We became good friends with Jopie and Izaak. We always enjoyed their company."

"Yes, but can you tell me something more specifically?" I ask. "Like a story, or something you did together, a joke she played, a favorite song?"

I see the consternation slowly spreading over their faces.

"Um," the cousin says. "I can't think of anything exactly. But, um, she was just so sweet. We all liked her a lot."

It's as if I've purchased a book and when I open it up, it's empty. Blank pages. I feel cheated. There's a safety in hiding that develops into a shelter. Somewhere along the line, Jopie learned this, too. Perhaps it became a method of survival as she capitulated to Izaak's strong personality. When did this change occur? When did this quiet hiding become her go-to? Before the children were born or after? Before Izaak became a dominee or later? I don't know. But as the years passed, Jopie divested herself. She'd always been kind and gentle. But it grew into more than that. Or less, as the case may be.

Can a woman resign from her own life? Can she *will* herself to evaporate? To dissipate and dissolve into time, and into herself, until she's no longer visible?

I ask Kristina what she remembers of her Oma Kandel.

"I remember she liked to wear scarves," Kristina says. "Sometimes I'd tie them around my head, and she'd play scarves with me. But then she'd get angry and pull them away. Sometimes she'd grab a cookie out of my hand and say it was hers. I was kind of scared of her. I think she already had a lot of problems with Alzheimer's. She was unpredictable, I guess."

I remember those pretty silk scarves. Jopie would take one from her neck and tie it around her head. She'd knot it under her chin like a babushka and shake her head at Kristina, who laughed and tried to do the same. But Alzheimer's was already changing Jopie's personality, changing everything. Although she delighted in playing with her grandchildren, her bursts of anger were erratic. We couldn't leave her alone with them.

I remember those visits. Izaak would pontificate and talk, the master of words, educated and erudite. Words were his power. Jopie would sit mute in her corner chair, scribbling words in a crossword puzzle book. We'd drink tea and chat, the kids playing around our feet, and Jopie would have a pencil in her hand, scratching at her paper.

She would sit, head bowed over her book, filling in the blanks. Like she'd retired from life, like she'd given up. She'd honed the ability to go silent, to go interior, to become invisible.

My mother-in-law was a woman who in many ways lost her voice. But still, she searched for words to navigate her silent life. I like to imagine her secretly triumphing over those crossword puzzles. Beating the game. Beating the odds. I imagine a smile sliding over her face when she fills in the last box.

A six-letter word meaning victory starting with the letter T: triomf.

Triumph! Here in this private corner of her house, in the quietness of her own world, inside her gentle mind, she's the winner. And when she turns the page, going on to another puzzle, I'm so very happy for all of her accomplishments.

Wrinkled, 1995

A couple of months after Jopie dies, Andrea gives birth to her first child, a son. It's a sort of miracle for Izaak. A new baby to love and dote on, to fill the hours that had been filled with caring for Jopie. Andrea sends us pictures of Izaak and his new grandson cuddling together. Izaak's smitten with the little boy, and I'm happy for them all. Happy that a tiny grandson has entered Izaak's life and fills him with joy and purpose.

A year after Jopie dies, Izaak decides he wants to come and visit us. He'll come for Johan's graduation ceremony. He wants to see his son earn his PhD in Agronomy from NDSU.

Johan's worked hard for three long years and I have, too. Besides homeschooling the kids, I've gone through a recertification program to renew my RN license. On Friday afternoons, once Johan returns from the university, I walk over to Bethany Homes, a nursing home just down the street from our house and work the 3:00 to 11:00 shift. I'm the RN on duty, in charge of Third Floor. We're chronically understaffed on weekends. Young CNAs calling in sick. Everyone knows they just want to party. I seldom get a break or time for supper; I seldom make it home before midnight.

As Johan's school winds down, I find myself forty years old and seven months pregnant with our fourth child. I work weekends, and I don't have the luxury of downtime. Each Monday morning, I wake up early and begin my other fulltime job, home-schooling our children. I know I need to work; it's financially smart. I also know it's temporary. We've walked through three years of skimping, long nights of study, and working weekends on mac and cheese, ramen noodles, and sheer determination. And now, the end's in sight.

It's May. The busiest season of the year for us. Kristina and Joren have their piano recitals to prepare. Kristina has a ballet performance and extra practices. Benjamin's a busy five-year-old, forever falling off his bike, bruising his knees, needing Band-Aids.

We're all tired. Very tired.

Izaak arrives a few days before Johan will defend his dissertation. Izaak settles into his room and seems to be getting used to the eight-hour time change.

"When is the ceremony?" he asks.

"I'm not going to walk down the aisle, Pa."

"Yes, yes. But the thesis ceremony?" he demands. "When is the ceremony?"

Izaak has come from the Netherlands to attend a thesis ceremony.

"Pa, when I go to defend my thesis, it will be a three-hour ordeal. In front of my thesis committee. It's not a public event. Afterward, I'll come home, and we'll have a party here. We're going to go out for supper."

"But . . . what about the protocol?" Izaak stammers.

The Dutch have a procedure for everything. Of course they do. How did we miss this?

In the Netherlands, a PhD defense is a very formal event with a protocol stipulating every single step, from how you address people, to the words you say at the beginning and the end. There's a master of ceremonies, the *pedel*, who carries a ceremonial mace and leads the external examiners, dressed in full academic regalia, to their seats. You and your family and friends attend. After you're through with the examination—timed to *precisely* one hour—there's a speech by your supervisor, a reception, and sometimes a party.

In the United States, a thesis examination's a different beast altogether. Johan will attend the grueling session alone. It's held in front of his thesis committee. No friends or family ever attend. It's not a public event. If he passes, he'll rework his thesis and submit it to the graduate school. They'll sign his papers when everything is finished. He can walk in the December graduation line if he wants to.

In the busyness of our lives, we completely missed the fact that what Izaak thought he was coming for, what he's expecting, isn't what this day is going to look like. Not at all. His expectations are totally Dutch. When we explain it to him, he's not at all happy, but there's nothing we can do about it.

The morning of the thesis defense, I decide to iron Johan's shirt. I want him to look special. I hardly ever iron. Who has the time for that?

I iron and simultaneously answer and ask questions as the kids run by, my house its usual commotion. I'm in a happy daze of thought. *We've done it! We've really done it.*

"Your shoes are by the back door, Joren."

"Has anyone put the dog out yet?"

"Ben, did you find your backpack?"

We're all excited and happy. In the past three years, I can count the number of times we've actually gone out to eat. We've chosen the Country Harvest Buffet. There should be something for everyone.

"Joren, stop pestering Ben! Why don't you get those breakfast dishes washed?"

Opa Kandel comes down the stairs and into the living room.

"*Goede morgen*, Opa," I say.

"Goede morgen, Yill."

He walks over to the ironing board as I go to grab a hanger.

He looks at me, his jaw tight.

"Yill!" he shouts. "There are wrinkles in this shirt. This, it is not ironed proper!"

I stare back at him, completely taken aback. I'm not much a swearing woman. But by all things holy. I've been up half the night with a fussy child. I'm exhausted. Deep within myself, I'm growing a baby who will be his grandchild. I've cleaned spittle and feces and blood and pus for three years at an understaffed nursing home, and he wants to call me out on my ironing?

"Jopie would never have let me preach in a shirt that was like this! This is not acceptable." Izaak's face goes red, veins stick out on his neck; he glares at me.

I feel his animosity like a slap across my face, the way he judges me. What a fool I've been. All this caring. All this wanting to please. No more. If this is the game he wants to play, then okay. Let's play.

Johan bounces down the stairs and into the room, interrupting Izaak and me. We stand like two bulls facing as Johan calls out, "Morning!" Smiling at me, missing the drama.

"Your shirt's ready," I say, spitting the words out of my mouth.

"Looks great, Jill. Thanks!" Johan says.

I stomp out of the room feeling Izaak's disapproving eyes sear into my back. My eyes well up. I can't believe he's ruining this day. I go upstairs shaking with anger and humiliation. He always does this to me. He makes me feel like dirt.

Ten minutes later, my tears dried, I put on a smile and go back downstairs. I'm not going to let him ruin this day.

Johan defends his thesis and comes home with a grin. I put on a dress and we gather up the kids and go out for our dinner celebration. I sit between the kids and we talk and laugh. They fill their plates over and over again, and I don't even care what they choose. We end the evening with heaps of soft ice cream covered in gooey layers of chocolate and strawberry syrup, topped with nuts.

Johan and I fall into bed that night happy and relieved. He's really done it! Dr. Kandel. We can begin to think about other things. We can job search and hunt and plan. These three years are nearly behind us.

Izaak stays two weeks longer and I'm courteous enough, but give him nothing of myself. I've put up my own wall, my own barbed wire barricade. I sigh with relief when he leaves. And sadness. And, I don't know, just sigh. I'm at my worst when I'm with him. Maybe he's at his worst with me, too.

The Man Who Lived a Continent Away, 1996

In July 1995, Johan takes a temporary extension job in Moorhead. Thirty days later, I go into labor and give birth to our fourth child, a little girl. We name her Anneke, spelling it the common Dutch way without a second thought. Not realizing that Americans won't know how to pronounce her name. That it will always be a reminder of her Dutch roots. If we'd have written it thinking about American pronunciation norms, we'd have spelled it *Anika*, for that is how it is said. Anika. Our perfect, deeply loved, beautiful Anneke.

In December, Johan is offered a permanent job with the University of Minnesota Extension, and I tender my nursing resignation. We'll be moving to a small town about a two-hour drive north of Fargo. There's only one house for sale so we drive up to Red Lake Falls and take a look; it has standing water in the basement. We give it a pass.

Johan commutes to Red Lake Falls for the next six months, four hours a day in our little white Honda Civic, through a winter that accumulates over 100 inches of snow. He leaves at 5:00 a.m. each day and gets home about 8:00 p.m. I spend the days homeschooling the oldest three and getting to know baby Anneke. On evenings when blizzards keep him from driving home, he rents a room in Red Lake Falls from an elderly woman. He drives back over the drifted roads when the winds die down and the snowplows have done their work.

While we're busy searching for a house, Izaak moves, too. It's been almost two years since Jopie died, and Izaak decides that his large house in Putten is unnecessary. He finds an apartment in Park Boswijk, a luxury senior residence in Doorn. The residence caters to people over the age of fifty-five and includes two-bedroom apartments, a park, a small lake, restaurant, and proximity to a forest. It sounds lovely. To make it even better, one of Izaak's lifelong friends will be living just one door down from him. Izaak writes an exuberant letter about packing, sorting, and moving. He seems thrilled with his new adventure.

Finally, in June of 1996, a colleague tells Johan that someone in Red Lake Falls is moving. We drive up and find a three-story farmhouse, built in 1890 and moved into the town in 1910. It's perfect. Big and architecturally interesting. It's also drafty, filled with old lathe and flax insulation. We put a bid in on it before it even goes on the market.

We'll spend eleven years in our Red Lake Falls home. My children will remember it as the house they grew up in. I'll remember it as the place I join a writer's group, take a graduate level writing class, attend my first writing workshop. Red Lake Falls is where I first dream of becoming a writer.

In the spring, I pick rhubarb from our yard. We eat it raw and dipped in sugar or I make rhubarb pies from my grandmother's old recipes. In the fall, we head to the hills and ravines, picking chokecherries, small and so dark they look nearly black. We eat them while picking, our fingers stained purple, our tongues dry and tingling.

In winter, the kids build snow forts against the window in the dining room. I look out the window and into the snow fort.

I watch my children, sitting in the igloo, drinking hot chocolate, and waving at me to come out and join them.

We raise hooded rats and build Lego mazes for them to navigate. Joren walks around the house doing his homework, with M&M—his favorite brown-headed rat—on his shoulder. We buy two purebred Bichon dogs. Anneke sleeps snuggled up with one dog on each of her shoulders.

Two years later, one of the dogs has a litter of eight little Bichon puppies. She doesn't have enough milk to feed them all, so I go to the vet and buy puppy milk and we bottle feed them. It works great. Except that they now need to be burped. We carry baby Bichons around the house, burping them over our shoulders. Anneke becomes quite adept at it and mimics the puppies. They burp. She burps. With time and practice, Anneke becomes a serious champion of burping-boisterously-at-will.

Izaak visits us once in Red Lake Falls. He comes the summer of 1997 to celebrate Anneke's second birthday. In all the photos, he looks happy. Dressed in khaki-colored slacks and short-sleeved dress shirts. I try. He tries. We travel to Winnipeg to go to the zoo. We take him out to western North Dakota to see the Badlands and Medora. We spend a weekend at my parents' lake home near Itasca State Park. He's seventy-three years old and has traveled across the ocean for a second time to be with his American grandkids and to see his son. I turn my life upside down to try to meet his expectations. Food. Mealtimes. Bedtimes. Coffee time. Tea. I'm sure he tries, too. It's just all too much. Too many mosquitoes. He can't believe they bite him! We check into the hotels too late. He's worn out. We need to stop every two hours so he can walk and stretch out his hips. Between the kids needing to pee and Izaak needing to walk and driving to restaurants and arriving at the correct time, it's just one thing after another. By the time Izaak leaves, I'm exasperated, exhausted, and relieved. I kind of think he is, too.

Why is family so difficult? Why do the people we're sup-
posed to be the closest to become the ones we can barely tolerate?
What's wrong with him? What's wrong with me?

Through all of our happy Red Lake Falls years, the children
write to Izaak every week. We mail fat envelopes filled with letters and pictures from each child. And just as Johan saved his
father's letters in Zambia, Izaak saves ours, too. He keeps small
thick photo albums, lining a shelf in his front room, and a box
neatly filled, in chronological order, of the letters he receives.
These letters document my children's lives. Their childish cursive
handwriting, their misspellings and enthusiasms. They are cheer-
ful, happy letters filled with stickers, drawings, and exclamation
points. Each letter so kind and sweet, yet, each letter a reminder:
you're not here. Letters that capture moments in time that Izaak
is not a part of.

That summer Joren falls in love with video, and he begins
tearing our house apart, making it into sets, writing scripts, and
talking his siblings into starring in his movies as Charlie Chaplain or Buster Keaton. In one scene, Ben chases Joren down the
main street in Red Lake Falls. Joren, the crook, wears a pink and
orange striped shirt.

"Orange and pink?" I question.

"It's a black-and-white movie, Mom! No one will ever know."

Ben, the cop, chases Joren with a homemade billy club,
threatening him with vile intent. Kristina—newly licensed—
drives the van, while eight-year-old Anneke hangs out the side
window filming. They hang Most Wanted posters around town,
pictures of a sneering Joren wearing an eye-patch and handcuffs.
I sometimes wonder what my neighbors think. The black-and-
white silent films grow into talkies as Joren buys better equipment. Joren recruits friends, neighbors, and family to play in his
movies. In one movie, Johan wears a toupee. In another, he grays
his hair with baby powder. The kids use makeup and imagination, shifting and changing into Lorna Doon, into Mustafa, into

Chief Inspector Croissant. I mostly clean up and play gofer, but I am in one movie. The one where I volunteer to have a whipped cream pie thrown in my face. The kids think it's the most hysterical thing they've ever seen. Mom wiping cream out of her eyes, leaving rings around them like a raccoon.

A year later, with a newly minted script, Joren *needs* someone to fall off a cliff, and the kids spend a day making a life-sized dummy out of old clothes. A papier-mâché head tops off the project.

"It will look real enough, Mom. You don't want me to throw Ben off, do you?" Joren says with a wicked grin.

The "stagehands" heave the dummy dramatically off the vertical sand cliff, above the Red Lake River, while Joren films. The dummy tumbles head over heels down the cliff and gets caught on a branch where it hangs upside down, halfway up the cliff, definitively stuck. It takes an hour for the boys to climb the sandy, steep hill and recover it for the second shooting.

I get used to my house being a stage and never quite know what to expect. I love the kids' mischievous fun, their creativity and joy. We are so full of ourselves, so happy. Izaak's existence is a tiny fragment in our lives. He's a man who lives a continent away. A letter, which requires half an hour to read once a week, after supper on a Monday night. He's a vacation. A month together, then gone for years and years. For all the benefits—to me and Johan and our children—of our cross-cultural life, it's no boon to Izaak.

Andrea and Bert send us photos of Izaak with his grandchildren. Three of them, two boys and one girl growing up in the Netherlands. I send pictures back. My four children growing up in America. I think of these *grandchildren*, these *cousins*, growing up continents apart.

And I think about Izaak.

I envision Izaak bereft of his son and only able to be with his grandchildren once every two or three years. How does he handle the emotions of saying goodbye, over and over again? How does he wrangle his thoughts and words and actions, knowing our visits are few and brief? He'll never really fit into our lives. We don't have the privilege of near geography, or the luxury of unbridled time or extraneous money.

As Izaak reads his weekly letters, more than half of his grandchildren live abroad. They play joyful birthday games, grow taller. They become teens, go off to school, graduate college, and begin careers. Mostly, without him.

When I say, "This is the life we choose," it doesn't negate the fact that it may not have been the life Izaak would have wanted, for us or for himself.

He's the outsider, looking in from a great distance.

A man at the window.

We stare at each other through fingerprinted glass. And I'm the one who knows each fingerprint by name.

Grandfathers, 1996

"Every child should have a grandfather," my mom used to say. "Grandfathers are magical people." These words are as familiar to me as the sound of my mother's voice. I'm forty-one years old and have always believed these words. Until now.

Until my mom looks me in the eye and says, "When I was a little girl, I was afraid of your grandpa."

I jerk my head up, staring at this woman I thought I knew.

"What are you talking about?" I ask confused. Wanting to know. Not wanting.

"I got some mail," she says, handing me a letter. "It's from one of your cousins. She asked me some questions about Grandpa, and I wrote back to her and told her what I knew. Now my family is all up in arms."

"Mom?" I ask.

My mother has always told a lot of stories; she is, above all else, a storyteller. I grew up hearing hundreds of her stories.

Her mother, my grandma Emma, grew up on a North Dakota homestead near Blue Grass, a town that no longer exists.

She passed eighth grade with honors. By the age of sixteen, she'd fallen in love with a young preacher. He loved her, too, said he'd marry her if she'd get one year of Bible School education. When Emma told her pa, he said, "You got more than enough education, girl. No gal of mine's gonna get more than that. Be glad what you got. Plenty work to be done round here."

When the young preacher left, Emma—out of spite to her pa—attached herself to the family farmhand, a hard-working man with a second-grade education. She'd show her pa what was what. So, they married. My grandma and grandpa K.

When they moved to town, Grandma got Grandpa into commercial house painting. She said, "In those days before paint mixing and matching machines, your grandpa could match any color perfectly! Women from all over town brought him a swatch of color they wanted, and he'd mix it up identical. He had an amazing eye for color."

Grandma Emma—always good with math—did his books and accounts, keeping track of expenses, payments, bills, and IOUs from families and businesses across the region. She bought and ran a boarding house where she also raised her seven children. My mother, the second from the youngest, was given the job of cleaning the spittoons. Later, Grandma decided to start a second business, wanting to buy into a newfangled franchise called Dairy Queen. And then, in her mid-40s, just before she was going to close the deal, she had a catastrophic stroke.

All of these stories happened before my time.

This is what I actually remember.

I remember rusty Red Owl coffee cans filled with marbles lining the floor of Grandpa's garage, leftovers from when my four uncles had been little boys. I loved sorting them by size and color pattern: shooters, steelies, cat-eyes, clearies.

In the late summer, I'd play outside by Grandpa's flower beds, abundant with his favorite flowers, California Poppies. The petals, delicate and thin, were the brightest orange I'd ever seen. I thought they were beautiful and exotic, coming to North Dakota all the way from California.

I remember Grandma. Grandma, sitting in a wheelchair, unable to speak. Uttering her inscrutable guttural noises. Tapping her cane against my skinny legs as I ran past. Always smiling her crooked smile, her eyes shining at me. I thought she must have been the happiest woman in the world. Her own silver chair with wheels. Her very own plum tree in the backyard. A little red bird, sitting inside a cuckoo clock, singing to her all the day.

When they came to visit, they never stayed at our house.

Mom said, "Grandpa and Grandma love hotels!"

I'm five years old, wearing a frilly skirted dress. I lie on my back and Grandpa K. holds my ankles. He drags me across the living room carpet. I laugh loudly. This is fun! My mother races into the room, shouting. My mother yells at Grandpa! She shrieks something that I don't understand. She tells me to stand up. She says the game is over. I'm confused by her quick entry, her anger. She hardly ever yells. Grandpa lets go of my legs, turns, and walks away.

"When you were very small," my mother says, continuing her story, gripping my cousin's letter in her hand, "A few years after Grandma's stroke, well, your grandfather was arrested. He had a court hearing and was found guilty. They sentenced him to prison, but the judge commuted the sentence. I went down for the hearings. It was all in the newspaper."

My mind fogs. I can't think clearly. *Grandpa K. was arrested?*

"He molested a little girl who lived down the block."

I shake my head to clear the jumble in my mind. *My grandpa was a pedophile?*

"I didn't want you to know," my mom says. "I wanted you to love your grandparents. I wanted them to be a part of your life. I never let you spend a minute alone with him. Never."

How could I not have noticed?

Grandma and Grandpa loved hotels!

"We're going to go visit Grandma and Grandpa, girls," I recall my mom saying. "Remember. We don't sit on Grandpa's lap." I thought I shouldn't sit on his lap because he was old. Because maybe in some strange way of old people it would hurt his bones.

Mom continues relentlessly. I don't want to hear any more. I don't want to know. I need to know.

"I told my brothers and sisters not to ever let Grandpa alone with their girls. I told them! Now there's all this mess." She waves the letter, pauses, and takes a deep breath while looking down at her hands. "I didn't want you to be involved. I just wanted you to be a little girl."

Are there other things she hasn't told me about? This is nuts. This is my family.

I'm staggered by my mother. Underneath the incandescent foibles of her life, underneath the exterior of her pheasant-feathered hats, her stylish silk scarves and matching heels, she held a sensibility, a practicality, a backbone that I never knew existed. I'd thought her a foolish woman. Flamboyant. Airy. But without her vigilant protection, who would I be?

I had always believed my mother's words. *Grandfathers are magical people.*

Those words influenced my thoughts concerning my grandfather, and concerning Izaak, too. I wanted Izaak to be fairy-tale like. To be special.

I wonder what my children will think of Izaak. Will they have fond memories? I've tried so hard to stay out of the way, to give them space to love each other. I wanted to give them the same gift my mother gave me. Innocence. Protection. Family.

Maybe that's partly what it means to be a mother, to protect both the older generation and the younger one. To stand in-between. To be the halfway point where generations come to meet.

I think about my years of being a mother. I wonder what kind of mothers my daughters might become. I think of my mother. And I'm reminded of an old verse in Ezekiel.

What was your mother? A Lioness!
Among lions she crouched;
in the midst of young lions
she reared her cubs.

Back in the Netherlands Again, 2002

In 2002, we decide to visit the Netherlands on a whole family trip. Kristina's just turned eighteen. Joren's sixteen, Ben twelve, Anneke seven. It's been ten years since I've seen the Netherlands. It's Anneke's very first trip there. We've been saving up for five years. Flying with six people is more than expensive.

The kids decide to make a paper daisy chain to count the days off until we fly. They cut out brightly colored strips of paper and loop them together. Circle after circle in all the colors of all the tulips. Each day, we pull one colored circle off the daisy chain.

"Only sixty-three chains left. When we get to the last one, it's Going to the Netherlands Day!"

They count and pull and dream over those chains. Each one coming off, a celebration. Each one a possibility of what we might do on our trip.

"We're going to the Netherlands!" they tell all their friends.

"I'm going on an airplane across the ocean!" Anneke says. "We're going to see Opa!"

"You aren't going to believe the tulips!" Kristina tells her little sister. Joren and Kristina spend hours telling Ben and Anneke about all the fun things they'll be going to do and see.

Sometimes, the preparation's as much fun as the adventure. We buy each of the kids a new backpack, and they spend weeks carefully choosing what to pack: books, audio tapes, headphones, coloring books, cameras. We plan our trip for months. And then the day arrives. We fly to Minneapolis, change planes, and fly KLM nonstop to Amsterdam. On the eight-hour flight, I settled my mind by reading a good old murder mystery: Agatha Christie's *And Then There Were None*. The kids are a bundle of en-

ergy fueled on free pop and peanuts, as they watch movies, walk
the aisles, take pictures out the window, and try not to fall asleep,
not wanting to miss anything.

Getting out at Schiphol Airport feels so familiar. We walk
through Customs and over to baggage claims. Fifteen oval con-
veyer belts carry suitcases in silver circles, while we look for ours.
The signs overhead, in English and in Dutch, welcome us. *Uitgang,
Vertrek, Laat bagagekar hier achter:* Exit, Departures, Leave baggage carts here.

We're finally here. Back in the Netherlands, again.

We pick up our luggage and breeze through Customs, and
there they are: Opa Kandel, Andrea, and her son. It's so nice to
see Andrea again. We've been writing more over the years, talking.
For years, she's been a good friend, but recently she's becoming
more like a sister. I can't thank her enough for all the care and
time she's taken to make this trip go well for us. Finding housing, renting bikes, arranging phones. She's been our own personal
tour operator.

Opa's hair has thinned to bald on top and sides, but there's
still a small mass of wild curly hair on the back of his head. His
paunch has grown a little bigger. He has tears in his eyes as we
greet in familiar pecking mode.

Stepping outside, the air's balmy, the sun shining. The Netherlands welcomes us with a brilliantly-green and floral spring.

We drive in two cars to Andrea's house while the tulips and
daffodils wave their breezy April faces at us. We have tea, try to
stay awake, and discuss plans for the next three weeks. The kids
play soccer with their cousins, getting to know them once again.

As the day winds down, we discuss how we'll bring all the
luggage and the bikes to our rented bungalow. The six of us can't
all fit into Opa's small car. Johan, Joren, and Ben will bike. Opa
will drive the girls and the luggage.

"Can we stop and get a few groceries?" I ask Izaak. "I'd like to
at least get some breakfast food."

"Ja, Yill. I can stop."

At the grocery store, I go to get a shopping cart, but they're locked. It takes a Euro coin to unlock and use them. I only have paper money. The girls and I each take a small hand-held shopping basket and walk down the aisles. The girls gape and dawdle, while I try to get my bearings. Opa comes in and walks beside me, tapping his hand on his watch, shaking his head.

"What's this?" Anneke asks.

"Ketchup," Kristina replies.

"In a tube?"

I point out various items to Anneke while Kristina takes photos of bottles in all their different colors, shapes, and sizes. Even the cola is interesting.

"Hurry now, Yill," Opa says, the frown on his face deepening. "I am waiting to bring you."

I try to negotiate the girls' questions and make decisions on what to buy. I can't quite find the things I want. It's the jet lag. And the different colored boxes and bottles with their Dutch labels. I'm trying hard to remember how to shop in the Netherlands. Where to find things.

"Yill, come now. What do you need?" Opa asks impatiently, glancing toward the cashier, trying to move us along.

Kristina and Anneke call out and point and laugh. They ask questions. I need cereal. And milk. And cheese. The labels are in Dutch, the quantities different. And the entire layout of the store makes no sense to me. I walk in circles, passing by items that I don't even notice, and coming back to find them.

"Yill. Come. It is long enough."

I find Kristina and Anneke. We head to the checkout where the woman at the till asks me several questions I don't understand. I shake my head. She speaks in English.

"Do you want coupons, Miss?"

"Oh!" I say grasping what she wants. "No. Thank you. I don't."

"Do you pay cash?"

"Yes."

The kids pack the groceries while I dig in my wallet, pulling out the brightly colored, glittery Euro banknotes and hand them to the cashier.

Izaak is right beside me, watching me sternly. *Does he never smile?*

She hands me my change and Opa hustles us out, leading the way, pointing to the car.

"*Hier.* Here we are. Get in now."

He has turned the adventure into an ordeal, sucking joy out of the day. All black and white and do and don't and just hurry up. *Is this man never spontaneous?*

Kristina sits up front with Opa. I sit in the back of the car with Anneke. I'm ashamed of my thoughts. We haven't even been here one day and already, yes, already, Izaak and I are at odds. I've never known anyone who can fluster me so completely, or so quickly.

Profound 2002

Unbeknownst to me, in April of 2002 while we're making plans to vacation with Johan's sister and brother, the Netherlands becomes the first country in the world to legalize euthanasia. They do this on April 1—April Fool's Day—2002.

The Dutch law states that patients must be adults, must have made a voluntary request, and must be facing unbearable suffering with no reasonable alternative.

There are 1,815 reported deaths by euthanasia the following year.

At first, unbearable suffering is the only acceptable reason to allow euthanasia, but definitions will change in the years ahead as the Royal Dutch Medical Association's guidelines for interpreting the 2002 Euthanasia Act become the protocol to follow.

I'm busy touring the Netherlands, a mother with four children, a wife, a daughter-in-law. I haven't heard about the euthanasia law. I've never considered the topic and I certainly haven't dreamt that in the years ahead this euthanasia law will come to affect my life profoundly.

Just Grand, 2002

We bike over to visit Izaak the next day. It's our first time to visit him at his new apartment in Doorn, and he's happy to give us a tour.

Park Boswijk, the elder facility he lives at, has a gorgeous entryway and large community areas. Izaak shows us his rooms and balcony. We tour the gardens filled with bright yellow daffodils and walk by ponds alive with ducks of all varieties. Back inside, my eyes light up when we walk past a black baby-grand piano. I've been hoping there'd be a piano. Kristina and Joren have been taking lessons for five years; they've prepared a surprise for Opa.

After the tour, at 10:00 a.m., Opa offers tea and cookies. I always forget this routine: visiting equals drinking tea. The Dutch are funny about their drinks. We have coffee and tea on ritualistic schedules, but when I sit down to supper, no water is ever served! I'm either drowning in tea or thirsty for water.

Anneke's enjoying everything, the tea and cookies, the balcony, little metal cars Opa sets out for them to play with. "When your father was a small boy, these were his cars," Opa tells her.

We chat but are interrupted by Anneke, "11:11 Make a wish!" she calls out.

"What is she meaning?" Izaak asks.

Anneke tells him about the magical power of making a wish at 11:11. She says, "Now make a wish, Opa, but don't tell me what it is. If you do, it won't come true."

Izaak smiles indulgently, closes his eyes briefly, and pretends to wish. He's smitten by his youngest granddaughter. Later, I wink at Kristina and Joren and point to their backpacks.

"Opa," I say. "Kristina and Joren have something special for you."

The kids open their backpacks and pull out some sheet music. "We brought some jazz music to play for you, Opa," Kristina says.

"So you can listen to our recitals," Joren adds enthusiastically.

"I do not have a piano," he replies.

"No, not here in your room," I answer. "That one we passed, down in the lobby. We can go down there so you can listen."

"No," Izaak said sternly.

"Why not?" I ask. "Is it broken?"

"That piano is for concert use only," he says.

"We won't bother anyone," I say.

"You must have permission. You must fill out the form to request such a thing. It must be approved."

"The kids just want to play a few songs," I say. "We thought you'd enjoy it."

"No," he says. "You cannot use that piano."

Stupidly, I don't let it go. "The other residents would enjoy the music."

Izaak scowls at me, shakes his head. The piano is sacrosanct. For approved concert use only. We are not approved.

I don't know how to respond. I'm completely blown off course. Should I try to make a joke? Should I let it go? I stutter something that even I don't understand and turn and walk away, my hands shaking. As I pass Kristina and Joren, I grab their sheet music so fast I startle them.

"I'll put this in my bike bag," I mutter as I head out the door, slamming it behind me. I stomp with searing indignation down the hall. My thoughts jumbled in anger.

Damn his rules and regulations, his superiority, his know-it-all mentality. Damn his approval, his approbation.

I'd wanted to be nice. I'd wanted to please him. To watch his pleasure, Kristina and Joren showing off their skills. I thought he'd enjoy it. I thought he'd smile.

Oh, just damn it all to hell.

I walk back to Izaak's room fretting, my neck tight with anger. *Lord have mercy.* I hate who I become when I'm near him.

Illogical

I once read a short story written by Lydia Davis—*The Bad Novel*—in which she brings a dull, difficult novel with her on a trip. She wants to like the story, returning to it with growing dread. She finds the story, each time, no better. Yet, she reads on, hopeful.

As I read Davis's story, I say to myself, "I have read novels like that, returning to them with an illogical hope that they will have improved overnight while lying on my table."

Later, I think, "Maybe this story is not about a book; maybe it's about a man." Perhaps Davis returns to the same man, again and again, knowing the truth, but unable to acknowledge it.

And later still, I think, "This is my story."

I view my life with Izaak with the same three Ds of Davis's story: dull, difficult, dreading. Each time we met, I thought it would get better. Maybe we'd get along. Maybe he'd be kinder or have something nicer to say. Each time I returned, I thought he might have changed. Grown softer. Opened up a little.

Pick up the book, continue reading the story. No matter how much time you put into it, the novel doesn't change. At what point do you stop reading?

Disillusioned. Disenchanted. Disheartened.

I've carried Izaak around in the suitcase of my life for decades. Izaak, Johan's father. Izaak, my father-in-law. Izaak, my children's grandfather. He's not the man I try so hard to find, try so hard to pretend he is. He is very much a fiction.

Curfew, 1941

Every other day we go over to visit Izaak. It makes me nervous. I don't want to be early; I don't want to be late. I mean, I'm *biking* with my husband and with four children. Kristina wants to stop and take a picture. Joren wants a video. Anneke and Ben are fascinated by the sheep and lambs. And all I want to do is yell at them. "Hurry up. Not now. We'll do that later. Opa's waiting for us."

Somedays, I just go with the flow and we're late and he's not happy. Other days, I push and prod them and live with their "Ah, Mom. Relax!"

Either way, I'm a mess by the time we arrive.

Izaak has always been concerned about time, but he's almost obsessive about it now. I wonder if his fixation began during the war. Began with curfews.

In 1941, when Izaak was seventeen, Nazi occupation had been going on for over a year. German patrols walked the streets, enforcing curfews. Radios, already confiscated by the Germans, no longer brought news or music into homes. Houses were dark and quiet in the evenings. How did Izaak spend those long evenings, week after week, month after month?

I imagine his mother saying, "Izaak, remember, you must be home by 6:00 p.m. Remember. The time of the curfew has changed again. You cannot be late. What time does your watch say? Is it correct?"

If he sneaked in late, did he find his mother agitated and fearful?

"I thought the soldiers had found you," she might have said with a tremble in her voice. Imagine her distress. Standing at the sink. Wringing her hands.

She thinks about her little grandson; what kind of world will he grow up in? She thinks about her oldest son, Wes, off to sea, somewhere, in the navy. She doesn't know where his ship is stationed. It's been so long since they've had a letter.

And then there's Izaak, a considerate and precise young man. He didn't want to add to his mother's sorrow. Didn't want to anger the German soldiers. Didn't want to break the law. Living within the structure of time—which was becoming an increasingly significant part of his life—soon became a protection. A protection for himself. A protection for his family.

Count You Did, 2002

I wonder if Izaak ever heard of W. H. Auden or read his poetry. They were contemporaries.

Auden lived an obsessively punctual life; some said he lived "a life of military precision." His most famous book, *The Age of Anxiety*, carried a title that might have defined Izaak's life.

Auden said, "The surest way to discipline passion is to discipline time." He lived his life frenetically checking his watch for eating, drinking, shopping, crossword puzzle work, the arrival of the mailman.

One of Auden's most well-known poems, "Funeral Blues," starts with this line: "Stop all the clocks, cut off the telephone."

A remarkable choice of words for a man who breathed time like air.

I can't imagine Izaak ever saying, "Stop the clocks."

I can't imagine Izaak living without their constancy. They were his daily bread. His communion. His prayer. Life and clocks all knotted together like macramé. Auden would have loved Izaak. Understood him. Neither of them knew how to survive without a tick-tock reassurance.

Maybe Izaak focused on time to relieve the other alternative: thinking primarily by events. Events and life occurrences were too changeable. He couldn't rely upon them. But if he focused on the day, on the clock, it remained solid. Each tick a progressive, steady heartbeat. The life of the day marching smoothly, steadily, precisely onward.

Clocks meant order and regularity. Clocks didn't throw curve balls. Time comforted. Tea was at 4:00. This was good. He could count on it. And count he did.

Family, 2002

Each morning, I wake up to the chatter of the kids and the smell of coffee. Our vacation cabin alight with joy. Kristina and Joren have introduced Anneke and Ben to their favorite breakfast foods: *vanille* vla, chocolate *haagel* sprinkles, thin slices of aged Dutch Gouda cheese.

Johan takes a bite of Gouda on bread and says, "*Alsof er een engeltje over je tong fiets.*"

"Like an angel is biking over your tongue?" I ask. "I don't think that's quite the way the saying goes."

"Yup," he replies. "An angel biking over my tongue."

He doesn't want to say it, but the real Dutch saying is *Alsof er een engeltje over je tong piest*. Like an angel is pissing on my tongue. One of those strange linguistic idioms that really doesn't make any sense at all but sure makes people shake their heads and laugh.

The ire of the past days, of trying to please Izaak, slips away as I find joy in the happiness and wonder of my children. Joy in being back in the Netherlands. Joy in a vacation so long planned and dreamed of.

We walk by thousands of bikes and cyclists each day on our way to the train station—few of them wearing helmets—the kids taking photos by the dozens.

Anneke asks, "Why isn't anyone wearing bike helmets?"

"In the Netherlands, everybody bikes," Johan explains. "Every car driver rode a bike before he got his car license. Dutch people understand biking and bike rules and, well, we're just good at biking."

Cars pass bikes without moving over to the other side of the road. Drivers trusting bikers and vice versa. It feels unsafe to us safety-conscious Americans, but it's normal to Johan.

Our days fly by. One day we travel to Haarlem and tour the Corrie Ten Boom House and Museum. The kids have read *The Hiding Place* and are eager to see the real thing. We take a two-hour tour, walk through the old watch shop, enter the parlor, and climb the steep circular staircase up to the top floor. The kids crawl into the tiny hiding space where the Ten Boom family secreted Jewish people away from the Nazis. The day ends with a walk to the harbor. We buy French fries, locally called *patat friet*. Johan gets a cone-shaped sack of french fries, a packet of mayonnaise, and a doll-sized plastic pink fork. I order *patat met satésaus*: fries with peanut sauce, another Dutch specialty. We stand next to a high outdoor table, eating our french fries with tiny forks. Johan dipping his into mayonnaise. Anneke bemoans the fact that there's no ketchup, but follows suit eating hers with mayo, too.

I think it's hysterical, eating fries with a fork. When we're done and dump our trash into a nearby receptacle, I pocket my tiny pink plastic fork to bring home as a memento.

We walk to a canal and take the most fantastical pictures of our family standing in front of a windmill with sunlit waters shining behind us.

Our days vacillate between tourism and family. One day spent at the fabulous tulip gardens of the Keukenhof. The next visiting a market with Andrea and her son. I begin to notice that Izaak's demeanor changes when he's with his Dutch grandchildren. He's more at home with them, surer of himself and less anxious. I think about my kids, Andrea's son, Bert's two children. Of course, there's a difference. Izaak sees them more often; they know each other. The language barriers melt away. The cultural coding syncs. And then there's all this stress. Since we're here for such a short time, the expectations and tension levels are enormous. Izaak wants everything to be perfect. He tries so hard. And that's the problem. All the trying, all the pressure, brings out the controlling side of Izaak. He's not the sort of man who rises up to meet the occasion, he's the one who tightens his grip and tightens his jaw. It's lovely to sit back and watch Izaak play with his other grandchildren. There's an intimacy and understanding. An almost carefree way he assumes when he's playing with them. It's something I'm an outsider to. Something my kids will never really experience.

Bert, who has worked for years high up in the government workings of Rotterdam, plans a wonderful day out for us. He takes us to *his city* with evident pride and a sure knowledge of the geography and sites to see. We walk through markets teeming with household items.

There are whole stalls filled with tiny pottery dolls dressed up in traditional Dutch clothing. Christmas tree ornaments shaped like little wooden shoes, whose pottery vanes turn round and round. Ashtrays. Milkmaids. Crosses. Salt and pepper shakers. Snow globes. Blue-and-white pottery everywhere. I wouldn't be surprised if some of them are stamped *made in China*. We walk by, smiling at the tourists who stop and buy.

The kids laugh at the stall selling nylons. Thirty or forty mannequin legs hang from the stall and blow in the breeze, each one decked out in a different stocking: polka dots, stripes, chevrons of every color. Draperies, purses, clothing, and watches give way to huge sections of fruits and vegetables, and finally the cheese market. Wheels of cheese as big as hubcaps. Everything from young cheese fresh and white to aged cheeses one or two years old. Cheese of every color—green, yellow, white, orange, speckled—infused with herbs and spices.

Bert and his family walk us through the market expertly. Stopping when we stop. Laughing at what we notice, what we take pictures of. We come out the other side and Bert points up. Yellow cubes tilt above us. The famous Cube Houses of Rotterdam! Bert buys tickets and we tour one of them, the walls tilted, the windows askew. It's like walking into an M. C. Escher drawing.

We walk with Bert into the belly of Rotterdam, under dark bridges, past gorgeously graffitied cement walls, coming out next to the harbor. Bert explains some of the workings of the harbor and hails a taxi. It's bright yellow, just like any old taxi, but it's a boat. A *watertaxi*.

We climb in and roar across the harbor, passing shipyards, thousands of colorful metal containers, and dozens of container lift stations. The kids move to the back of the boat where they sit splashed, wet, and grinning.

We end the day at Bert's house with a fancy homecooked meal. He lives in a three-story home next to a canal. From the top floor we look down on the small boats sailing by; from the bottom floor we look up at the boats. I'm astonished by his home. The modern art, the clean white openness of it. It's so, I don't know, *European*. I love the curved stainless lighting above the table, the rounded edge of the seating nook, the comfort of the minimalist chairs. Bert's home seems like a masterpiece. This whole day does. We've seen parts and pieces of this city we'd never have seen on our own. We've been invited in. We've been made to feel like family.

Part 6: MOORHEAD, 2007—2011

Warren Robert Jensen leaning against a birch tree near his property on Little Man Trap Lake, Minnesota. Circa 1990.

Hat Trick, 2007–2008

We've been living in Red Lake Falls for eleven years and start to feel hemmed in. We're outgrowing our little town. Kristina's living at home, studying towards her BA in history, and runs her own photography business. Joren's moved to another state, studying toward a BA in film. Ben's seventeen and Anneke eleven. It's time to think about moving on.

Johan applies for several jobs, and when NDSU offers him a job, we accept. We'll be moving back to the Fargo/Moorhead community where he did his graduate work. Now instead of studying at NDSU, he'll be a professor.

Joren graduates from college and gets engaged. On a cold March day, flurries in the air, he marries his childhood sweet-heart—a gem of a girl that we've known for over a decade—and they pack up and move to Chicago. A month later, we put our house on the market, and start driving down to the FM area to look at housing.

We sell our old house and buy a rambler. I choose a corner at the foot of the basement stairs and set my computer below the tiny window. I get up each morning at 5:00 a.m. and go down-stairs to my desk, writing for four or five hours. I write my way back into the years we spent in Zambia, the heartache, the joys, the confusion.

Kristina's photography business flourishes. Ben joins a wood-turning club, buys a lathe, begins learning the art of woodturning, making pens, bowls, and boxes from any wood he can find. His lilac wood pens are stunning. Anneke takes ballet classes, twirl-ing her way into adolescence. She leaps—wearing pink tights and soft leather slippers—through the front room and the kitchen. There are so many opportunities opening up for each of us.

Johan digs into his new job at NDSU. He'll be helping mas-ter's and PhD agronomy students with their research and thesis work. He'll be out in the fields and on farms since his job includes teaching extension staff and farmers all across the state. A perfect non-desk job. It feels to all of us like we've come home.

I attend writing workshops and conferences and join an online critique group. We read each other's work and submit essays to various literary journals. I take a freelance job writing for a local women's magazine. When *Image Journal* accepts an essay of mine, I'm beyond exuberant. When *Under the Sun* accepts an essay, I can hardly believe it. Two essays coming out. Then, I get an email from *Brevity.* They're sending me a *yes* on an essay. I have three essays forthcoming. After all these years of writing, it looks like it might finally be going somewhere.

I can't wait for Johan to come home for supper, so I give him a call. "Hey, guess what? I say. "*Brevity* wants one of my pieces. *Another* acceptance!"

"It's a hat trick!" Johan crows.

I know enough soccer to understand. A hat trick: three goals in one game.

As we settle in, Izaak and Johan begin to Skype weekly. Izaak also continues writing to us, once a week as always. Johan reads the letters to the kids, and then he puts the pages into a large black three-ring binder. We have a dozen of them on the back of a closet shelf gathering dust.

It's Only Talk, 2008

In the early spring of 2008, Johan's brother calls and says, "If you want to see Pa alive, you'd better fly home." Johan, my husband of twenty-seven years, drops everything and flies out from Fargo to the Netherlands. Hoping his father, Izaak, will still be alive. Hoping to see his father one last time.

When Johan arrives at his father's house, jet-lagged and exhausted, Izaak, greets him at the door. Pa is not only alive; he seems to be fine. Before Johan can step over the threshold, Izaak blurts out, "I have asked you to come here because I want to end my life. The euthanasia rules state I have to tell my children before I can do it. So. Now you know."

He was always one to follow the rules.

Johan spends a surreal week with his father. He can't see anything that causes his father such distress that he wants to consider euthanasia. Izaak still drives his small red car, goes to the library, reads extensively, goes to concerts and museums, and travels across the Netherlands to visit family and friends. One of his lifelong friends lives a door down from him.

Johan is as baffled as is his brother, Bert, and his sister, Andrea. In the end, they conclude that Pa's just talking. Nothing will come of it.

"The Dutch system has many laws and multiple preventative measures," Andrea says. "Pa will never get permission. He's too healthy. He doesn't meet the medical criteria."

When Johan arrives back home in Fargo, he tells me all about Izaak's declaration and the family conversations. I listen, stunned.

"Euthanasia?" I ask repeatedly.

"Pa's only talking," Johan says. "He won't find a doctor to agree with him."

I'm a North Dakota prairie girl, a nurse married to a Dutch agriculturalist, staggered by the very word euthanasia, let alone the concept. It must be a mistake, a misunderstanding.

"Dr. Death" comes to mind. *What was his name? Jack Kevorkian, I think.* There are no other thoughts or images.

It's legal in the Netherlands?

I'm as ignorant of euthanasia, its laws, precedents, and uses, as I am of the surface of Mars. I know nothing of the pros, the cons, the controversies. The statistics, types, abuses, or misuses. The nuances, the complex grief that follows. I have no knowledge of the guilt or the relief it brings. No stories to think back upon. No foundations against which I might throw my circling questions.

A Little More Time, 2008

In the weeks that follow Johan's trip to the Netherlands, he talks with his father weekly via Skype. The Dutch euthanasia law clearly states that two doctors need to agree on a euthanasia est, before it will be considered, before the applications are set in motion.

Izaak says, "I went to another physician, and he said I wasn't ready."

He still wants euthanasia. He doesn't provide any explanation or reason. He's past reasoning, his mind made up. I don't understand why Izaak's so adamantly pursuing euthanasia. It's true he has prostate cancer, but it's been in remission for years. He says he doesn't sleep great, but he's far from ill.

On the Skype calls, Johan asks his father about his daily life. He's still doing his own grocery shopping. Andrea said she'd be glad to help, but he said he can manage. He can take care of himself.

Johan thinks that Izaak is afraid of having a stroke and being unable to articulate his own wishes. In the Netherlands, you can choose euthanasia if you are lucid. But you can't sign the papers ahead of time saying you want euthanasia *if* or *when.* The Dutch thinking is that someone might change their mind, and there's no way medical staff would know it. You can't sign up for it ahead of time *in case* of dementia, in case of this, or in case of that.

Andrea says he's afraid because of what he saw Jopie go though, her slow and needy death.

"It was horrible watching Ma die," she says. "Pa never asked for any help when her Alzheimer's got bad. We didn't know how hard and desperate it was for him all those years. Nights he couldn't sleep because Ma would stay awake wandering the house. He couldn't leave her alone for five minutes. He never said a word. He took good care of her, but he didn't ask for help. He never told us anything much."

Izaak's fears—from the war, from Jopie's death, from a lifetime of taking control— have gotten the better of him. He's afraid of the future and what it might hold. He's afraid of the unknown, the uncontrolled, the possibility of dementia, senility, dependence upon others, the years ahead. He's unable to visualize any-thing in his future except worst case scenarios.

Izaak doesn't seem to be able to enjoy what he has. His sight and hearing. His reading, music, concerts, friends. His daily walks, driving his car, the voluntary preaching he still does. The activities he attends. None of these ongoing accomplishments offer pleasure or joy strong enough to scratch away his all-con-suming fear.

Izaak wants to die.

A few weeks later, Johan and Izaak Skype again. Izaak says he has news. He's searched for and found yet another doctor—this one a proponent of euthanasia—who agrees with him. Izaak has signed all the euthanasia paperwork. His doctor has signed it, too. They've agreed.

Izaak's euthanasia request is in the system. It's a matter of time.

"Do you want to know the day or the hour?" Izaak asks.

"No," Johan says, "I don't want to know."

Johan and I are both horrified. It's as if we've entered some sort of futuristic time warp. Some dystopian novel. The solid prairie land under my feet has given way and I can't seem to find my footing.

Andrea and Johan talk. Andrea says, "It's not the norm. Most Dutch doctors would never do this. They'd be afraid to. It's just . . . not usual. But you know how Pa can talk and talk. You know how he charms people. He knows how to get his own way."

It's June. Summer days of gardening and tomatoes, the first hot days of outdoor swimming pools, picnics, and puppies. We're reveling in life and Izaak is planning his death. *Has* planned his death. How can this be happening?

Johan tosses and turns all night long. I feel so bad. Nothing I say can help him. He's lost in his own grief and confusion. I'm mostly angry. I can't believe Izaak's going to carry through. Does he really want to die? Like this? Now?

Neighborly, 2008

A week later, on a Sunday morning, I grab some coffee, and go outside to walk through my front garden. A large note is taped onto my garbage bin. It's written in bright red marker, or lipstick.

> Please clean up your garbage.
> A disgrace + detriment to our neighborhood.
> This area is not a slum!

I read it several times, confused, then turn and look at my home. We've lived here for just over a year. Our garbage bin sits *beside* the garage, not *in* it like the other houses up and down the street. Our silver Honda's parked on our driveway. Our small garage—still a mess of miscellaneous stuff we aren't sure what to do with—has just enough space for one car but can't hold our two large garbage bins. There's a wheelbarrow tipped beside our garden and a pile of wood that Ben collected to turn on his lathe. To my eye, it's normal life. We keep the grass mowed. I've planted pink and yellow begonias in the brick flower planter by the door. It's not like we have old sheets hanging in the windows or rusted junkers parked along the street.

I wonder which of my neighbors put this note here, and why didn't they just talk to me?

That afternoon a neighbor—possibly the same one—yells at me over our shared back fence. It's a three-foot chain-link fence. Not like she has to yell. I can see and hear her clearly. She demands that I take my greenhouse down.

"It's against city regulation to have a structure within three feet of my fence," she shouts.

I look at my greenhouse, my pride and joy giving me an extra six weeks of garden time in our harsh climate. It's six feet by six feet and at the peak about nine feet tall. The design's magic: lightweight, covered in sturdy clear plastic, neat and efficient. We've been eating spinach and chard since April.

I tell my neighbor I've never heard of that regulation. Can it wait a couple of months? It's June. My tomato crop's climbing up the interior twine.

"I'm going to call the police if you don't take it down today!" she yells.

I don't want trouble. We're leaving the day after tomorrow for a long-awaited vacation in the Black Hills. I envision the police coming while we're gone.

As the tomatoes fall into heaps on the organic soil, as they bend underneath the weight of their stems and break, I pull the anchors and drag the greenhouse three feet.

Three feet away from her fence.

When we got the greenhouse, I'd placed it strategically, thinking about what we saw of each other's backyards. Now, since it's moved, I look directly onto her backyard patio. I could watch her drinking coffee each morning if I want to. She's got a great view, too. A direct look at my washing line and Ben's woodpile.

Hope you enjoy the new view, I think to myself, wiping tears from my face.

I thought we were neighbors.

To Become like God, 2008

Later that afternoon, Johan has his weekly phone call with Izaak. There's something about Izaak's voice, his finality, that startles Johan. Something's wrong. When they hang up, Johan calls Andrea and she tells him.

"Tomorrow. The doctor's coming tomorrow."

Johan calls his father back, pleads with him, knowing it will be their final conversation, and what can you say when you've been given this awful power, this knowledge of the future?

Later that night, we tell Kristina and Joren about Opa's decision. We tell them that Opa Kandel has chosen euthanasia. They are heartbreaking conversations. We don't tell the two youngest children. I don't know, we just can't bring ourselves to do it.

It will be four years until we learn the details of the day. The minute-by-minute happenings, the food eaten, the carefully chosen music, the actions of the people present, Izaak skipping down the hallway to his bedroom as if going on vacation.

For four years, I will only know this: On Monday, June 23, Johan does not stay home.

He goes to work, restless, agitated, and inconsolable.

Today. At 1:00. Looking at his watch.

Today. At 1:00. Waiting.

Today. At 1:00.

Johan waits, four thousand miles and seven time zones away. It breaks a heart. It shatters a world. This is a knowledge not to be borne. To become like God is not a gift to be coveted.

Complicit, 2008

Anneke is our youngest, my baby, not yet a teen. How can we tell her that Opa *asked* to die? Do we want her to know the cause, the method? What would such knowledge do to her? Would it shatter her childhood? Give her nightmares? Does she need to know? Johan and I agonize over the decision, over the implications.

"Let's give her a few more years of just being a little girl," I say to Johan.

"She's smart," he says. "She'll figure out something's off."

"You want to tell her that her grandfather chose to die?" I ask. "And just how do you plan to do that? What would you even say?"

"I don't know," Johan answers. "I don't know what to say."

Perhaps it's not the children we're protecting, but ourselves. I've lost all of my words. I stand mute before Izaak's decision. I don't know what to say. Time slips by. I don't have a handle on it at all.

What day is it? How long ago was it that he died?

"We have some sad news," we tell the youngest kids late Monday night. "We got a phone call your Opa in the Netherlands passed away."

We skim over the details and fudge the facts. *It was his heart.* They look at us, tears swelling up in their eyes. They don't ask too many questions, just cry as we hug them.

"Are you going back for the funeral?" Kristina wants to know.

"I don't think so," I say. "Dad's swamped with work and a plane ticket is expensive."

I say this as if these facts are the only truth. But facts and truth are seldom the same thing. I don't want to see the Kandel family. I don't want to listen to their discussions, to walk down the memory lane of Izaak's life. I have enough memories of my own.

Johan barely talks about his thoughts, let alone his feelings. He walks around in a daze of confusion and shock. The last thing he wants is to go to his dad's funeral, to talk to family, to discuss what, for him, is incomprehensible. His father is dead. Of his own choice. How could he do that to himself, to us, to our children, to *his* children?

We need some space. We need some time.

Izaak was a pastor of the Dutch Reformed tradition. He'd spent his life saying, "If God wills." It came out of his mouth like the refrain of an old, all too popular song.

See you tomorrow if God wills.

I'll go to the concert if God wills.

I hope to come and visit you in England if God wills.

Where is *if God wills* now?

And the date he chose—just two weeks before Andrea's wedding—how could he? His only daughter. She's getting married in two weeks. What was he thinking? My thoughts are a mess, colored by an anger I don't understand. How can I be so angry at him and at the same time be sad that he's gone?

Late that night, I sit on Anneke's bed, and she whispers, "I wish I could have seen Opa, just one more time."

They'd written letters back and forth since she was little, but hardly spent any time together. He visited her twice in the United States; she visited him twice in the Netherlands. Extended vacations to be sure, but still, infrequent at best. Sporadic and expensive trips that encompassed years of living apart.

"I wish you could have, too," I tell her and squeeze her hand three times—*I love you.*

She squeezes my hand back four times—*I love you, too*—our secret code.

I go to bed thinking about my four children. Two of them in the know. Two in the dark. I think about this man who was my father-in-law and lives no more. This man I've lied for. This man I've broken trust with my children over. I never wanted to keep his secret, but that's what Izaak's choice has become, a secret to keep. A secret from my children. His final betrayal.

I wonder how it will play out. If we've done the right thing. Maybe we should've told them? I just don't know anymore. I don't have any answers. I carry a vague fear of what's ahead and go to sleep shouldering a weight that wasn't there yesterday. There's an uneasiness in my new knowledge. When we finally tell Ben and Anneke, what will they think of us? Will they wonder what else we haven't said?

Suddenly, unexpectedly, I'm back in my mother's kitchen, a dozen years ago. I'm forty-one years old and sitting on the red Formica counter.

"I slept with a knife under my pillow," my mother is telling me. "I didn't want you to know about your grandfather, so I never told you. I just wanted you to be a kid."

I stare at her in disbelief. I have no idea what she's talking about. She's kept this secret for forty-one years?

"I always thought," she continues, "That grandfathers should be magical people. I made the decision not to tell you. About his arrest, the prison sentence, the little girl down the back alley. I thought, it was better to wait, till you were older."

I want to throw up. Even the memory of this conversation with my mom and its ramifications makes me sick to my stomach. Forty-one years old and slapped across the face with a family secret so hurtful and hidden that it's still tearing my mother's siblings apart.

I hate family secrets. I said I'd never keep or have them.

When I was ten, my mom went in for plastic surgery. We were told to tell people, if they asked, that she was on vacation. She came home, her face black and blue and swollen, and hid in the house for weeks. Until she looked back to normal, okay to go out.

"No one will ever know," she said smiling a Cheshire grin.

When I was in junior high, she went into the hospital for psychiatric care, weighing less than ninety pounds. She was gone for weeks and Dad told us the same thing. "Tell people she's on vacation."

I wasn't any good at lying.

All those years, if Dad was home but not on medical call, we were told to answer the phone and say, "Dr. Jensen is out. Call the hospital if you need a doctor." There was only one phone in the house, at the foot of the stairs, between the kitchen and the den. A little nook with a desk. By the time I was in high school, I refused to answer the phone. No more lies for me. I swore if I ever had kids, I'd never ask them to lie. I'd never lie to them either. But all of this changed today.

Today, I'm actively keeping information away from my children. A woman with a secret.

I sing myself to sleep that night with the poetry of Dylan Thomas.

Do not go gentle into that good night,
Old age should burn and rave at close of day;
Rage, rage against the dying of the light.

Where did you burn bright, Izaak? Where was your rage against the dying light?

I sing myself to sleep, sing the poetry of our tight secret. I rage against Izaak who put me in this position. I hate him for it. And I hate myself for my own complicity.

This Thing Called Family

What had I expected from Izaak? What does a daughter-in-law want from her in-laws?

A little flexibility. A little kindness. I'd envisioned *niceness.* That good old North Dakota and Minnesota word. A sort of general agreeableness.

Most of all, I imagined that Izaak would be happy for us. Happy that I loved his son. Happy that I pleased Johan. That Johan had found somebody who'd go to Africa with him, working by his side. That his son had found someone to love.

These were the things I expected. Not so grand. Not so needy, not so greedy. To laugh a bit. To enjoy some kindness along the way. A bit of shared meaning. A feeling that we were all in this thing together. This thing called family.

A Baffled Bereavement

There've been many griefs in my life: the deaths of friends, co-workers, grandparents, neighbors. Everything surrounding those deaths *normal.* Understandable. The feelings came and grew and dipped and slowly muted. A natural progression.

This death from euthanasia leaves me confused.

Why did he choose this? What if he hadn't? Why that date? What if he'd waited?

My mind's a hurricane of questions.

Whose fault was it? We should've talked him out of it. Johan and I should've been there. Would it have made any difference?

Izaak's death is a prolonged grief, a prolonged anger. I can't seem to move away from it. I function. I laugh. I love. I go on vacations, write, sleep, eat, find joy in life. But Izaak's death lies shallow beneath it all. A burial that isn't quite finished. A toe sticking out of the ground.

I don't even understand why I care so much. We weren't on the best of terms.

Why does it hurt like this? Why can't I just let it go?

I rear up ready to fight and there is nothing to strike at, just a mirage of pain that flickers and fades. I've never known such a complicated grief, such a baffling bereavement. I want to stop him. To change the outcome. I want to yell at him. To rage. But I cannot. He isn't here. Not anymore. Not ever again.

The Love of Life

Izaak and I tolerated each other for the sake of family. I didn't connect with him, nor he with me. After years of interactions, vacations, and time together, I didn't understand him, or, for that matter, even like him very much.

So why has his death hit me so squarely? It should be easier, but I can't seem to move on. What the heck is going on with me? What am I *really* circling and fighting and stewing over?

Looking back, it makes more sense to me now. I grew up swimming in an ocean that valued the very idea of *life*. An idea which held me, molded me, thrummed through my veins.

I grew up with hardworking virtues: never quit, work hard, keep on keeping on. We were homestead stock, solid as the land beneath our feet. I watered my horse in the winter when water froze overnight, and I needed an ax each morning to chop a hole through the ice. I ran track and field, got straight As, never turned in an assignment late.

My dad kept people alive: by profession, by the medical decisions he made, and by sheer effort of will, heading off to the ER night after night dead tired in twenty-below weather. Throughout my childhood, I heard his footstep on the stairs in the dark of night, the car starting-up and driving away. Off to an emergency. Off to save another life. Off to birth a baby. Men pulled from grain bins. Children pulled from swimming pools. A woman needing a Cesarean section. He'd returning hours later and when I got up for school, he was always already gone, 8:00 a.m. sharp, back to the clinic no matter how short his night had been.

As a teenager, I was drawn toward activities that honored life. Once a week, I'd get together with a group of my friends and we'd go to ARC events where we volunteered to work with dis-abled kids. Dances or hayrides. Swimming or just hanging out. I tussled the hair of little boys who walked crooked through life, went bowling with Down Syndrome children who threw their bowling balls straight up into the air and laughed at the thud of them falling hard onto the golden wood floor. I coached Special Olympics, preparing little girls for gymnastics events, teaching them to touch their toes, to balance standing on one foot. Their laughter so contagious, they couldn't continue, falling on top of each other in pure joy.

I headed up an Easter Seal's summer camp day program, 'disabled' latchkey children doing belly flops into swimming pools, watching movies, producing artwork, spilling glue and glitter and popcorn, their smiles the stars in the night sky of my teenage years.

And later, my education trained me towards life-giving skills. I chose the profession of nursing and learned the art and science of caring for, treasuring, and saving lives. I worked ER, intensive care, pre and post-op. I spent one year in a huge hospital on an IV. Therapy Team, carrying a beeper and roaming the hospital starting IVs in emergency situations, in cancer wards, in pediat-rics. Fixing, healing, and curing formed me through four years of school and three years of work.

After nursing school, I did a year of postgraduate Bible study. I was taught that life is sacred. That a God who *is* life, *gives* life. And even though many of my beliefs and thoughts have matured and grown since then, still, it was my faith training, my kinder-garten, my foundation. *We are not our own.*

I gave birth to four children, two girls and two boys, and took joy in their every delight. We raised Bichon puppies by the dozen and giant French Lop rabbits that bit us when we weren't care-ful. We rescued robins, raising them in the kitchen and releasing them to the wild, where they would fly off, and later return and sit upon our shoulders.

All those years, without realizing it, I'd been living with a laser focus on life's enchantments, glories, beauties, responsibilities, and value.

Izaak's decision to take his own life shook me to the core. It took the oxygen out of my lungs. Tossed me onto dry land and left me gasping. His death raised a thousand questions that I didn't know how to face.

Did life have value in and of itself? Is anything sacred? Are there any limits? Should there be?

His choice of euthanasia opened up a black hole of questions, a fathomless frightening abyss, a Pandora's box that I reared back from, afraid and uncertain.

It also placed Izaak upon that sacred stage where the dead are enshrined. Beyond reproach and conversation. He glowers at me from there, his new position, his posthumously high pedestal. Set in stone. Elevated. Ennobled. Enthroned.

Here we stand. Me with my innumerable, unanswerable questions. My shaken beliefs. Izaak upon his dais, still and impenetrable. He's done it again. Made his point. Had the last word. Taken his final canonized stance. He is become now a high and holy relic, calling us to come and admire, come and cherish, come and agree.

I am no worshipper. And he is no god. But still. Who am I to speak against the dead?

Forgive Me

My mother, Betty Lou, and my Dutch father-in-law, Izaak, were both accomplished wizards when it came to words. My mother used her words to cling and wrap, hold tight and reward. Izaak used his to be in charge, to keep himself distant and above.

My mother's words overflowed and flooded my life. A tsunami of needy love. I was six or seven, perhaps eight years old and fast becoming her little confidant. Her go-to talk-to on days she felt sad, bad, and blue. On days she wouldn't eat, we'd sit at the red

Formica kitchen counter—she with her black coffee and me with
a mug of milk—and she'd talk. And cry. How confusing it all was.
Her warm love wrapped up and tangled in such need. In the face
of my mother, I drowned. The flood of her words, her yearnings,
and appetites—something she herself did not understand—both
overwhelmed and attracted me. I was too young to contain such
knowledge. Nothing could have quenched the flow of her hunger.
But oh, how I tried.

Izaak's words, by comparison, were a desert dry, a sandstorm
devoid of affection. In the face of Izaak, I covered my face against
the flying grit. I bowed before my father-in-law's stark controls;
his dry bones hollowed by fear. Nothing could appease his relentless requirements. Do this. Don't do that. Now. Later. Never.

I could breathe in neither parental space. Wet with emotions
or blasted dry by the dearth of them. Lost between the drowning and the drought. Yet there I existed, in a land shredded by
their brilliant histories, devoid of moderation, both soaked
and parched.

Is it any wonder, my great need for language when much of
my life had been inundated by such power? All *my* words pent up,
a riot within, kneeling and bowing before others.

I will wait a decade, and then another, before my own needs
burst: the research culminates, the reservoir overflows, the dam
breaks, the words spill. Perhaps someday I can forgive myself for
the destruction my words will bring.

Letter from the Dead

A week after Izaak's death, Johan goes to get the mail. He comes
back and holds out a letter.

"It's for you," he says. "From my dad."

I'm momentarily confused and can only stare at the envelope.
My name's written across it in Izaak's distinct cursive. There's a
Dutch stamp in the upper corner.

"He's dead," I say stupidly.

"Apparently, he wrote it before he died," Johan answers, still holding out the letter.

In that instant, I see my husband—just six days ago—talking to his father via Skype. I hear them say good-bye. I see his shoulders convulse. As the memory fades, I look up into my husband's sky-blue eyes, but do not take the letter from his hand.

"I don't want it," I say quietly.

"But he wrote it to you. He must have wanted you to have it." Johan shakes the letter slightly, wanting me to take it.

Since the day I met Izaak, he has told me what to do and how and when and where. My Dutch father-in-law, the man with all the answers. The patriarch who always had the final word.

I don't want Izaak's words in my ear anymore. I don't care what he thinks, what he writes. I don't want his explanations, his justifications, his verbosity. I'm exhausted by his voice.

"I don't want it!" I yell at Johan.

He stands quietly in front of me.

My shoulders tighten. My jaw compresses.

"I'll put it in the file cabinet," he says. "It'll be there when you want to open it."

"You can damn well burn it for all I care," I shout at his back, and it isn't Johan that I'm angry at.

I am through with Izaak.

Steady Hands, 1976

My dad calls a few months later, in December. He hasn't been feeling well and went in for several tests. The doctors found five tumors on his liver. A few weeks later, on the day after Christmas, his biopsy reports arrive. Three of his tumors are cancerous. There're too large for any kind of successful surgery. His advanced cirrhosis, due to undiagnosed hemochromatosis, has no cure.

I think about my dad and all he has meant to me. Back in 1976, when I was in my third year of nursing school, I went home to visit my folks. During the visit, Dad said, "Well, I guess you're almost a nurse now. Want to come with me on my rounds?"

We walked in the side door of the hospital and he grabbed his white doctor's jacket, *Dr. Warren R. Jensen* hand-embroidered in a cursive red stitch above the pocket. He strode down the hall; I followed as he went room to room, talked to patients, read charts, and gave orders that nurses jotted down. In-between the patients, he turned and talked to me about decisions, diagnoses, changes in medications, new technologies.

When he was called to the delivery room, I came along and watched my dad deftly wrestle and coax a reluctant life into this world. A mother gritting her teeth and bearing down, legs parted high in stirrups, panting, cries, and at last my dad's declaration: *It's a boy! Congratulations.* The mother pale, sweaty, wrung out, delighted. The first birth I'd ever seen. The cut of the umbilical cord. The squirt of blood. The red and sloshy placenta bowl. Above it all the newborn wail. There's no sound like it. Indignant. Hungry. So sweet it made me ache. The cry of life.

The last stop of the night was oncology. My dad sat softly on the bedside of another boy; this one eighteen years old and all used up. He was pale and sweating like the mother I'd just seen. The boy's father stood in the corner, his red-rimmed eyes pleading with my dad.

My dad took the young patient's hand and stroked it lightly, asked if he was comfortable, bent down to listen. The boy didn't respond. My dad had no encouraging words to give the father, nothing to say or do. And yet, he sat—comfortable with the dying, gentle in its presence—and held the boy's hand. Death hung there, in that room, quiet enough, but relentless. Close enough to touch.

We were quiet on the way home.

I went up to my room and wept. I wept for the glory of a new life, and for the great aching hollow of death. For the speed at which we'd walked from one to the other, just going down a hall. I cried for the father who stood beside his son's bed. For my dad's gentle goodness.

I cried because my dad had spent long hours every day of my growing up years in his own private world—the hospital—and tonight, he'd invited me in. I'd never been in such a place before. I felt it sacred, this place where life and death kissed each other in the hall, and how my father held them both in his strong and steady hands.

Falling to the Ground, 2009

Being an RN, I have seen my share of births and deaths. I have seen people die in agony and others who passed so quietly that the mystery of it all left me wordless.

In the last year of his life, I watch my own father soften. A surgeon with magical hands, he can fix anything, build whatever my mother wants. He's not much of a talker, never has been. When he's diagnosed with terminal liver cancer, knowing the heavy toll treatments would inflict, Dad chooses not to undergo the extensive, invasive procedures. He talks about his decision with several specialists. The procedures would lay him up for months and the results would be questionable at best. He wants to finish his garden, work in the woodshop, be outdoors.

When we come to visit, I see him out puttering in the yard, pulling up weeds or planting bulbs, and I can't help thinking about the cancer, about him dying. When I ask him how he's doing, he knows what I mean.

Dad looks up at me and says, "Me? Look at me. I'm not dying. I'm living. I'm just going to keep living every day I've got."

Toward the end, there are days when he's confused, and I spoon feed him like a child. We sit side by side on the couch, me with Cream of Wheat covered in milk and sprinkled with brown sugar. He looks over at me with a question in his eyes. I hold up the spoon, and he opens his mouth like a little bird. Then he swallows and looks at me again and smiles. Those beautiful eyes lock onto mine and he smiles and smiles.

There are days when his mind works fine and he whisper-talks about his life. How he regrets having to leave the pond in his yard unfinished. How there are so many things he still wants to do. An unfinished painting to complete. He talks about much he loves us, and how infrequently he's said so.

"Take care of Mom," he'd say.

My dad says things in those last weeks that he's never been able to say before. He holds my hand unashamed and unabashed. Just quietly holds my hand as we sit beside the lake.

He cries, too. Easily. Openly. I've never seen him cry in all my life. He cries over movies, and things he reads, over petting his dog. He cries when the sunset glows pink and orange above the calm waters of Little Mantrap Lake.

The day before he dies, I wash his hair. He lists to one side while sitting in a wheelchair that hospice gave us only two days earlier. I place a large towel over his shoulders and let the warm water wash over my hands, over his silky white hair so fine. I take another towel and pat his hair, his forehead, his neck, and brush his hair into place. My brother uses the electric shaver, tiny hairs falling to the ground. These days. These moments. I wouldn't give them up for the world.

We bury him to a twenty-one-gun salute. I wince at every shot, tears unstoppable, stoop and pick up an empty shell and put it in my pocket. My father, a captain in the United States Army, lies under the prairie soil just south of Bismarck, the town he grew up in after he'd left the farm, the town where he met my mother.

American Man, 2010

Over the years, Johan's talked about becoming an American citizen. Because he lives in the United States and has an American wife and children, there wouldn't be any legal complications. He's reluctant, however, to give up his Dutch citizenship. It's a part of his identity, but also, he likes to think that someday we might work for the Dutch embassy again.

"Maybe when the kids are older, we'll move back overseas,"

he says. "If I have my Dutch citizenship, there'd be more job opportunities."

Sometimes, in what seems like a fruitless effort, I ask him questions.

"If you become an American, would you still get your Dutch pension for the years you worked for the Dutch government?"

Over the years, he's sent letters to his previous employers and letters to the Dutch pension services asking about what benefits he's entitled to. They send back long, convoluted, vague answers. They won't know until he applies. He can't apply until he's sixty-five.

"What about having dual citizenship? Can you carry two passports?" I ask. "Some people do. Don't they?"

"That varies from country to country," he replies. "Two passports are recognized in the Netherlands; America only recognizes one."

We go back and forth. More questions than answers.

Right now, Johan is considered a Permanent Resident. He's required to carry his US Permanent Resident card with him at all times.

Living with a person who isn't a citizen has some worries of its own.

What if, God forbid, he's accused of breaking a law, charged with drug related crime, or who knows what misdeed or offense. He could be sent back to the Netherlands, transferred, deported. What would I do, mother of four children, without his presence, his income? How could I raise my children without their father?

We both know it's highly unlikely—he's the most law abiding of men—but we also know justice isn't always just. There are people who get caught in the cracks of the system, mislabeled, misjudged, wrongly accused, wrongly convicted.

We've been married for twenty-seven years, when in the winter of 2009, Johan makes a decision. He's tired of the ongoing situation of being foreign. He's going to become an American.

I don't know how to feel about it. I mean, it will certainly be easier. I'm relieved that we won't have to worry about his status. But I also feel sad; it's like he's giving up a part of himself.

We've stood side by side at airports, in Zambia, Indonesia, Malaysia, The Netherlands, the UK, and I held out my blue American passport and he held out his burgundy Dutch one. Funny the details you don't think about that are just a part of your life. The color difference of our passports one of those things. Just one of those things.

Johan writes to the US Citizenship and Immigration Services (USCIS) requesting information on citizenship. As an individual born in a foreign country and already immigrated to the United States, he will be a citizen through a process called naturalization.

It takes months of paperwork. Johan fills in the N-400 Application for Naturalization. He appears at the USCIS to be fingerprinted and has photo ID pictures taken. He pays $675 to the Department of Homeland Security. He passes the tests of English and US history and government. And finally, in the mail, he receives a letter: *Congratulations! Your application has been recommended for approval. If final approval is granted, you will be notified when and where to report for the Oath Ceremony.*

On Friday June 18, 2010, Johan and I and three of our children drive to the International Friendship Festival at the Historic City Hall in Pelican Rapids, Minnesota. Johan sits up on the stage with twelve other people from multiple countries: Iraq, South Africa, Canada, Nepal, Belarus, Serbia, China, and Mexico. We listen to "The Star Spangled Banner," and then an officer from the Department of Homeland Security speaks. Afterward, the soon-to-be citizens stand, raise their right hands, and the presiding judge administers the Oath of Allegiance.

> I hereby declare, on oath, that I absolutely and entirely renounce and abjure all allegiance and fidelity to any foreign prince, potentate, state, or sovereignty of whom or which I have heretofore been a subject or citizen . . .

and that I take this obligation freely, without any mental reservation or purpose of evasion; so help me God.

Each new citizen is presented his or her naturalization certificate, an American Flag, and a Pledge of Allegiance card. President Barack Obama speaks to us via video. The ceremony ends with the song "America" and the reading of Emma Lazarus's poem "The New Colossus."

> Here at our sea-washed, sunset gates shall stand
> A mighty woman with a torch, whose flame
> Is the imprisoned lightning, and her name
> Mother of Exiles.

I have never thought of Johan as an exile. He is, it's true, an expatriate. But exile brings to mind refugee or outcast, someone banished, expelled. I wonder if he feels these things today.

> Give me your tired, your poor,
> Your huddled masses yearning to breathe free,
> The wretched refuse of your teeming shore.
> Send these, the homeless, tempest-tost to me,
> I lift my lamp beside the golden door!

And so the golden door opens. We watch the other families exuberantly waving their flags, broad smiles lighting their faces. We take a lot of pictures, too. Johan waving his flag. Johan with the children. Johan and I side by side.

Johan hands me his Certificate of Naturalization. It looks like a fancy graduation certificate. Dates, places, official signatures. His is signed by the Director of the US Citizenship and Immigration Services. In the lower left-hand corner of the document are these words: Country of former nationality: Netherlands.

Former. Who he was. Who is he now? Has anything *really* changed? Yes. And no. Our life will go on much as before. He won't have to carry his registration card, won't have to go every five years to reapply. Maybe we'll feel more settled. More like we belong. Like this is home.

We drive back to our house where a small party with friends joins us. I've made a red, white, and blue dessert: strawberries, whipped cream, and blueberries. I serve it on plates and hand out red-and-white-striped napkins. The evening ends with talk and laugher and game after game of Dutch Blitz.

That night, when I get into bed, I sleep for the first time in my life beside an American man.

Part 7: UNSPOKEN, 2012

Jopie and Izaak Kandel's wedding day. The gymnastic girls Jopie taught all line the steps of the church. Dordrecht. The Netherlands. August 8, 1951.

My Children's Anguish, 2012

Four years after Izaak's death, Johan says he's ready to go back to the Netherlands. The country entices us, calls us back. It's been too long since we've seen Johan's brother Bert and sister Andrea. Since we've seen their children. We've never met Andrea's husband or his daughter. Our children barely know their cousins.

We know we'll have to tell Ben and Anneke the truth about Izaak's death before we go. We don't want them learning from the odd comment from a cousin, from overhearing a conversation. We want to give them time to process the information before our trip.

The time has come. We call a family meeting.

"Anneke, Ben, Kristina. Can you all come to the living room? Dad and I want to talk to you."

Here it comes. God, I wish I could stop this conversation. I never asked for it. I certainly didn't want to be smack-dab in the middle of this.

"Before we go on our trip to the Netherlands, there's something we want you to know. In Holland, well. I don't know how to say this," I stammered.

Once spoken, these words can't ever be taken back.

I try again. "In Holland, they have a new law, that if you are tired of living, you can, um, you can decide . . . It's legal to . . ."

Johan interrupts me. "What Mom's trying to say. Is that. In the Netherlands people can decide to end their own lives if they want to."

The kids have that *don't tell me; I don't want to know* look spreading into their eyes. But we continue talking.

"We're saying. That's a choice that Opa made. When he died, it wasn't because he was sick. It wasn't his heart. He made a decision. He didn't want to live anymore."

Their eyes widen and they look away from us. As if trying to grasp and trying to push away at the same time.

"It's legal," Johan continues. "There are doctors who come to your house, when that's your decision."

Kristina is not surprised. But Ben and Anneke look like they want to cry, like they want to run away and never return. We're breaking their hearts.

I watch as my kids' faces crumple into tears and questions and confusion. I watch as a knowledge forms inside of them. I watch a part of them die. They've lost a part of their innocence and it will never be restored.

I hate what Izaak's decision is doing to us. I hate what we're doing to our children. In my wildest of dreams, I never thought euthanasia would be a part of my life. I'm a North Dakota girl! A solid-footed prairie woman. How did this happen? How did legalized killing gash its way into *my* family?

I go to bed that night with the worst taste in my mouth, sick at heart for what we've introduced into the thoughts of our children. I hate what I've done, and I hate the man who brought this anguish into the lives of my children.

Later, Anneke will ask why we didn't tell them sooner. Why we waited. There's no easy response. No clear explanation to give. There isn't a right answer; it's all so wrong. Nothing I do or say will change it. What's done is done is done.

This is what I know. I have betrayed my children's trust.

Gone Too Far, 2012

The work and research of writing about Zambia winds down and I begin to send it—my Zambian manuscript—out. As I wait for responses, I begin to think more and more about Izaak and his death. There's so much I can't get my head around. I keep circling back to the day Izaak died. I circle round it like a moth consumed by the flame that attracts her. I can't seem to step away.

I don't want to write about Izaak. I just want to try to understand what he did so that I can move on. Maybe if I learn more, I can let go. A little research is a good thing, right?

With those mixed emotions and jumbled thoughts, I begin. One day I work on submitting my manuscript to an agent, a publishing house, a contest; the next day I read articles about euthanasia or WWII. I doubt I'll ever write about any of it, but I need to understand. If I'm ever going to move on, I need to understand. As the days pass, I spend a lot of time wondering about Izaak. Sometimes I talk to him in my mind.

Let me remind you of our history, Izaak.

After I married Johan in 1981, you saw your son once a year, at most, for the rest of your life. Sometimes, three years would pass before you set your eyes upon his face. This was the life he chose. I used to think, *this is the life he chose the day he married me.* I used to think, *I guess I'm not your favorite person since I took your son away.* But the truth's different. Johan chose to leave you before we ever met, working three years in Zambia in his early twenties.

You lived in the Netherlands the entire length of your life. Over these decades, you visited us once in England. Twice in America. A trinity of times. Your totality.

We visited you so many times I can't keep track of them all. We came to the Netherlands and visited you in Hardenberg, in Putten, and in Doorn. We stayed with Andrea, or in rented cottages, bungalows, caravans, and once on a sailboat. We spent our primary vacation time and money, year after year, to be a part of your life. It wasn't easy or cheap.

I've seen many places on this exquisite blue marble of a globe, but there were more I wanted to see. Still, we came to the Netherlands, time after time. Vacation after vacation. Our days spent with you, our vacation time used up, our bank account dwindling. I came because Johan wanted to be with you. Share time. Talk. How he loved talking with you. I came out of deference. Out of wanting our children to know their grandparents. In retrospect, I don't know if it was worth it.

You met us with controls and smothered us with fears. Fear of what others thought. Fear of getting it wrong. Fear of not being in control. Fear of being late. Fear of making a bad impression. Your blind, broken, stubborn fear. Correcting and criticizing.

Still we came.

The final time Johan went to the Netherlands to see you, I didn't come along, busy with the kids in school, our days full and booked tight. Not enough money in the bank.

But Johan came. He cancelled meetings, bought a ticket, booked a plane, left his family, missed his kids' soccer games, flew across the ocean, just to be with you.

On that spur of the moment occasion, your son's final visit— *If you want to see Pa alive, you'd better fly home*—you hammered a wedge—*The euthanasia rules state I have to tell my children before I can do it. So. Now you know*—that broke my husband's heart. This is what you did. And nobody could stop you. After all those years, and all those trips, this was how you treated him, Izaak.

You didn't take anyone into consideration except yourself.

As I said, Izaak, this is the history that we share. A history that ended with your final act: the point where our lives separated. A day of your own making. The day that altered the course of our history. There are no returns, no remakes, no do-overs.

One of the things that hurt me most, that still goads, was the date you chose: two weeks before Andrea's wedding.

You couldn't even wait two weeks, attend her big day, wish her joy? Your only daughter.

You stole a time of fun, excitement, and preparation from her. You turned her wedding month into a deathbed, a funeral, a time of mourning. She should've been out choosing her dress, instead she was choosing what she'd wear to your funeral. She should have been planning flowers and desserts for her wedding. Instead, she was writing up an obituary, shopping for funeral announcement cards, planning your funeral service. How could you have done this? I hate you for it. For how you treated Andrea, my sister, my friend. This fact alone is incomprehensible. I've never known such blatant stubbornness. In timing. In execution. In silence. In selfishness.

Selfishness, the word I keep coming back to, yet shrink from. But there it is. I wonder if you ever considered anyone other than yourself. Did you think about the day after? The ramifications of your choice? Did you imagine the outcomes or consider the emotional slurry you so easily flung at us?

You can tell so much about a person by the way they leave you.

Your son was considerate and caring towards you all his days, Izaak. A daddy's boy most of his life. He adored you. He'd have done anything for you. How he loved you.

I want you to know this, Izaak. Your choice changed the world. It changed me. It changed your son.

Your son did not attend your deathbed.

Your son did not return home for your funeral.

April Fool's Day, 2012

We want our trip to the Netherlands to be in time for tulip season and decide to fly out on April 1, 2012.

April 1, 2012. Ten years to the day since the implementation of Dutch euthanasia laws.

Although Johan's been back to the Netherlands multiple times, I haven't set my foot on her soil for ten years. Ten years! Anneke was seven the last time we came. She has very few memories of her father's homeland. She's almost seventeen now. How did ten years pass by so quickly? Joren won't be coming along; he's a working married man. So it will be Johan and I, along with Kristina, Ben, and Anneke.

Andrea goes overboard to help us out, letting us stay in a camper trailer she owns, getting us bikes to rent, stocking our trailer with wonderful Dutch treats. We arrive to rainy, foggy weather. I'm so dizzy and disoriented from the jet lag that I refuse to ride a bike for the first day and a half, afraid I'll fall off or make a fool of myself biking right into some unsuspecting person.

It's great to be back! There's something solid about walking down the cobbled streets that have been traversed for hundreds of years. There's a continuity in houses dating back to the 1500s and 1600s that are still used as homes. We bike by castles and statues and landmarks and museums; I feel wonderfully at home in that land of grass and water, surrounded by much of the history of Johan's life.

We eat locally grown vegetables and freshly made breads. Markets overflow with the flowers. We watch fishmongers and cheesemongers sell their ridiculously gorgeous food. People ride on bicycles with more children aboard than seems quite believable. Babies wiggle in seats attached to front bike handlebars, while their toddler siblings sit neatly in seats attached in back. Some bikes have a sort of big cart in front. I see mothers with four small children in one bike-cart. We laugh and say, "Look! A Dutch minivan."

Pedestrians walk by, jog by, or hop on the tram. It's delightful to be in this land filled with people who are tall, fashionable, and slender.

We spend every other day with family. The in-between days, we play tourist and visit Amsterdam, Rotterdam, and fantastical tulip gardens. Johan's cousin gives us an inside tour of the famous flower auction houses at Alsmeer where he has worked for twenty-five years. We walk by signs that say, "No tourists beyond this point," and laugh about our insiderness. We crisscross the country with ease, hopping trains and taxis, trams and buses. We visit the Rijksmuseum, the stormy coast. We bike along the canals for miles, passing fields alive with spring lambs, newborn Lakenvelder calves, and working windmills that twirl overhead.

We do all of this while simultaneously not bringing up *the topic.*

But Andrea and Bert, our niece and nephew, and even some of the cousins, all want to talk about Johan's dad. Every time we sit down—for *pannekoeken* at a restaurant along the canal in Utrecht, in a fancy Chinese restaurant with incredibly colored sushi and fresh seafood, eating apple tart on Andrea's patio—everyone brings up the subject we have so studiously avoided.

Why did he do it? Do you think he was depressed? He was a pastor, for God's sake! We've never talked to anyone outside of the family about it. It's been four years and we still don't understand.

Finally, on a walk through the forest on a foggy afternoon—when Johan and I are finally alone with his sister—she tells us about the day Pa died. She is reduced to sobs, but she talks on through her tears, through her anger and anguish, through her confusion. All the little details come out. She talks and talks until I can see it. Until I feel as if I was there. Maybe that's what she needed. She needed us to be there, and we weren't. But we can be there for her now. We can listen to her, our sister, our friend.

Oh, God.

All the details. All the little details.

House Call, 2008

The doctor agreed to the house call. He would come to Izaak. They got out their agendas and chose a date and time. One that Izaak thought would work for his family. No one would be on vacation. They'd be able to come.

Jopie died on March 23. Perhaps that also had something to do with the date Izaak chose. He always did have an affinity for dates and calendars. For linking things together by number.

The doctor marked his calendar.

Monday, June 23, 2008, 8:00 p.m.

Izaak served coffee at 7:30 p.m. that night. With cookies. He tapped on his wristwatch and looked at the door. "The doctor's late." Izaak, the precise man, chose the music with care. Mozart's *Requiem Mass* playing on CD.

The doctor arrived twelve minutes late. He took two minutes to shake hands around, and then asked Izaak the question required by law. "Are you sure?"

"Ja."

Izaak jumped up, ran down the hall to his bedroom, and lay down on his bed. Later, it was said that he lay down on the bed with all the excitement of a kid going to a fair, off to the beach, going on vacation. Have a nice trip.

Izaak's oldest son held his hand.

The lawful questions asked and answered, the doctor set up all the equipment and started an IV.

Izaak's soon to be son-in-law looked away, out the window, remembering a different land of pain.

Izaak's daughter, so not wanting to be there, so not wanting her dad to be alone, so brave, so kind, so sweet, so sad. His daughter.

Here's where the facts jumble with the tears. I lose sight of the scene, blurred into stupor and oblivion. But Andrea's words, the details of that day, march on. Like soldiers, like minutes, they march on to the grave.

His grandson cried.

It took the doctor one minute to slowly inject all of the poison, then he walked over to the window, turned his back to them, and stood looking out at the view.

It took less than half a minute for Izaak to stop breathing.

One good deep breath.

And his oldest son, the one holding his hand said, "Is this all? Is this it?"

The room sucked in its breath, hollow with the void.

"It was what he wanted," they said to each other. Nodding. Together.

The doctor signed the required papers.

The sister-in-law called the undertaker.

And from that moment on, Izaak was referred to in the past tense.

The *is* of his life, in a blink, in a breath, became *was*, and *has been*.

The deed was done and all in all, it went rather well. Smoothly, you might say. No kink in the procedure. Routine.

Doctors in America no longer provide house calls. They still do in the Netherlands.

It's a matter of courtesy.

Free Fall, 2012

As we walk, Andrea talks and sobs, and talks some more, I can't comprehend the details of Izaak's death. I can't shake the images that fall into my mind. We're walking through a lovely Dutch forest near her house, our feet trod a solid pine needle covered ground, but I'm unmoored. Untethered.

How could you? What have you done? Who were you, Izaak?

I'm free-falling through fleeting images. Time moves too slow; moves too fast. I can't order my thoughts. I can barely walk. The sound of Andrea's sobs drowning out sense and reason. We finish our walk and return to the trailer. I try to keep it together, talk to the kids about their day, and finally crawl into my pajamas. I lie in bed restless, Johan tossing and turning next to me.

When I finally fall asleep, my dreams frighten me. They're full of large red buzzers set atop black boxes. Red buzzers pushed, slammed, beaten down by men wearing white-lab coats, all of them with smiling clownlike faces. Each time the buzzer depresses, it blares a siren wail. My dreams are black and white and red. Corpses zipped in plastic bags. Andrea's face. Cookies and cups of coffee. The doctor shaking hands. My dreams wrap and wrestle me, trip and tangle me. We tussle through a long night. Blurry thought and painful flight.

Weeks later, when we leave the Netherlands, my dreams travel back across the ocean, follow me home. For the next five or six months, I can't escape them. They stay and stay and finally, when I'm strong enough, weak enough, tired enough, when I've run enough, fought enough, cried enough, my dreams reach in and grip me till I can no longer look away. Until I'm able to stand quiet before them, ready to see.

Ash Upon Ash

You lie dead upon your bed, Izaak. I can see you now, see through your suit, your tie, your unwrinkled starched shirt. I always could. Beneath the silent blaring music, Mozart's dead. A requiem Mass.

You were so afraid of brokenness, it broke you more. Until you were nothing but fractured fear, glued together with stubborn pride. Together they destroyed you.

As surely as the bombs rained down on Rotterdam.

As surely as the planes sped away.

As surely as the fires burned for days and the Black Snow fell sixty miles around.

At your death, the ashes of that Black Snow were still falling, dark and unrelenting, gritty upon your cold unmoving lips. The ashes fell and fell. Until they became all that was visible. Your body only an outline.

Ash upon ash.

Though they muted the noise of our weeping, we never did know how to stop them.

The Rule, 2012

There were so many rules in Izaak's household. Bert often got into disagreements with Izaak and was the only one of the three children who openly defied Izaak.

"Father forbade us to go to pubs," Bert told me one day. "It was not allowed. What would his congregation think to see his sons drinking in public?"

Bert, off on his own going to college, didn't care. He enjoyed his student life, drank when and where he wanted. Drinking is one thing; a live-in girlfriend is another.

"Ja," Bert said. "Somehow Father found out and the next time we came home he called us into his office."

Izaak sat down behind his big desk. Bert and his girlfriend sat on the other side. The inquisition began.

"Well, son," Izaak said glowering at Bert then turning his gaze. "Well, Lady. It is forbidden, what you are doing!"

Bert told Izaak to mind his own business. He was paying for his own schooling and holding down a job. He lived an independent life. It didn't matter to him what Izaak thought.

After the encounter, Izaak never visited Bert's student flat again.

"Mother came," Bert said. "But Father said as long as we were *living in sin*, he would not ever come to visit. And he never did."

Years later, just before his death, Izaak made another declaration. He told Bert that he could not talk about his choice of euthanasia. It was not allowed.

"After I die, you must tell people that I died from cardiac arrest. My heart will stop. You will NOT tell them anything else."

In the days that followed his death—when Johan's brother and sister phoned family members and friends—everyone seemed astonished, saying they didn't know he'd been sick. Asking what had happened. The siblings answered vaguely. Hung up quickly.

Izaak's best friend said, "I saw him the morning of the day he died! He came over for a visit about lunchtime. He returned a book that I'd lent him. He didn't look ill. What happened?"

Izaak hadn't said a word about euthanasia to his lifelong best friend. Simply returned a book, had a cup of tea, and walked away.

At the funeral, when people asked what had happened, the family simply said, "It was quite sudden. His heart has been bad for years, you know."

Because the family couldn't or didn't answer questions honestly, they lived with a sort of deceptiveness or falsity. The words they said didn't line up with the kind of death they'd witnessed. White lies and cover ups. Izaak controlling their words even after his death. Izaak in charge. Deferred to as usual.

Later, they told an extended family member about Izaak's choice. "My cousin's a member of the Evangelical Church in the Netherlands, which is pro-palliative care," Andrea said. "When I told him the truth, he was just so shocked. He could barely take it in. He said, 'You don't have to keep people alive with all the bells and whistles, but you don't kill them!'"

Izaak had been his dear friend. His uncle. And a pastor to boot.

"They were so stunned," Andrea said. "It was all very painful."

After that, they didn't tell any more people.

You Did This, 2012

What if you hadn't chosen June 23, 2008, to die, Izaak?

What if you'd waited just one month? You'd have seen your daughter married, your only daughter, the one you always wanted even when son number one and son number two were born; you always waited and longed for her, but you didn't wait for her wedding day, and I can only wonder why.

And what if you had waited longer? You would have seen a grandson enter medical school, that grandson who went to Montessori and did school his own way and loved to run so much that he started winning medals. You would have seen him streaking by and standing on the podium: first place in the Baanloop Aalsmeer 5K, first place in the Sylvesterloop 6K, second place in the CPC Aramco 10K. But you chose not to wait. You left him, too. Fourteen years old, still a boy and you could have been there. He was there for you.

What if you had waited a few months more? You could have held your first great-granddaughter and two years later her sister. And then your first great-grandson. And your second. You left them, unseen.

What if you would've left well enough alone, not chosen a day, not called a doctor, not gotten those papers signed, not lain down on your bed and exposed your arm to the doctor's needles. We'll never know. There are so many things we'll never know.

There are days and times driven deep into us now, just as there were dates and times pounded into you. You circled May 10—the

day Germany invaded the Netherlands—all the days of your life.
You circled February 16—your first date with Jopie—too. But this
is the date we circle: June 23, 2008. The day you chose to die.

You did this.

This isn't an accusation. Just a fact. Like so many other facts
in the long list of facts that resided inside your brain, and you
should appreciate this: that finally and at long last there's a date
that I remember and remember all too well and can't seem to
forget. This is the date stamped in my brain. Inked over my husband's heart. Tattooed on the inner arm of my memory.

June 23, 2008.

When we lived in Indonesia, our Dutch neighbor—head of
coffee production and Johan's boss—had a number tattooed on
the inside of his forearm. He usually wore long sleeves. But one
muggy, sunny day he rolled up his sleeves and there they were:
blue ink numbers. A list of them walking up his arm. He saw me
looking.

"From the Japanese concentration camp," he said. "I was living in Indonesia when the Japanese invaded. They put us behind
barbed wire and took away our names. For years, I was nothing
but a number."

His name was Jan: the kindest of men, generous and smiling.
His wife, Pief, taught Kristina and Joren piano lessons. We were
neighbors and friends for three years on those glorious volcanic mountains on the island of Sumatra. Jan and Pief meant the
world to us. I'm so thankful he survived. I'm so thankful he found
his way.

This is what I keep coming back to, Izaak. When did you get
lost? Why is it that you couldn't find a better way? How could you
survive the war but not survive yourself?

What if your life had lived out its role, its fate, its faith, its
natural end?

There wouldn't be so many questions now. There wouldn't be
this nagging, *what if*. Nothing can put this question to bed. This is

what you gave. Your legacy, the memorial you left behind: a date and an unanswered question.

June 23, 2008. What if?

And here's the deeper question.

If you had died naturally, slowly, within Andrea's home and care, would you have softened enough to say goodbye? Tell her just once that you loved her.

Could you have opened your heart enough to show your hand? We will never know. And the sadness is, neither will you. It wasn't only us you hurt.

It's been four years now. Enough time to bear the facts. Enough time to read the epilogue. Still, I live with the residual. It never goes away.

I'm tired of the dregs, the leftovers, the reminders, the aftermath. I'm tired of your choice. I'm tired of my anger. I'm just plain tired.

Keys, 2012

Anneke has a new interest in WWII after our trip, and I get out the old family history that Izaak wrote to Kristina. I make four copies of it. I dig through old Kandel family photos and make copies of them, too. Several are of Izaak's family while they were living in Indonesia, before he was born. Two are of parachutes dropping over the city of Dordrecht the morning Nazi occupation began. Two are of Izaak's and Jopie's wedding day. I intersperse the photos and the story and put everything in three-ring binders. One for each of my children.

I think Anneke will enjoy reading some of what Izaak has written, but not all of it. So much of it reads like an end-of-year church board report. I just can't understand him. Who would want to write to their granddaughter about the hierarchy of church decision-making, the organizational models of youth group growth? What kind of person would·write about conferences, courses, and lectures, including techniques to stimulate conversations, didactics, and methods of teaching catechism?

There's one story in the lot that makes me curious. After pages of writing about his work, why does Izaak include this story? What merit does it possess?

Kristina, when you were eight months old, you came and stayed with us in Hardenberg/Heemse. Your parents and Andrea went to the second morning service which started 10:45. Jopie offered to babysit. I was in the middle of the sermon, when behind me the door opened to the pastor's room. The caretaker walked into the church. He passed the pulpit and he went in the direction of the bench where the family was sitting. I saw he was talking to Jill.

As I continued preaching, I realized that Oma had called for assistance because she could not manage Kristina. Jill and Andrea got up and left the bench.

As I was preaching, I put my right hand into my pockets and got the car keys. I continued preaching while Andrea and Jill walked under the pulpit and I dropped the keys. Andrea got them as if we had rehearsed it. I continued preaching as if nothing had happened and nobody in the congregation noticed anything. After the service, somebody picked me up from the church.

It's a cute story, a fun memory. Izaak at his professional best, carrying on, no big deal, but it makes me uncomfortable. The story isn't really about Kristina. It's about Izaak again. Izaak the one who saved the day. Izaak, the hero of his own story.

Look how I handled that situation so smoothly!

Look at me shine.

Safeguards, 2012

In 2002, when euthanasia was first legalized, I didn't have any idea about it. Oblivious has many meanings. Lacking awareness of, unsuspecting, not ready. I was all of these things. I lived my happy, ordinary, daily life in Red Lake Falls and later in Fargo, oblivious to the happenings on the worldwide stage. I had no premonitions, no bad dreams, no forebodings or presentiments. I had no hunches or suspicions. I raised puppies, brought my youngest children to orthodontics appointments, piano lessons. I watched them play soccer games and dance in spectacular ballet recitals. My life had become typical upper-midwestern: mother, wife, cook, chauffer.

It's not until now that I begin to understand what went on behind the scenes of my life. In other places. On other stages. Things I didn't know. I wade into this dark world, this world of death and dying and medicine dragging my courage behind me. Determined. Unsuspecting.

I start with dates and locations and right off the bat there's some confusion. The Netherlands passed a law to legalize euthanasia in April of 2001, but it didn't "come into vigor" or practice until a year later, on April 1, 2002. Either way, 2001 or 2002, the Netherlands was the first country in the world to legalize euthanasia. Belgium became the second country to follow suit in May of 2002. Six year later, Luxembourg became the third.

What surprises me most is that these three countries all border Germany and were under Nazi occupation in WWII. Why would countries, doctors, and medical systems that were forced to carry out euthanasia laws under Hitler be among the first to enact them for themselves? It makes no sense. I check euthanasia laws in Germany itself; euthanasia is strictly illegal.

The Termination of Life on Request and Assisted Suicide Act has strict criteria including five stipulations necessary for euthanasia to be considered.

- Patient must have made a voluntary, well-considered request to die
- Patient must be facing a future of unbearable suffering
- There must be no reasonable alternatives
- A second doctor must be consulted, see the patient, and give a written opinion
- Life must be ended in a medically appropriate way

The law permitted sixteen- and seventeen-year-olds to make euthanasia decisions for themselves, although their parents had to be involved in the discussions. The law allowed twelve- to fifteen-year-olds to request euthanasia but required parental consent for euthanasia to be performed.

This Dutch law is long and includes the following safeguard: In the Netherlands, five regional review committees—each consisting of a lawyer, a physician, and an ethicist—are charged with keeping an eye on and assessing whether a case of assisted dying complies with the law.

In 2003, 1,815 deaths by euthanasia were officially reported in the Netherlands.

In 2004, the questions of newborn euthanasia came to a head when the University Medical Center Groningen called for the formation of a national committee to draw up a protocol for life-ending treatment for newborns. The hospital's guidelines, which created a legal framework permitting doctors to actively end the life of newborns, were referred to as the Groningen Protocol for Neonatal Euthanasia. Again, there were five criteria.

- Diagnosis and prognosis must be certain
- Hopeless and unbearable suffering present
- Confirmation by a second doctor
- Both parents must give informed consent
- The procedure must be performed with accepted medical standards

Children euthanized for presumed poor future quality of life included, for example, those born extremely prematurely; children with brain damage, severe spina bifida, or anencephaly; and children with epidermises bullosa, commonly known as Butterfly Children.

Once death becomes an *answer*, it doesn't take long for it to become prescriptive.

In 2005, there were 2,297 euthanasia deaths.

To be fair, Dutch doctors don't rush into using euthanasia. They wouldn't want to, nor dare to. They are a rule-abiding culture. To be fair, the vast majority of deaths by euthanasia follow

Dutch medical protocols exactly. To be fair, Dutch doctors use euthanasia sparingly and only in acute circumstances. Patients near death in excruciating and unrelenting pain.

I try to be fair.

Even the looking and learning hurts my heart and my mind. The examination, the statistics, the facts. I've begun a long and arduous trek into a world utterly new to me. It bruises me to simply pay attention. There are days I can't do more research. Can't handle more information. Wonder what I'm even doing.

On those days, Johan's words, "Just let it go, Jill," seem like good advice.

But I can't stop myself. This compulsion to understand stems from a deep place. I know I won't be at peace until I understand, and I won't understand until I go under.

Playing Her Part, May 1940

I can't decide if it's worse to study euthanasia or WWII. It seems like everything I drop down into carries pain. Izaak had written about the day the Nazis invaded the Netherlands, but I didn't really know much about what happened after that, except that Rotterdam had been bombed before capitulation. I wondered what else was going on right around that time period. So, that's where I began.

The Nazi commanders projected that the invasion and total occupation of the Netherlands would take just one day. May 10. That should be it, such a flat country, such a small amount of terrain to cross. The invasion, however, dragged on into a second, a third, and then a fourth day. Hitler, stewing over the slow progress, decided to bomb Rotterdam.

The official Capitulation of Dutch Forces in The Netherlands was signed and countersigned on May 15, 1940. The occupation of the Netherlands had begun.

Hitler appointed Arthur Seyss-Inquart, Austrian-born like himself, as Reich Commissioner of the Netherlands. Behind his back, the Dutch people called him Manke Poot, Lame Leg. They drew cartoonish pictures of him, laughed at his limp.

Seyss-Inquart held the post Reich Commissioner of the Netherlands for five years. Today, Dutch school children are well aware of his name. Their own version of Benedict Arnold.

The Dutch five-day war against Germany is too often over-looked. Considered by many to have been a straightforward Germany victory against a flat and unprotected nation. But the German victory came at a cost. The five-day war left 7,000 Nazi soldiers wounded, 2,000 killed, and 1,250 German troops and trained pilots captured.

When WWII began, the German Luftwaffe had an operational air force of 1,000 fighters and 1,050 bombers. Of these, three hundred airplanes were destroyed during the fight over the Netherlands, equaling more than 10 percent of the German fleet of airplanes destroyed in five days. A significant amount. Hitler's existing plans to invade Northern Ireland and England had to be altered.

The Netherlands had played her part, and played it well.

Talking, 2012

I begin to talk openly about Izaak's death. It's hard on Johan. He adored his father. I know it hurts him, but I'm done with secrets. No more hiding. No more fudging the facts.

"Do you still visit Johan's parents in the Netherlands?" a friend asks me.

"No. They've both passed away now," I say. "His mother died from Alzheimer's. His dad chose euthanasia." This information makes people ill-at-ease or curious. It's usually one or the other. I'm comfortable with either response.

"He must have been very ill," my friend responds.

It's a common assumption.

"No, not really," I say. "Izaak was mostly healthy. Still living on his own, cooking, going to concerts, driving."

These are hard words to say; they are also hard to hear. She appears confused and puzzled. She looks stricken. I understand. I've spent four years trying to come to terms with Izaak's choice, trying to find words to explain it.

At this point, the conversation usually ends abruptly or veers into questions of legalities and doctors and methodologies. We haven't even touched the sorrow. Or the anger.

I used to think of the grief following euthanasia in the same terms as that of suicide. I've learned that this is partially true, but not completely. I have a dear friend whose brother took his own life, jumping from a bridge, a rope around his neck. She always says, "I should have known. I didn't pick up on the clues. I wish I had been there. I wish he hadn't been alone."

Her grief is tied to her brother's solitude on that day. Her grief is that she didn't know. We knew about Izaak's choice. He didn't just give us clues; he signed the damning paperwork and handed it to us. There were people with Izaak the day he died: a doctor, his daughter, one of his sons, a grandson.

I turn in smoldering circles, bruised by both the passivity and the acquiescence. I'm stunned by the okay-ness, the pallid looking-on-ness of the Dutch and their system.

His grandson stood and watched.

My friend wasn't expected to agree with her brother's choice. Society gives her that. She's left to her questions, her wishes, and people (rightly so) tell her how sorry they are. I have no such cushion. I'm expected by polite Dutch society not to question, but to agree. There is little space given for hesitation. Little room for misgivings, second thoughts, or doubt. We don't grieve. We don't get angry. We accept. This pressure to accept is a part of my anger, too.

The Kandel family ends nearly every discussion with the same words: *It was what he wanted.* Their magical incantation. "Well," they say looking at each other. "After all," they nod in unison, waiting for their shared benediction. "It was what he wanted."

The catchphrase. The pat answer. The zipping up of the plastic bag that held his corpse. It is so easy to say. *It was what he wanted.*

But here's something more bothersome, something that rankles and gnaws. There were no real conversations, no consensus even vaguely thought about or talked through. Izaak's pronouncement swift and final.

How do you live when decisions concerning death are commandeered? How do you survive when euthanasia smacks you flat, and you don't know how to breathe anymore? Your air gone. Your answers gone. Your assumptions buried.

No one knows how to talk about it. No one knows. Yet, people still come up to you, people still ask, and you? You still try.

Eugenics

Researching WWII, I come across the idea of eugenics and follow it down a trail that leads to a Nazi Euthanasia Program. I'm completely caught off guard. There's a Nazi euthanasia program? I didn't expect the subjects of euthanasia and WWII would ever connect. It's a remarkable find.

Hitler's Germany grew first and foremost out of ideals and ideas. Early on, Hitler wrote about eugenics, praising the idea. He thanked the United States for its eugenics programs and for promoting the idea of making a better race.

American ideas fueled Hitler's desires?

Wow. I don't remember reading that in my history classes.

Eugenics—literally *good creation*—is the science of improving the human species by selectively mating people with specific desirable hereditary traits. It aims to reduce human suffering by "breeding out" diseases, disabilities, and so-called *undesirable characteristics* from the human population.

The American Breeder's Association, established in 1903, was the first eugenics body in the United States. A year after its founding, Indiana passed the first compulsory sterilization legislation law in the world. Thirty states soon followed: sterilizations forced upon Black women, Native American females, Hispanic women, patients in mental hospitals, those who were prostitutes, unfit, mentally defective, and prisoners.

Hitler wanted a master race; he liked what he read about and saw happening in the United States. After his election in 1933, Hitler issued an order to medical personnel compelling physicians, nurses, and midwives to report newborn infants and children under the age of three who showed signs of mental or physical disability. A secret order. *Start registering the disabled children.* Any disability would do. Lame. Blind. Disfigured. Low IQ. Deaf.

Hitler's secret Nazi Euthanasia Program went by the codename Operation T4. The actual innocuous legal name was Reich Work Group of Sanatoria and Nursing Homes. The headquarters stood at Tiergartenstrasse 4, Berlin. Thus, T4.

As the program grew, parents were encouraged to admit their disabled children to designated *pediatric clinics*. In reality, the clinics were killing wards, gassing stations for German children. Hitler built six of them.

Transported by bus and rail, the young *patients* were sent to these *clinics*. The gas chambers, disguised as shower facilities, used carbon monoxide gas. The bodies of the children were cremated. Urns filled with their ashes were sent back to parents with fictive causes and dates of death. As time passed, the age requirements broadened until children up to the age of seventeen were included.

Hitler's goal—to restore racial integrity to the German nation and eliminate *life unworthy of life*—took a drastic step forward in 1939 when he told Dr. Karl Brandt to expand the authority of physicians. They were encouraged to grant *gnadentod*, a mercy death, to patients considered incurable according to the best available human judgment. It was no longer just the deformed children; adults were included as well.

Who wasn't worthy to live? Those with psychiatric, neurological, or physical disabilities, those who constituted a genetic or a financial burden on Germany. They—*those people*—were given various names: *unworthy lives, burdensome lives, useless eaters, embarrassment to the master race.*

The Nazi T4 Euthanasia Program pre-dated the Jewish genocide by two years. It wasn't the Jewish people, but the disabled German children who were out of time.

In August of 1941, Hitler halted the T4 program because of public awareness and protest. According to internal calculations, the program claimed 70,273 lives before Hitler disbanded it. In actuality, Hitler didn't stop T4; he just moved it underground. Behind the scenes. It would resurface soon enough with another face.

As Thin as Breath, 2012

I need to articulate and know the basics of euthanasia. I expect it shouldn't take too long to understand the terminology of death, to get a handle on it. I take the dive: Euthanasia 101.

There are two primary types of euthanasia: active or passive. Active euthanasia brings death about by an act. Passive euthanasia brings death about by an omission, a withdrawing or withholding of a treatment or medication.

Within these categories, euthanasia is further broken down into three types: voluntary (performed with a person's consent), involuntary (performed against a person's will), and non-voluntary (performed when a person is unable to either give or withhold consent).

There's one more common delineation: self-administered euthanasia or physician-assisted euthanasia. The administering person is defined specifically as the self or the physician.

And then there's suicide, the act of taking one's own life voluntarily and intentionally. If a person wants help to kill him- or herself, that's called assisted suicide.

And last of all, physician-assisted suicide. A physician assists the person to obtain the necessary items, but doesn't administer them. The person administers the drug, or pushes the button that releases the medications, by him- or herself.

For the life of me, I don't understand the demarcation between self-administered euthanasia and suicide. I don't understand the difference between non-voluntary physician-assisted euthanasia and killing.

Does the patient swallow by himself or with the aid of a glass of water the physician holds and tips? Does the physician hold the trembling hand while it pushes down on the button? The human heart can't measure the differences and distances between the definitions.

The deeper I fall into the words, the tighter they become. The line between the meanings less than a Planck length apart: deci, centi, milli. All these scientific prefixes for measurements that get tinier and tinier. Nano, pico, femto. Yet none of them are small enough. Atto, zepto, yocto. The differences between these words, the spaces between them, that our lives hang upon, as thin as breath.

Merely a Rehearsal, 1941

One of the byproducts of the ongoing T4 Program in Germany was the staff it produced and educated. The cooks and housekeepers, doctors and nurses and orderlies, grounds keepers and custodians, secretaries and clerks who carried out Hitler's plans. Somebody brought the children to the basement. Somebody turned the gas on. Somebody removed the bodies. Somebody signed the papers and licked the envelopes shut and put them in the mail. Somebody changed the linen on the bed.

Let's get ready for the next child, shall we?

These workers had names. Hermann Schwenninger headed the transport squadron bringing victims to Grafeneck. Josef Oberhauser was responsible for burning the bodies. Christian Wirth forged the official death certificates. T4 employed forty physicians. Hanns, Otto, Walter, Ernst, and Oskar. Arthur, Theodor, Carl, Kurt. Rudolf, Wilhelm, Valentin, Franz.

Hitler built an efficient staff that soon had two years practice under their belts.

A noticeable change came on March 13, 1941, when Seyss-In-quart—Reich commissioner in German-occupied Netherlands—spoke in Amsterdam saying, "The Jews, to us, are not Dutch. They are those enemies with whom we can come to neither an armistice nor to peace. We will beat the Jews wherever we meet them, and those who join them must bear the consequences. The Führer declared that the Jews have played their final act in Europe, and therefore they have played their final act."

T4: Hitler's rehearsal. The real show hadn't begun. It waited in the wings. Hitler would promote many of the original doctors and staff from T4. Promote them right into the new and expanding concentration camp system. It was logical. They had the necessary skills set. Experience was everything. Success even better.

Let the main show begin.

Changed, 1941

Izaak once told me that his life didn't change much after Nazi occupation began. Not at first. The thing that jolted him into the new reality had to do with his drum and fife group, Jubal. When the Nazis officially disbanded them and destroyed many of their instruments, Izaak knew his life had changed forever.

Soon, foreign radio stations were forbidden. The Dutch language broadcast from BBC London, Radio Oranje—Radio Orange—continued in secret, but the freedom of the press and of the airwaves no longer existed. The freedom to *know*, suspended. Nazi radio consisted of strictly Aryan propaganda and music. And who wanted to listen to that?

It must've been quite a dilemma for Izaak. As a child, he'd been taught to obey the laws of his country. To obey his father. To respect his teachers. When he did things, he did them correctly, as expected. The Dutch are a law-abiding people.

At some point, Izaak grew concerned over the new laws and asked his father about not listening to the radio.

"Should we listen to Radio Oranje when it is forbidden, Papa?" he asked.

His father replied, "This is a German law. And we are not Germans."

Imagine the Kandel family sitting furtively beside their radio, 9:00 sharp each evening, turning the dial to Radio Oranje, turning the volume down, listening for hope.

In the first years of the war—with so much bad news coming their way—much of the fifteen-minute Radio Oranje broadcast focused on boosting Dutch morale. Sometimes they heard news of British soccer matches, or the lovely refrains of forbidden music. Occasionally, they heard the familiar voice of their Queen Wilhelmina, speaking from her exile in London. What a reassurance it must have been.

Later, as the war broadened and resistance groups in London coordinated, the broadcasts instructed the Dutch how to battle against their German invaders. They carried more news of the war and coded messages to resistance members.

In 1943, Dutch citizens were ordered to hand in all radios. Izaak's mother, fearful of German retaliation, convinced Father Kandel to hand over their radio. Now, there wasn't even a radio to fill the Kandels' long evening hours at home.

A Yellow Rope, 2012

I can't get Izaak out of my mind. I remember my friend whose brother died by suicide. The two stories merge and I dream about them, night after night. Izaak and my friend's brother.

In one dream, Izaak and I stand on a bridge high above a wide and raging river. A yellow noose rope circles my friend's brother's throat, but he morphs into Izaak. The rope around Izaak's throat while he stands, balancing on a thin metal rail, staring down into the murky water.

"What do you want?" I ask Izaak.

"I'm finished," he replies.

"It's your decision," I say, trying out the grand gesture, the magnanimous reply.

"I want it all to end," he says as an ambulance pulls up. In the dusky light, a doctor emerges, white coat and stethoscope. He carries coffee and a cake.

"Have a piece," the doctor says in celebratory tones, holding out a chocolate wedge.

"Eet smakelijk."

Then he walks over to the railing of the bridge and reaches up to place a hand on Izaak's shoulder. It looks as if he wants to pat Izaak on the back, or possibly hold him back, prevent him from jumping, but instead, he gives a sure and certain push. As Izaak falls, strangles, lurches below us, the doctor walks back beside me. We sip espresso and nibble chocolate cake.

"Well," the doctor says, smiling kindly at me, "That's done." Mozart plays on his phone.

"After all," he continues, "it's what he wanted."

I push him away, shivering, and the dream morphs into a young Bob Dylan rasping out the old soul tunes in my ear of "License to Kill."

Distribution, 1941

The German war machine needed bike tubes and tires and fuel. Nazi soldiers needed food and lodging and clothing. Whatever the Germans needed, they confiscated. Anything and everything that helped promote and sustain their war.

When choosing between the Dutch people and the Reich, there wasn't a choice. Just an army to feed and fuel. "Reducing the consumption of the [Dutch] population in order to obtain supplies for the Reich," as Seyss-Inquart said, became a common practice, helped along by the distribution ration card system.

Dutch people weren't allowed to purchase just any item, not anymore. A *stamkaarten* book had to be presented at a Distribution Office, where citizens were then given *bonkaarten*, ration cards used for in-store purchases.

I've seen Jopie's *bonkaarten:* small, perforated squares printed on one sheet of paper; ten squares across and seven rows down. It's hard to image her, going to a store, ration card in hand, waiting in line, hoping there were supplies. The cards specified commodity and quantity. Some women tore the cards along the perforated lines and stored them in shoeboxes with divided compartments named *rijst, suiker, jam, zeep, vermicelli, havermout, aardappelen:* rice, sugar, jam, soap, pasta, oatmeal, potatoes.

Just *having* the ration cards wasn't enough. The German occupation authorities reserved the right to decide *when* the ration cards could be used. Announcements were aired on the radio about when certain numbers could be used. If you missed the date, tough luck. Wait till it comes around again. Pay more attention. Get it right.

Among the first items rationed were coffee and tea. Next came textiles, followed by meat, then natural gas and electricity. And later, fuel. Gasoline shortages meant few Dutch citizens could drive cars. Bike tires were impossible to find. Soon bikes with wooden tires were seen clumping along the streets. Trams and trains ran less frequently.

As people spent longer and longer hours standing in lines, queuing up to get rations when they were announced, stomachs emptied. Houses grew chill and cold. Electrical light shone intermittently. This was only the beginning.

Dark and cold and hungry soon became a way of life. By 1941, milk and potatoes were rationed. Then the Dutch were called upon to turn in all nickel, lead, tin, and copper materials. Church bells stopped ringing, the Germans confiscating and melting them down into war machinery. What could a country do? A cold, dark, hungry country where even the bells were silent?

Three main choices existed: resist, collaborate, or hide.

Many Dutch became invisible, silently hoping to outlast the war. They hunkered down, rationing out their own personalities, their own thoughts. Afraid of their colleagues, neighbors, and friends. Even their own families.

I can't imagine such fear. Such hiding. How much depended upon you keeping your mouth shut, your eyes down. How the fear must have wrung you dry and left you gasping.

Kisses, 1941

It was February 1941. You were seventeen, Izaak. Every day you heard airplanes overhead. The noise from newly built Luftwaffe air force bases—staging areas for attacks on Britain—a normal part of life. Throughout the war, over six thousand airplanes were shot down over Dutch land, approximately three planes per day. You didn't know that yet. But still. You heard the planes. Maybe you even saw them fall.

At night, when you could, you snuck over to a friend's house to listen to the forbidden Radio Oranje. Queen Wilhelmina told the Dutch people to keep the faith. She believed in a free Netherlands. The news always on your mind. But, more than that.

There was this girl.

You were working as an apprentice in a department store in Dordrecht, responsible for—of all things—the window displays. I have a hard time imagining you doing that work. Changing mannequin's clothing, artfully arranging a scarf, or a shoe. You made just over two guilders a week. In the evenings, you attended business school.

On a Saturday night, you walked out of the department store with a girl named Jopie. Out into the evening air. As you walked together toward the bicycle rack, you picked up your courage and blurted out, "Would you be my friend?"

The words just out of your mouth, your heart pounding, your question thrown to the world, open and exposed, when nearby German air defense guns started firing at Allied planes passing overhead. The noise terrified you both, standing as you were out of doors, in the dark.

Jopie jumped onto the back of your bike and you pedaled furiously, bringing her home. She talked over your shoulder, loudly into your ear, above the sound of the flak: *I'll give you an answer. Tomorrow. After church.*

The next day, you hardly heard a thing the pastor preached. The service lasted forever. You watched the church empty and saw Jopie walk out, arm in arm with her best friend, Beb. Shyly, a bit forlorn, you headed after them. And then, grace and mercy. Beb went her separate way. Jopie walked over to you.

She said, "Yes. Yes, I'll be your girl." As easy as that.

Later, after an afternoon walk in the forest, you said your good-byes and received something new. A little kiss, in the midst of the war. You were so young, Izaak. In love and moonstruck. You could hardly think of anything else. The sweetness of that first kiss stayed with you the rest of your life. Even as an old man, you still tasted it upon your lips. She was your first and only girl and would always remain so.

It was February 16, 1941.

You will celebrate February 16 for the rest of your life. You and your Jopie.

Post-Euthanasia Syndrome, 2012

Even now. Even after four years. I still fall asleep and there he is. Izaak. Izaak on my mind. I can't stop the images, the noise, the memories, the questions.

I wonder if there is such a thing as post-euthanasia syndrome. I search for any kind of information that might be helpful and find a hollow of data. How do families respond in the weeks and months, the years, following euthanasia?

I did find one article. The woman writing it said, "The guy who came to pick up the hospital bed that Mother had used, told us, 'Normally, I would say I'm sorry, but I guess this is what she wanted.' He didn't think this was a loss for us."

When Izaak died, I said, "I'm so sorry." But what I meant was, *I'm sorry for what he chose. I'm sorry for the pain he caused. I'm sorry that he hurt Johan.*

I grieved the method, the timing, the decision, but not the man.

Johan and I didn't talk about memories of his father. We didn't reminisce. We didn't pay for a flight to the Netherlands to attend the funeral.

I think about our recent trip to the Netherlands. Our Dutch relatives didn't want to talk much about Izaak their father, their grandfather, their uncle. They did, however, talk endlessly about the what and how and why of Izaak's death. The rules and signatures required, the details and specifics. The doctor, the timing, the decision, the date, the method.

Euthanasia took away more than Izaak's breath. It stole our communal memories. Our shared stories. Our remembrances. Euthanasia stole our mourning.

The Atlantic Wall, 1942

In March of 1942, with England proving evasive and America joining the war effort, Hitler released his Führer Directive 40. A bullet-point message, demanding the construction of a defensive line from the tip of Norway all the way down the European seaboard.

He called it the Atlantic Wall.

Hitler knew that if his Third Reich were to be invaded, it would be by sea, and his answer was to build a three-thousand-mile-long chain of fortresses, gun emplacements, tank traps, and obstacles. Over the course of the next year, 9,671 bunkers were built, spreading throughout Norway, the Netherlands, Belgium, and France.

Izaak wouldn't have needed to travel far from Dordrecht to see some of the building in progress. The Hague—a mere thirty-five miles away—had numerous Atlantic Wall fortifications, anti-tank ditches, and anti-tank walls. One hundred thirty-five thousand people in The Hague had already been forced to leave their homes for the project. Two thousand four hundred buildings demolished. Beaches, coastal promenades, and large parts of the city became an occupied wasteland of bare space, bunkers, checkpoints, and military personnel. The largest fortification in the history of the world.

Hitler, disappointed with the slow progress, appointed General Rommel to take over construction. Rommel ordered fifty million mines be laid on land and on sea. He ordered row after row of steel barriers—Belgium Gates—to block landing craft at low tide. He ordered the placement of thousands of ramrods with steel-bladed ends to rip open the bottoms of landing boats at high tide. Rommel ordered. People complied.

To do this work, the Germans began pulling men from concentration camps. They used POWs, but it wasn't enough. They grabbed men off the streets: the French, the Poles, the Dutch. Thousands of old men and young boys seized and forced to labor. In total, over 32,000 civilians provided forced labor for the seaside construction works of the Atlantic Wall.

Barbed wire played an enormous role in all of this, the Nazi fortification of Europe. On beaches along the North Sea, barbed wire was erected in straight lines, parallel to the shore. Between fortifications, the lines of wire jutted out at right angles toward the sea.

Barbed wire allowed the Nazis to create large empty spaces around the perimeters of camps, forts, pillboxes. As the war progressed, the Germans began to use a new type of non-corrosive wire: twisted and square with three-quarter-inch barbs placed four inches apart. The Dutch aptly called barbed wire *prikkeldraad*. *Prik*: to sting or prick or poke. *Draad*: thread.

Perhaps, it was during this time that Izaak began to put up his own defenses of prickliness and barbs. A wall of wire used to create his own space, his own wasteland of self-protection.

It's easy for me to look back at it all, to look back across this history, knowing Izaak will live, knowing the Allies will win, knowing the Netherlands will be freed. But Izaak didn't know that. Nobody did. He lived in a time of gigantic upheaval, saturated with moment by moment fear. The world was up for grabs, an idea that Hitler keenly understood.

Lucky Ones, 1942

What was it like to be a young man in the Netherlands back then? Your country under occupation for nearly two years? In January, bronze and silver coins were hardly to be seen anymore, zinc versions were put into circulation. There wasn't any coffee in your kitchen. No cigarettes, chocolate, butter, fats, or cheese. The Nazis declared the coastline of the Netherlands closed to everyone—all beaches off limits. No more seaside jaunts. In Amsterdam and Rotterdam, Nazis began to confiscate bicycles. They stole your grandfather's boat. The metal one he built and welded all by himself. He and his boys. The one he was so proud of. And then, they begin to steal the boys and the old men.

Germany offered enticements to Dutch citizens to travel east. *Work in Germany! Work for the Fatherland!*

Dutch citizens who went willingly were promised premiums, rewards, and extra distribution coupons for their families. But this harvest of Dutch men was not enough. Germany needed more workers in their factories and in their fields. As German soldiers were sent to the frontlines by the thousands, the need for manpower in Germany grew. A quota to fulfill.

July: 40,000 men.

September: 40,000 more.

November: add another 35,000.

This quota for forced labor had to be met or heads would roll. Better Dutch ones than German ones. Soon it wasn't just men, but boys.

In 1942, Izaak began having trouble with *netelroos*, a red, itchy skin condition. His doctor tried several cures, including taking his blood and then injecting it back into him. Izaak went in for injections every fourteen days. Not having any success, he went to a dermatologist who diagnosed him with *urticarial lesions*, also called hives. Those red raised welts, triggered by food, pollen, or dander, easily exacerbated by stress.

Called for a pre-transport medical checkup, Izaak provided a letter from his dermatologist saying he was *unable*. Izaak's rash, his thriving nerves, kept him from being conscripted into the German labor force. His brother, Piet, deemed fit to work, spent one year in Gelsenkirchen. Given a short leave after one year, he came home, and for one reason or another, was never picked up or forced to return. He fell through the cracks. It's not known why or how.

Most Dutch men forced to work in German factories, farms, and camps never returned home. Izaak and Piet were two of the lucky ones.

Grave, 2012

I'm not particularly sentimental about gravesites, although I grew up visiting my grandparents' graves, my mother buying plastic wreaths once a year—great gaudy flowered rings—to lay upon their graves. My dad's parents, Nels Peter and Sophia Jensen, buried in the Jensen family plot at the Hazen City Cemetery, lie next to five of their sons. On my mother's side, Grandpa K and Grandma Emma, are buried in the Sunset Memorial Garden in Bismarck. The tombstone carved in relief, bouquets of Emma's favorite flower, Lily of the Valley, surrounding their names.

My dad is buried in the North Dakota Veterans Cemetery south of Bismarck/Mandan. We visited his grave once, but that was a fiasco. A busy Fourth of July with crowds of people, a planned program, a speaker, taps playing over the prairie. A regular show. My brother and sister, their spouses, and the grandkids. We were all there. The Jensen clan.

My mother loved it. I felt bereft.

I miss my dad tremendously. Sometimes it's difficult to comprehend he's really gone. On a whim, I take a day off and drive out to Bismarck. I want to visit his grave. Alone.

I walk the straight military lines of the graveyard, searching for his name. When I find it, I sit in the grass beside my dad's grave, then scooch over and lean my back against his tombstone. Looking across the rolling hills, I can see the Missouri River and the high bluff on the far side. I went to college on the top of that bluff. When I stare into the distance, I can see the outline of the Bell Tower at the University of Mary and I remember those happy college years.

My dad's tombstone—sun-warmed on this bright April day—makes a perfect backrest. I take out a piece of paper and write a letter to my dad. I tell him about the last three years, what's happened in my life. I write about his grandkids; he'd be so proud of all of them. He'd love to see the woodwork Benjamin's turning on his lathe.

I write about my sorrow. How I miss him. How visiting his house in Hazen—when I go out to see Mom—still hurts. I keep expecting him to walk through a door, expect to hear his voice, deep and soft calling my name. I miss the sound of his voice. I miss his wit, his intelligence, our conversations. Walking through my parents' home, every room a memory, pains me. Their garden is no different. Each apple tree, every lilac bush, his handiwork.

When I'm done writing, I pat his tombstone, then rub my palm across the soft green grass, remembering the feel of Dad's fine white hair. I notice a gap between the tombstone and the ground, a little hole right at the base of the stone. I roll the letter into a scroll—a tiny cigarette of a paper—and stuff it deep into the hole, pulling the edges of the grass up and over it. I don't know why I do this. I just want to leave something for him. My words. My love.

This place feels unexpectedly hallow. Somehow sacred and meaningful. I couldn't be more surprised. When I stand up to leave, I lay my hand on top of the tombstone, bend over and kiss it lightly.

Warren R. Jensen
CPT
US ARMY
KOREA
May 31, 1929
October 17, 2009

My father died one year and four months after Izaak decided to end his life. My father's been dead for nearly three years. Izaak nearly four.

My father's death feels sad, but natural, normal, ordinary in the sense that we all die. It wasn't unusual or unexpected. My dad had cancer of the liver; he died. As hard as that is, I'm able to process it. It makes medical sense, a straight logical line. There's nothing to reconcile, question, examine, or rethink.

Izaak's death—even though I've had a year longer to deal with it—still feels mistaken or incorrect, somehow unfinished. I don't know how to reconcile his choice with how he hurt his son, how he hurt his grandchildren. I don't know how to square the facts with all the questions.

Izaak is buried in the New General Cemetery not far from where he died in Doorn. We never considered going to visit it on our last trip to the Netherlands. None of the kids showed any interest. It seemed more like something to avoid than to embrace. I had nothing I wanted to offer Izaak. There wasn't any comfort to be given or taken.

One night not long ago, I ask Johan about Izaak's tombstone.

"What does it say on it?" I ask out of curiosity.

"I have no idea," Johan replies. "I'm not even sure he has one."

"Why wouldn't he have a tombstone?" I ask.

"Well, in the Netherlands, people don't stay buried in the same place," he replies.

I don't have a clue what he's talking about.

"You can check out the facts, but I'm pretty sure after twenty years people are dug up and the graves are reused. I don't remember ever visiting my grandparents' graves," Johan says.

I can't believe it. It's too crazy. After thirty-some-odd years of marriage, I thought I'd heard it all. A little bit of fact checking quickly shows me that Johan is right.

Izaak will stay buried in the New General Cemetery for ten or twenty years. Or possibly thirty. It depends on the cemetery and on the contract that the family signs. It depends on how long they have paid their fees for.

Grave sites aren't purchased in the Netherlands. They're rented.

It's hard to grasp. All these years, when I've thought of my grandparents, they have a place in my mind, a spot of ground, a patch of earth with their names above it. And when Johan thinks of his grandparents, there are no graves. No sites to visit. No Memorial Day flowers. This simple, normal discussion hits me hard. Reminds me again how very different we are, one from the other.

In the Netherlands, there's a gross lack of cemetery space. Once the term of a burial contract is reached, bodies are exhumed and reburied in mass graves.

Your final resting place isn't your final resting place in the Netherlands. There are exceptions made for religious reasons with people of Jewish origin, but for the average Dutch citizen, no matter how permanent death is, the grave is not.

Prins van Oranje, January 11, 1942

She was laid down on September 20, 1930, in the dockyard Slikkerveer de Maas. From that day—the official commencement of her building—the ship builders worked on her until launch day, July 10, the following year. She took ten months to build. Commissioned on February 2, 1932, she bore the name the *Prins van Oranje*. The *Prince of Orange*.

She left the Netherlands under two triple-expansion engines, with a maximum speed of fifteen knots. She was a minelayer, one of two built in the Netherlands, and among her 121 sailors was one who bore the name Wes Kandel.

When Queen Wilhelmina declared war on Japan on December 8, 1941, the *Prins van Oranje* received orders to station in Tarakan, an island in the Dutch East Indies. She'd be laying defensive minefields against a Japanese attack. Since the Japanese attack wasn't considered imminent, she sailed to Tawao first, took fifty-six Japanese fishermen prisoner, and captured the *Borneo Maru* and three other vessels. She sank seven smaller vessels, then returned to Tarakan on December 12.

The *Prins van Oranje* spent the next three weeks—frequently a target of Japanese bombers—with no direct hits and several near misses. On January 9, she was damaged lightly and a few of her crew were wounded. She laid low in the Sesayap River, then withdrew upstream attempting to reach the Java Sea through another part of the complex delta area.

On January 10, 1942—with Japanese troops landing on the nearby islands of Tarakan, Celebes, and Menado—Lieutenant Commander A. C. van Versendaal, on the *Prins van Oranje*, received permission to attempt a breakout. He delayed, wanting to take advantage of the expected poor visibility, rain and heavy clouds. Sadly, shortly after she sortied, the weather cleared.

Sighted by the Japanese destroyer *Yamakaze* and the Japanese Patrol Boat P-38, the *Prins van Oranje* was outgunned and quickly overwhelmed. Returning fire, she was hit and started to burn. Then the Java Sea opened her arms and the *Prins van Oranje* sank into them, her fire doused as she settled, taking most of the crewmen down with her.

Sixteen survivors rescued by the *Yamakaze* were ushered ashore under gunfire, onto the island of Tarakan, as prisoners of war. Wessel Gijsbertus Kandel was not among the survivors.

Although the Netherlands had declared war on Japan back in December, Japan wouldn't officially respond with its own declaration of war on the Netherlands until the next morning, January 11. When they did, the *Prins van Oranje* already lay at the bottom of the sea.

Wes died not far from the lovely harbor his father helped to build decades earlier, not far from the island paradise of his own beloved boyhood. The Java Sea gave Wes a sailor's burial, and his bones still lie there, beside his fellow mates, in the turquoise, pristine, and hallowed waters of his childhood.

As his ship flailed, did Wes think of his baby brother, Izaak, sleeping obliviously in their attic bedroom in Dort?

As he gulped his last breath, did he reach out to touch his bride one last time?

As his lungs exploded and there wasn't any more air, was it then that he reached out and touched the dreams of his mother?

Death on Wheels, 2012

My dad used to make house calls. Mostly to the elderly, those who couldn't or wouldn't come to a clinic. The hermit, the recluse, the old bachelor homesteader. If Izaak would've chosen to die ten years after legalized euthanasia began instead of six, he might not have needed a housecall. He could have gone to a clinic instead. He was, after all, ambulatory and in decent health.

The first Levenseinde Kliniek—Life End Clinic—in the Netherlands opened in The Hague in March of 2012, ten years after the first euthanasia bill passed into law. The clinic cared for all patients seeking euthanasia but was specifically helpful to those whose family practice doctors refused to help them die, thus neatly filling in a gap within the euthanasia system. The clinic operated on site. People could walk in for their prescheduled euthanasia appointments.

Soon after opening, the clinic launched six mobile euthanasia teams. These Levenseinde Housecall Units offered services to those who might be disabled or frail or lacking mobility. The program, referred to by some as Death on Wheels or Death by Delivery, provided the service of coming to the housebound, free of charge.

The Housecall Unit consisted of a doctor, a nurse, and all the necessary medical equipment. In the first six months, 456 people registered to use the clinic. Of those, fifty-one were assisted in death and ninety-four were refused. Fifty-four people died of natural causes before their paperwork had been processed. Two hundred and fifty-seven remained waiting for the availability of a team.

The teams couldn't keep up with the work; this was partly due to the strict protocols they followed. According to the standards used, "Teams will be limited to one house visit a week, in order to minimize the psychological burden placed upon them."

War for Words, 1942

As the occupation continued, the Dutch people hunkered in for the long haul, and the Germans began another invasion. A paper one. Color posters, pamphlets, and brochures popped up on walls, on billboards, on doors, on posts around the cities.

I have seen some of the originals, the posters and pamphlets housed in the Dutch Resistance Museum in Amsterdam and in the National Liberation Museum in Nijmegen. I have been there, walked down the halls, read the brightly colored propaganda. Masculine strength is a common theme, as well as anti-Bolshevism, anti-Judaism, depicting the Allies as brutal enemies, and telling the Dutch people that the New Europe under Hitler is a wonder to behold.

> A Nieuw Nederland in een Nieuw Europa. Strijdt Mee in de NSB
> A New Netherlands in a New Europe. Join Us in the National Socialist Movement.

One of the posters stands out in my mind, a typical 1940s poster printed in two colors, an Art Deco image of streamlined power. A crowd of men, wearing blue work overalls stand against a bright yellow background. They look identical. Lined up, shoulder to shoulder, one foot forward. I remember the men's jaw lines. Each man's overly large square jaw jutting out into the world. Facing forward. Chin up towards the sky.

Wie in Duitschland Werkt Dient het Nederlandsche Volk
Those Who Work in Germany are Serving the Dutch People!

Next to it, a powerful blue poster shows yellow search lights revealing a bomb falling over a darkened city skyline.

Engelsche Vliegers kennen geen Genade voor Vreedzame Burgers
English Pilots have no Mercy for Peaceful Citizens

Propaganda posters depicting power and speed with angular, sleek letterforms cover the walls of the museum.

Come Work on the German Farms in the East!
National Socialism is Unstoppable
The Allies are not Your Friends

Along with all these posters promoting work in German and the untrustworthiness of the allies, Germany begins to circulate posters with another message.

Jews are to be Avoided
Jewish People are the Enemy
Bolsheviks are the Enemy

All those hate-feeding signs and posters and leaflets. All those fear-feeding words. Will the hungry little country eat what it's being fed?

Lies proliferated. Life lied. Words lied. Your neighbors lied. Radio stations flitted between the words of the Nazis and the words of the Radio Oranje. Ordinary Dutch citizens tried to make up their minds, tried to see through the dump of messages, the din of war.

The Nazis flung their words out like candy, and the Allies followed suit, dropping their share of words, too. Paper falling from airplanes. "V for Victory" pamphlets fell, floating down from the sky like angels; they dropped, scuffed and dirty, into canals and onto orange-tiled rooftops.

This war for words etched itself upon the cobbled streets. What did these neat Dutch women think of their streets littered with propaganda? Did they still clean their stoops each day?

Did Jopie pick one up and hide it in her purse? Did Izaak step on one, bend over to pick it up, and read it eagerly? Would there be a victory? Would Nazi Germany survive?

The Germans noticed the increase in Allied propaganda and stepped up their game. They commandeered the V for Victory and made a new series of posters: V for Victory because Germany is Victorious on all Fronts!

As the German papers fell, the Dutch countered. They scribbled out the German words but left the Vs untouched and scrawled their own messages:

V for Verlies
V for Lose

Sometimes the Vs were vandalized into Ws.

W for Wilhelmina

All this war fought on paper with pen and ink. So much of war has always been battled this way.

Of all the men who knew the power of words, Winston Churchill was unsurpassed. His whole persona exuded confidence, from his black Homburg hat to his famed fat cigar. His pudgy fingers flashing V for Victory, a symbol he flaunted like a badge.

In November of 1942, after defeats from Dunkirk to Singapore, Churchill finally stood before the House of Commons with some good news. "We have a new experience. We have victory. A remarkable and definite victory." Alexander and Montgomery had turned back Rommel's forces at El Alamein, the Battle of Egypt a success.

Churchill continued with his now famous line, "This is not the end, it is not even the beginning of the end, but it is perhaps the end of the beginning."

Margriet, January 19, 1943

One of the great celebrations in the Netherlands during WWII occurred on January 19, 1943. Such a happy day, a respite of a day. The day Princess Juliana (daughter of Queen Wilhelmina) gave birth to her third daughter.

Princess Juliana—living in Canada during most of the war—miraculously gave birth to her daughter on Dutch soil, a requirement for lineage to the throne. Princess Julianna produced a seven-pound five-ounce little princess, fourth-in-line as heir to the throne.

How could this be?

Canada. Oh, Canada! Your government declared the birthing room, on the third floor of the Civic Hospital in Ontario, to be extraterritorial. A sort of embassy-zone for the time needed. A Dutch spot on foreign soil. The Dutch tricolor flew. The Dutch National Anthem played. People in Canada celebrated, eating traditional *beschuit met muisjes*—dry rusk crackers sprinkled with sugar-coated anise seed. These sugar-coated sprinkles were a long-standing tradition, eaten on beschuit to celebrate a birth. Normally, the sprinkles were pink, but on this day, on January 19, the anise candies were bright orange to honor the birth of a princess, a new addition to the Royal Dutch House of Orange: Her Royal Highness Princess Margriet Francisca of the Netherlands, Princess of Orange-Nassau, Princess of Lippe-Biesterfeld.

The news of the new little princess spread around the world. A Dutch underground newspaper told the story. "Little Margriet, you will be our princess of peace. We long to have you in our midst . . . come soon Margriet. We are awaiting you with open arms."

For this one moment, a hungry little country overrun, occupied, discouraged, cold and hungry, looked out at the world and smiled.

Princess Margriet's birth united the war-weary country. Her birth offered a breath of celebration, a glimmer of hope. And you,

Oh Canada, you will never be forgotten for what you did that day. After liberation, when Princess Juliana and family returned to the Netherlands, they sent one hundred thousand tulip bulbs to Canada in thanks for their wartime refuge. The Netherlands continues to send ten thousand tulip bulbs every year.

I wonder how Izaak responded to Margriet's birth. Was it then, upon the birth of that little girl, that Izaak first internalized a desire for a daughter of his own? Was it there, in the middle of the war, in January of 1943, that he began to dream of his own little princess?

Everything begins somewhere. And after a beginning it grows and continues to grow until it's more than a dream; it becomes a need. And somewhere, somehow, it crosses a line, and grows to be a burden. A burden that's loaded with anticipation and expectation and innuendo.

More than any little girl could ever be able to fill.

More than a little boy could ever fill, also. Especially, if you *want* that boy to be a girl. and tell him so and give him a girl's name. Your desire, your words, your naming will not matter, Izaak. Your first child will be a boy. A boy with a girl's name and long blond curls. Your second child a boy. Your third, a girl, your princess at last. All your expectations piled upon her. All your dreams waiting to be fulfilled.

Queen's Day, April 2013

On April 30, 2014, as I study Queen Wilhelmina's reign and the beginnings of WWII, the Netherlands celebrates Koninginnedag: Queen's Day. It's a Dutch national holiday referred to by some as The World's Greatest Party. Celebrations include giant city-wide rummage sales with people setting their wares out on curbs, on blankets, in their yards, on the street. Crowds of people dress in orange and throng around bargain hunting, listening to music, dancing in the streets. Boats festooned in orange—filled with people dressed in orange, drinking beer, singing lustily to loud music—crowd the canals. It's not about patriotism or nationality. It's hardly even about the queen. For some reason, it's a day the Dutch, traditionally stoic rule-followers, let loose, celebrate, sing, party, and carouse.

Nothing seems too absurd. Orange wigs, orange hair. People dressed in orange clothes head to foot. Faces painted orange. Dogs sport orange tutus and party hats. Even though it's always a fantastic party, today's Queen's Day tops them all.

First of all, it's Queen Beatrix's seventy-fifth birthday.

Second, it's also coronation day! Today, Queen Beatrix is abdicating the throne to her son. King Willem Alexander will be the first king in the Netherlands since 1890.

In brief, The Netherlands had three King Willems between 1815 and 1890. After that queens reigned. Queen Wilhelmina carried the Netherlands through WWII, abdicating to her only daughter, Juliana, in 1948. The year I met Johan, 1980, Queen Juliana abdicated to her daughter Beatrix. Queen Beatrix has been queen of the Netherlands since just before I got married. Her profile's as familiar to me as my own, almost every letter Izaak sent stamped with her image on it.

Next year, the national holiday will change its name from Queen's Day to King's Day. The date of the celebrations will also change, from April 30—Beatrix's birthday—to April 27, Willem's birthday.

Surfing the web, I look at drone pictures showing streets a throng of brilliant orange. It makes me both happy and sad to see the pictures. I miss the Netherlands and hate living so far away from Andrea and Bert and their children. Wouldn't it be something to be able to hop in a car and drive over to share a day, a party, a cup of coffee? Wouldn't it be something, to have the money to go as often as we wanted? My cross-cultural, cross-Atlantic life has its joys. But sometimes, I wish the world were a tinier place.

Happy Anniversary, 1943

By 1943, Izaak and Jopie have been seeing each other for two years. Two years of dating, waiting, loving, hoping, and war.

Life in 1943 Netherlands included the rounding up of university students in Amsterdam, Utrecht, and Delft. Many students went into hiding. Universities closed. Physicians were arrested by the hundreds. Pastors and priests, also. Anyone with a moral objection, a different notion, an unwillingness to comply to the Nazification of their respective professions.

And, oh, the mistakes that were made that year. Mistakes that proved costly.

On March 31, 1943, American planes left England to bomb submarine pens, dry docks, warehouses, and rail lines in and around Rotterdam Harbor. Thick clouds and gusting winds and who knows what and suddenly, swiftly, 198 bombs missed their mark. Those one-thousand-pound bombs fell on residential sections of Rotterdam, killing 326 civilians and injuring another 400. That evening left ten thousand people homeless. After the war this incident would be called The Forgotten Bombardment.

Allied planes missed the Fokker Aircraft Factory and hit Amsterdam instead, killing 157 people. And a month after that, an error caused a misidentification of a target resulting in the bombing of Enschede and the deaths of 151 people.

The Dutch resistance movement derailed trains, passengers onboard injured and killed, both German and Dutch alike. At some point, it became difficult to discern who was inflicting the damage, those occupying the Netherlands or those trying desperately to free it.

In March of 1943, the Germans lengthened the Dutch work week to fifty-four hours. Don't complain. Don't even bother getting used to it. In August, it increased again. Soon, there was a seventy-two-hour work week. Every day there were new commands, orders, directives, and demands.

Men between the ages of eighteen and thirty-five must report for work in Germany.

Round up Dutch men in the countryside, not just the city!
Rations began to include razor blades and all textile products. Fruits and vegetables, too.

Begin deportation of spouses involved in mixed marriages with Jewish people!

Five thousand seven hundred Jewish people were caught in large-scale sweeps of Amsterdam. A month later, the Nazi doubled that number, brought in over 10,000 Jews, and deported them.

The number of Jews in the Netherlands decreased.

The number of German soldiers increased.

The number of dead, exponential.

The Netherlands shrinking and expanding and heaving its way through war.

Only One Essay, 2013

I wake up one morning with Izaak on my mind and have a brilliant idea. I could write about Izaak and his choice of euthanasia easily. I just have to write fiction. Writing memoir is too vulnerable. I can't go there. But fiction. That's a great option. In a pinch, I could tell people I made it all up.

I begin to write a YA story about a preteen girl whose grandfather chooses euthanasia. I name her Eloise. Perhaps she can say what I cannot.

A year later, even though I love how *Eloise* is coming along, some of the topics I need to broach feel too heavy, too mature for such a young audience. I begin an essay about euthanasia.

When it's done, I enter it in The Missouri Review Jeffery E. Smith Editor's Prize Contest. Months later, I get an email. My essay, "Paying the Piper," won second prize! First prize dishes out $3,000. Second prize only $200 and publication. I'm disappointed about the money, but ecstatic with publication. Johan isn't. He doesn't understand why I'm delving so deeply into euthanasia. Into his dad. He doesn't want it "out there." I understand. I wish I could *not* write it.

I cover and protect myself with this idea: *It's only one essay.* I'm primarily busy writing *Eloise*, writing fiction. I fool myself into thinking it's true. Into thinking *Eloise* will be enough.

I'm excited to see my essay in print, but hope my Dutch family never comes across it. When the journal arrives, I put it on the shelf alongside my other publications and go back to *Eloise*, but I can't get that essay out of my mind.

The essay comes back to me, sentence by sentence, thought by thought. In my dreams and daydreams, my sleeping, and my waking. I push the thoughts away, unwanted alleys I don't want to walk down. Clues, I'd rather not follow, not yet, but the day is coming.

Identity, 1944

Germany required each Dutch person, over the age of fourteen, to apply for and carry an identity card called a *persoonsbewijs*. The Germans were fingerprinting, photographing, and numbering each Dutch citizen.

Jopie and Izaak each received a notification. They went. They stood in line. Were they humiliated? Defiant? Did they go together? There are so many unknowns.

In 2016, when I go to the Netherlands on a research trip, I'll go through old family records. My niece, a keeper of history, has one of Jopie's *persoonsbewijs* cards, a tri-fold card stock, with a photo on the inside page. The photo sits inset, in a cut-out like frame, blue ink stamped over the corner of the photo and onto the paper. The photo shows a dark-haired young girl, looking slightly down, her eyes not focused on the camera.

The identity card states her birthdate and place.

Her nationality: Nederlander.

Her job: *typiste vliegtuigfabriek*, airplane factory typist.

I've never heard anything at all about Jopie's war years. She was a typist. At an airplane factory. Forced to work for the Germans. I wonder if she was paid, or conscripted. If she liked it or felt it a great burden. I don't even know how many years she worked there.

Jopie's twenty years old, the same age as Izaak. The authorities signed and stamped the card, and a *controle* stamp was placed above her photo. Her signature sits near the top of the page. On the bottom of the next page: two fingerprints. One of them blackened onto a light blue fifty-cent stamp attached to the card. The Nazis not only introduced the indignity of registration cards, they made each person pay for their own card. Fifty *centen*. In some locations, the price doubled, costing one *gulden*.

Go get your card. Pay for it yourself.

From 1941 onward, each Dutch citizen was required to carry this paper, at all times. Stop and search. Stop and identify. I picture them, those young people, opening and closing their wallets. Pulling the cards out of their trouser pockets or purses. Their identities tied to a small trifold, scrutinized, and questioned.

When your identity rests within a piece of paper, controlled at will by an invader, who do you become? You are a photo. You are a fingerprint. You are a number. You exist on a folded card, 4 x 9 inches. Show on demand.

Who are you really? What are you becoming? When you pull your card out, and show it to a Nazi soldier, even as you are revealing yourself, you are simultaneously drawing inward, veiling and self-protective.

And when the soldier looks you up and down, nods, agrees that you are you, and hands back your identity card. You take it from him. You put it away.

When was it in this process, that Izaak began to put away more than his card?

When did he begin to put away his personality, his laughter, and the carefree youthfulness that he'd barely even tasted?

In the Beginning, 2014

When the Dutch first legalized euthanasia, unbearable physical suffering was a necessary condition. But over the years the definition of suffering came to include suffering of either a physical or mental nature. "Mental and psychosocial ailments" such as "loss of function, loneliness and loss of autonomy," incorporated into the understanding of unbearable suffering.

In 2013, the number of people choosing euthanasia jumps up to 4,829. One in every twenty-eight deaths in the Netherlands. Triple the number of people euthanized in 2002. In 2014, the number rises to 5,300. The uptick in numbers comes as no surprise. It seems inevitable, but the reasons people are choosing euthanasia are changing, too.

The boundaries of acceptability extending.

Slowly, unbearable *physical* pain as requirement came to include unbearable *mental* pain, and now, unbearable *sociological* pain is being added to that list; all are considered grounds for euthanizing. Doctors connect the dots. A patient's lack of "social skills, financial resources and a social network" might be included in their "unbearable and lasting suffering," opening up the possibility of legally assisted death based on psychosocial factors alone.

The medical community considers your request with a mind toward your status in life, your financial stability, your social isolation. They wouldn't want to underestimate your pain.

From 2011 through 2014, 110 people were euthanized for mental disorders.

In 2014, forty-seven-year-old Gaby Olthuis—a woman who didn't want to live because she suffered from severe tinnitus— was euthanized at the Levenseinde Clinic.

Afterward, the clinic received an official reprimand.

D-Day, June 1944

Growing up I thought of D-Day as the end of the war. In my youthful mind (knowing the end would ensue) I imagined the war "over." My youthful thoughts were in fact, far from the truth. On D-Day, my future father-in-law and mother-in-law were barely out of their teens. The war for them had a long and frightening time to play out.

D-Day, originally planned for June 5, delayed at the last minute by bad weather, took place on June 6, 1944. The Allied assault on Nazi-occupied France, set troops on the ground in Europe and led, eventually, to pushing Hitler back. Back through Europe. Back to Berlin.

Nine million tons of supplies and equipment crossed the Atlantic, from North America to Britain, in preparation for the invasion. Two million troops arrived in Britain. American, British and Canadian troops made up the majority. There were also Australian, Belgian, Czech, Dutch, French, Greek, New Zealand, Norwegian, Rhodesian, and Polish troops.

D-Day: the largest land, naval, and air operation in the history of the world. Pictures show the sea and sky so full of ship and plane that it's a wonder more of them did not simply crash into each other. Over six thousand ships, and nearly twelve thousand aircraft, supported the invasion as 150,000 Allied troops landed along a fifty-mile stretch of French coastline, on beaches named Utah, Omaha, Gold, Juno, and Sword.

By the end of the day, more than nine thousand Allied soldiers had died or been wounded. But, by day's end, Allied troops had successfully stormed Normandy's beaches, not only securing them, but digging in and setting up camp. A first toehold in Europe, and they were there to stay.

News of the invasion was carried live on NBC, CBS, and the BBC. And the Dutch people, at long last, had something to cheer about. D-Day. A day that would go down in history. The beginning of the end for Hitler.

The slow, cold, deadly slog across Europe and into Nazi Germany had begun.

Tragic, 2014

Every year people in Fargo partner with the American Foundation for Suicide Prevention hosting an Out of Darkness Walk. Hundreds of people walk to raise awareness, raising thousands of dollars. A local women's magazine I write for asks me to cover the story.

I quickly learn that family members who've lost loved ones to suicide don't like it when I say *committed suicide*. They prefer *died by suicide*. There's less stigma, less finger pointing with these words. Families are also adamant that suicide is tragic and should be prevented. The AFSP website's tagline says it succinctly: Together we can . . . put a stop to this tragic loss of life.

As I write the story, I meet mothers and fathers whose faces and eyes are marked by grief and longing—marked by heartbreak—and I'm so conflicted as I try to meld my thoughts on suicide with what I'm learning about euthanasia. When Americans talk about euthanasia prevention or stopping euthanasia, they're often perceived as fundamentalist loonies. But don't euthanasia and suicide boil down to nearly the same thing? Personal choice. Personal autonomy. I don't get it. Why is death by suicide considered to be a preventable tragedy while death by euthanasia is acclaimed and lauded, almost applauded? I feel like I'm reading Lewis Carrol and all my words and thoughts are absurd and nonsensical.

> 'Twas brillig, and the slithy toves
> Did gyre and gimble in the wabe;

The words that parse suicide and categorize euthanasia make as much sense as those of Carroll. I'm lost in the midst of it all. Lost and tumbling down a hole.

Keeping up with Success, 1944

As the summer of 1944 progressed, the radio and underground were full to bursting with news. Japanese troops surrendered Saipan. There was an attempt to assassinate Hitler. The Allies liberated Florence and recaptured Guam. And then, on October 25, Free French forces and Allied troops liberated the City of Light; Paris was free.

Did you dance, Izaak, the day you heard the news? "Paris is liberated!" People in France took to the streets by the thousands as Germans fled in panic. Did you weep, when you heard the news, Izaak? Did your mother sing? Did Jopie give you another kiss? Did you talk about your wedding plans? The Germans retreating! After four long years, it must have felt like a miracle.

If only war were not so chaotic.

War on a map is not war on the ground. War on a map looks straightforward. Follow the road. Cross the bridge. Keep pushing north and east. War on the ground, however, includes unexpected bottlenecks. An American infantry division required 150 tons of gasoline per day. An armored division twice that. After Normandy, vast divisions advanced across France and Belgium. As the Allied troops pushed north and east, their supply lines grew longer and thinner, reaching hundreds of miles from the beaches of Normandy up towards the Netherlands.

The German Army retreated so rapidly that the Allies had to scramble to keep up with them. The Red Ball Express, a 24-7 trucking operation, moved provisions and munitions across thousands of miles of supply lines. And still, the Allies struggled to keep up with the enormous needs of its quickly moving troops. Motors burnt out for lack of oil. Drive shafts fell off for lack of tightened nuts and bolts. Batteries went dry, tires burst, fenders fell off. Trucks ran for miles on flats, no maintenance point in sight. They drove all day long, then continued on at night with or without lights, hauling the necessities of war.

In those heady days, just before September, the Allied offensive began to falter, bogged down by terrain, hedgerows, mud, and a tightly stretched supply line. Out of gas. Out of munitions. Waiting for food. In response, the German retreat slunk to a halt and Hitler's armies stopped and dug in with vengeance. The Allied advance slowed to a crawl because everything had gone too well, progressed too quickly. The Allies couldn't keep up with their own success.

Opa and Grammar, 2014

Johan and I get a phone call on a Monday in early summer. Our first grandson has just been born. We drive the five hours to our son's home and meet the new baby. He is perfectly, altogether gorgeous.

I hold my grandson in my arms and marvel at the weight and heft of his body. The solidness of him in my arms. I kiss the top of his head, his fine hair silky against my lips. His chest rises and falls with each in and out soft breath. He is both marvel and mystery.

"What name will you choose?" my son asks Johan.

"Opa," he replies without hesitation. "I want to be called Opa."

"And will you be Oma?" he asks me.

"Nope," I say. "You all called my mother, Oma. I don't want to be her. How about Grammie?"

"That's what his other grandmother has chosen," our son replies.

I try a few names.

Grandma. Nanny. Nonna. Gram.

Nothing feels right.

"I'll think of something," I say.

It takes me three months. But when I find my new name, it fits perfectly. *Grammar.*

I tell our son, "I want to be called Grammar," and he laughs.

"That's perfect!" he says. "I love it."

Crazy Tuesday, September 5, 1944

On Monday, September 4, 1944, the Allies liberated Brussels, advancing north at a breakneck speed, they were within forty-five miles of the Dutch border by the end of the day. That evening, on Radio Oranje, Dutch Prime Minister Pieter Gerbrandy sat down in London to speak to the Dutch nation. Before going live, he read through his announcement and decided to change a few words. The announcement said *advancing near*; he changed it to *have passed into.*

Gerbrandy stepped up to the microphone, "Now that the Allied forces *have passed into* the Netherlands, I will, in the name of all of us, welcome the Allied forces onto the soil of the Dutch Fatherland. The hour of liberation has tolled."

The news didn't come as a total surprise. The Dutch had heard of Allied victories and followed news of the troops racing up through France and into Belgium. Pictures of the liberation of Brussels showed streets so congested with people, there was barely room for the jeeps and trucks to inch their way through. The Dutch people went to sleep that night with the taste of liberation in their mouths. Just one more night.

The next morning, Tuesday, September 5, the Netherlands came to a standstill: offices closed, check points were abandoned, stock market trading ceased. Dutch flags were pulled out of dusty attics and flew triumphantly in the clear blue sky.

In some Dutch towns, the Germans were still shooting people and arresting them. In other towns, people dressed in the colors of the Dutch national flag: colors of red, white, and blue. Or they donned bright orange—that gaudy Dutch color long sported in honor of William of Orange—and lined the streets in anticipation of seeing the liberating Yanks and Tommies. Holland was ready to welcome the Allied Forces. The nation stood prepared to cheer their liberators on.

Three days earlier, Seyss-Inquart, watching the fate of the German army in France and Belgium, had ordered the evacuation of German civilians, telling them to relocate closer to the Nazi border. Ready to flee across if necessary. Besides these Germans, approximately 65,000 Dutch citizens—those who'd been Nazi sympathizers and collaborators—joined the throng, further clogging the already congested roads. They marched and plodded and ran. They stumbled under their burdens, threw suit-cases to the side of the road, clung to their dearest possessions. All of these people fleeing the Netherlands, going north and going east, going back toward Germany, ahead of the expected Allied advance.

The Dutch, awaiting liberation, threw stones and jeered as the bedraggled German soldiers retreated in chaos, streaming back to the Fatherland, disorganized, shambling, on foot, on horseback, on wooden-wheeled bicycles, on anything they could find. Chaos on the roads. All those trucks belching black smoke, little diesel available, running on make-shift wood-burning gen-erators. Germans, wearing ragged uniforms, pushing carts and baby buggies, riding stolen horses, clinging onto overfull carts.

Their world in disarray.

In one month, Izaak would turn twenty-one years old. It would be his first *free* birthday since he had been sixteen. Twenty-one and free. And only days away.

Did you run in the streets that day, Izaak? That day when thousands of your emaciated fellow countrymen took to the streets, shouted themselves hoarse, fell upon their knees and wept. Did you climb up on your roof and watch the parade below?

German tanks and trucks and soldiers headed helter-skelter east. You can practically hear the Allies coming. Did you buy an orange ribbon for your Jopie, shape a pretty bow and pin it on her coat? Did you splurge and buy an orange button for yourself? Did you throw your caution to the wind, for just a moment on that crazy day? That day-long celebration for an event that had not and did not occur.

September 5. The day the Dutch waited. And waited. By nightfall, the Allied liberators had not crossed over her border. As evening fell, they simply, clearly, and plainly had not arrived. The difference between *advancing near* and *have entered into* more than evident. The Allied troops, less than fifty miles away, were held down by heavy fighting. Held down by bottlenecks, and a need for gasoline and munitions. Held back by war.

September 5. Dolle Dinsdag: Crazy Tuesday. Mad Tuesday. *The troops have arrived! Welcome!* Oh. Sorry. Guess not.

I can't begin to imagine the bitterness you were forced to swallow that day, Izaak. You thought the war was over. Freedom in sight. Your uncertainty returning as darkness fell, draping the night, thick and heavy. Your fear escalating. It must've made you sick. To have been so close. And you had no choice, but to crawl back into your protective shell and hide.

Years later, on the phone or in letters, you'd say, "I'll see you next month," and then you always added, *if God wills*. You lived with perpetual disbelief and liked to call God into your equations. A type of belief or mistrust, I never could tell the two apart. *If God wills*. You tacked those words onto the ends of your sentences like a petitioner making the sign of the cross after a prayer. "I'm going to the concert next week, if God wills." Trying to make sense of your life. "I'm preaching next week at Doorn again, if God wills." Not sure. Thrusting that responsibility upon someone else, someone you called God.

On Dolle Dinsdag, September 5—while the Dutch were pre-emptively celebrating in the disarray of war—Anne Frank arrived at Auschwitz Concentration Camp. She had already endured two years of hiding and a month of imprisonment at Westerbork Camp in the Netherlands. She'd spent the three previous days on a grueling Jewish transport train before disembarking in Germany. Her mother, Edith, would die at there in Auschwitz within four months. Her father, Otto, would survive and be liberated by Soviet troops. Anne and her sister, Margo, would be transferred to yet another camp, Bergen-Belsen, in October. They'd survive for several months, and both die within a few days of each other from typhus. They'd die just two weeks before British troops arrived and liberated their camp.

The arrival of the troops—*Welcome! Enter in!*—a matter of life, a matter of death.

Age Limits 2014

In 2014, the legal age to consider euthanasia in the Netherlands remains at twelve years old. That year, neighboring Belgium becomes the first nation in the world to legalize euthanasia by lethal injection for children under the age of twelve.

This is so absurd, so unbelievable to me. When I read this news, I feel like I've fallen into a dystopian science fiction novel. But I haven't. This is the new reality of euthanasia in the world in which I live.

By a vote of eighty-six to forty-four (with twelve abstentions) the Belgian lower house of Parliament approved the law previously passed by the Senate. Under the law, children will be allowed to end their lives with the help of a doctor. There's no age limit to minors who can seek a lethal injection. It won't take long before an eleven-year-old is serviced. A nine-year-old, too.

I am horrified. *Children? Eleven years old? Nine?*

I stop writing, reading, and researching. *No age limits?*

I don't want to know any more. I want to curl up and pretend. Pretend this isn't true. Pretend I never met Izaak Kandel. Pretend anything, but not this.

Weeks later, when I step back into my research, I'm confounded by what I find.

In Luxembourg, where euthanasia has been legal for over a decade, only seventy-one people have chosen to end their lives. In total. Seventy-one people euthanized in over ten years.

How can this be true? In the Netherlands, there were over five thousand deaths from euthanasia in 2014 alone. Why do two countries, in such proximity to each other, who both legalized euthanasia, have such extremely different outcomes? I don't understand.

I hate what I'm learning. At the same time, I'm honestly fascinated. There are days the dark waters I swim in feel warm, almost inviting. Other days they're cold as ice.

Part 8: MY STORY, 2015—2016

Betty Lou Jensen with with her daughter Janet at White Sands, New Mexico. 1954.

Fictitious 2015

I spend much of 2015 working on my forthcoming book, *So Many Africas: Six Years in a Zambia Village*. Cover art, dedications, acknowledgements, blurbs, proofreading, pre-sales, publicity. After it's published, I'll do 186 events, everything from throwing a book launch party to making a book trailer, to being on radio and television. I begin doing public speaking events and readings at a furious pace: bookstores, women's groups, libraries, book clubs. As great as it is, it's also exhausting. I'm used to being in my basement, quiet and writing for hours every day. And now I'm what, a public speaker?

I need some quiet time, some time away. I've been working on my fictional euthanasia manuscript. *Eloise* sits unopened on my computer desktop, gathering dust. I've rewritten the story four times. Each from a different point of view with narrators of various ages. All of it fictitious. Nothing seems right. It all feels like I'm throwing empty words against a cold wall.

I find a writer's retreat near Lake Michigan and am accepted to attend. Five days with twelve women, Leslie Leyland Fields our host and teacher. In the mornings, we workshop each other's chapters, Leslie leading and teaching us. There's time to write, ride horses, walk the beach, and even take an afternoon class on bookbinding.

On the third day of the conference, I walk along the shores of Lake Michigan, and Leslie joins me saying, "I have a question for you, Jill. You've written a successful memoir; it's won some awards. You know how to write nonfiction and you're good at it. So, why aren't you writing memoir?"

"I'm not sure," I say. "I'm going to have to think about that one."

I spend my free hours walking the shore of the lake, looking out over the cold whitecaps, listening to the roaring waves. I ask myself Leslie's question over and over.

Why not write memoir?

The seagulls squawk around me. The clouds darken; it rains. The answer comes to me after two days of confusion and contemplation.

I'm afraid.

Afraid of hurting Johan, afraid of hurting my Dutch family, afraid of getting it *wrong*. I'm frightened of being too liberal. I'm terrified of being too conservative.

I'm afraid to tell this story.

This revelation is so clear to me, I can't believe it's taken this long to see. Of course *Eloise* isn't working. Her story is fiction; mine isn't. That's the sad truth. My story is real.

I come home from the conference and take out that euthanasia essay published last year. I riff off of it, expanding its themes and questions. I write about my relationship with Izaak, our hurdles and hang-ups, the confusions and misconceptions, the expectations. It's hard to write. But deep down I know this: there's an honesty in these new words, a truth I need to follow.

I didn't ask for this story. I didn't want this story. I would've never chosen it, either. But the truth is this. It's the story I was given, and it's mine to write.

Apologies, 2015

The more I study, the more I feel a need to apologize to Johan. It's his family, after all, that I'm digging into.

"I'm sorry," I tell him one night. "Really, I am. You shouldn't have married a writer."

"You weren't a writer when I married you," he replies. "I married a nurse."

"I know," I answer. "Tough luck, right?"

I mine his family. Whether that refers to digging holes or laying out explosives, either way the result is nearly the same: scarred land, exposed pits, the tearing up of our memories.

I'm driven and curious. I can't let things go until I understand them.

Why euthanasia? Why 2008? Why am I so angry? In truth, I am a writer. And what I know how to write is creative nonfiction. I'm a storyteller after an elusive truth, the big picture, searching for a little honesty, a little clarity, some unveiling of the soul. Don't put up your walls; I'll only knock them down. And for Pete's sake, no matter what, don't hide. I'm a genius at shining the light.

So, yes, after all, it was pretty darn crummy luck on Johan's part, on my family's part, on his family's part. Pretty darn crummy luck for us all.

I apologize for that.

Izaak's Family Practice Doctor, 2015

On November 6, my thirty-fifth wedding anniversary, Johan gets an email from Andrea and forwards it to me. The doctor who euthanized Izaak has died. A heart attack. She says he'd been involved with some lawsuits for malpractice, the inquiries ongoing. When Johan forwards the email to me, he writes in the subject line: Murderer died. I guess it's not hard to guess, even seven years later, how Johan feels about that man.

I go on the web and find a photo of the doctor. I find the address of his practice. His office, attached to his home in common Dutch fashion, is called a *huisartspraktijk*: House Doctor Practice. What we call *family practice* in the United States. I find his wife's name. She's a psychologist who also works in the practice and a famous artist who creates colorful, simplistic abstracts and bleak, black and white sketches. Their medical practice specializes in "all of life and death." They use art as therapy and are interested in depression and wholeness.

On January 2, 2014—a year before the doctor died— he received a medical reprimand. His name is listed on the webpage, "Black-Listed Doctors." There is some vague information about an ongoing court case.

I look at the doctor's photo, read about his work, browse his website, look at the art hanging on his office walls. He looks so genuinely normal. Like a man who knew how to relax. How to laugh. I feel sick. What would happen if I looked his widow up? What would I say?

"Hi. Your husband killed my children's grandfather."

Perhaps that's too harsh. Perhaps not. Who's to say?

Someday, when our grandchildren are grown and look back, what will they think of us and the world we have created? How will they judge the decisions we've made? Will they have a need to build a memorial to these, our dead? How will they view our morality, our choices, our swift acceptance to follow a doctor's decision?

Watching the Crabapple Tree, 2015

In 2013, after living on her own for five years, my mother moves into an elder care facility in Moorhead. One week after she moves in, the corporation that owns the facility changes hands. It goes downhill from there.

Her once-a-week room cleaning changes to every two weeks. I begin to notice little things and things not so little. Small shards of glass underfoot from a cup she's dropped.

"Mom, why didn't you call someone to help you clean up the glass?" I ask.

"Oh, they came and swept up," she replies.

"They might have swept, but they didn't get the glass under the microwave, or under the stove. I just stepped on some," I say.

I begin keeping track. The every-other-week clean slips to three. When I talk to the person in charge, she says, "Oh don't worry about it! I'll check into it."

But she doesn't.

The kitchen staff become slower and slower at setting tables, taking meal orders, bringing the food.

"Sometimes we sit here for an hour waiting for our food to come," Mom says one day. "They tell us that we don't have anything to do anyway, so stop complaining."

I don't believe her. I think maybe she is confused, but she isn't. She tells me stories about how staff talk to residents. About accidents that are reported and not taken seriously. Residents complain of missing money.

As the number of opportunities and activities decline, the rent Mom pays goes up significantly. Long-term staff are fired. The person in charge of activities resigns. Pretty soon, I hardly recognize any of the staff when I walk down the halls. We're paying over $3,000 a month and I begin to wonder why. Mom isn't receiving much more than room and board. The night staff dwindles. When people walk in, there isn't even a receptionist. The front desk sits empty, no one to talk to, no one to answer a question. No phone. No nothing.

One evening I walk over, and the front door of the residence isn't locked. Normally, I need a code to enter. But there it sits, wide open, the automatic shutting mechanism stuck. When I hunt down one of the few night staffers, and he says, "Oh, it's nothing. Don't worry about it. The maintenance man can have a look at it in the morning."

Here is an elder care facility, wide open to anyone walking in off the street, at night.

The next morning, I call social services and ask for someone to talk to about options. We tour other elder care facilities in the area. When we walk into Riverview Place, a retirement community started by the Presentation Sisters in 1987, we're impressed. The Sisters dreamed of creating an environment that nourished body, mind, and spirit. Written upon a wall are these words: Reverence, Integrity, Compassion, Excellence.

Mom and I both like the facility, and she signs the papers. We joke with her, a staunch-Lutheran-sometimes-Baptist, moving into a Catholic facility. Within two weeks, everything's arranged, and she's all moved in.

Two months after moving to Riverview Place, Mom has a heart attack and requires the placement of a stent. The surgery goes well but leaves her too weak to care for herself. She moves, within the Riverview complex, to a floor specifically designed for residents with more intensive needs. The floor, called Crosshaven, has twenty-four-hour medical staff, its own dining room, and private apartments for twelve residents. We thought the move would be temporary.

Mom doesn't bounce back and within a month, with a prognosis of deteriorating congestive heart failure, she's put into Hospice care. No one expects her to live much longer. After six months, she moves from a studio room to a one-bedroom apartment just down the hall. She especially loves the outdoor balcony attached to her room, and sits out there each morning, drinking coffee. I join her there. It's fresh and she has a lovely view over a landscaped garden.

The hospice staff includes a chaplain, a nurse doing biweekly assessments, doctors who prescribe her meds, a CNA who gives her biweekly showers, and volunteers who visit and send her greeting cards. Mom begins using oxygen, then small doses of morphine to ease her pain.

Still, we go on the occasional shopping trip, on wheelchair rides through flower gardens, out for coffee. We watch the crabapple tree outside her window come into glorious pink blossom. Months later, we watch snow fall over the small, reddened berries, and later still, after she's been in the hospice program for fifteen months, we hear the return of the robins.

Research Trip, 2016

In the summer of 2016, Johan decides to go on an agricultural trip with Farmer to Farmer to teach subsistence farmers and agricultural extension staff. He's gone back to Africa once a year for the past five years, visiting Ethiopia, Kenya, and Uganda. He asks me if I'd like to fly to the Netherlands and meet him there on his way back. We could vacation together, and I could stay longer and research my book. I'm thrilled about the whole thing—a vacation, time with my Dutch family, and research, too. I make plans and book a flight. I'll stay with Andrea for a few days before Johan arrives from Africa. I'll be gone six weeks.

The day before I leave for the Netherlands, my sister and I plan an outing for Mom and take her to Itasca State Park. She'd lived near there for ten years. Her happy place. The boardwalk down to Itasca Lake is bumpy but manageable in her wheelchair. She looks at the lake, but what she really wants to see is the gift shop. I push her slowly through the shop, and after an hour she chooses a bright green plush frog to buy. We eat lunch at the lodge, and two of the waitresses call Mom by name, "Betty Lou! It's so good to see you again!"

Mom loves all the attention, the shopping, the small talk, and eating out. The whole day is right up her alley, fills her joy bucket to the top. When we take her back to her room, she's perfectly content and happy.

As I leave, Mom says, "See you when you get back! But if I pass, don't you come home for the funeral. It's okay, you know."

The day of my flight, I put on light weight gray pants, a t-shirt, and a charcoal gray hoodie. When I find my seat by a window, I put on noise-cancelling headphones, pull my legs up into a ball, and lean against the window. The hoodie covers my face as I scrunch down, put eye covers on, turn on some soft music, and fall asleep.

The stewardess wakes me an hour before we land. I freshen up, feeling great. I'm ready for the Netherlands! It's my second time to come back since Izaak died eight years ago. The last time I was here was four years ago, back in 2012.

Sisters, 2016

Every time I've been in the Netherlands, I've come with Johan and/or with kids. Now, I have five days alone with Andrea before Johan comes to join us. She's fixed up a room in her attic and gives me time to get settled. I come downstairs after unpacking, a little bleary from the time change. We have tea and talk about the week ahead and things she's planned.

That evening, Andrea talks about the home she grew up in. "We didn't learn to easily make decisions. Our opinions weren't asked for or wanted. It's hard now. I'm always second guessing myself," Andrea says. "Ma wasn't really there. She was sick a lot, vague stomach issues. She was in the hospital off and on for it. She modeled quietness and hiding. That's what we saw. That's what I became. Johan, too. He and I are always asking ourselves, what does the other person think? What does the other person want?"

Andrea and I spend the week talking and walking and getting to know each other. One afternoon, we hike for five hours, passing cows and goats and sheep. We walk by blooming gardens and then back into the woods.

After her brothers both went away to college, the church called Izaak to work in the small village of Laren as pastor, and he said, "I want to go." He didn't ask Jopie. He didn't ask Andrea, who spent her high school years as the only Kandel child still living at home.

Izaak wrote of that time, "Laren was a rural agrarian village and 95 percent of the inhabitants were on the roster as members of the Reformed Church." Even though almost everyone belonged to it, many did not attend services. They expected a visitor from the church, however, when they were sick. If there were festivities, they expected that Pastor and his wife would come to the reception."

Izaak spent nearly five years in Laren, a village of three thousand, with farming families who'd known and depended upon one another for generations. Duty, honor, and tradition reigned large. Izaak loved Laren. As the only pastor, he was automatically granted status, prestige, and power.

"Did Jopie like it there?" I ask Andrea.

"No. Not really," she answers. "She just wanted to fit in, to be a friend. Everyone was kind to her as the pastor's wife, but she had a role to play. That just wasn't her way. I think she gave up in Laren. Just quit being present to herself and to us."

"And you?" I ask. "What was it like for you?"

"Everybody watched me," she said. "Being a pastor's kid is like growing up in a fishbowl. I didn't really have any close friends. I had to behave you know, I was *the Pastor's daughter*! Sit in the front pew at church. Always do everything correctly, properly. The girls in my class were afraid to be my friend. What if I told my father what they were up to?" she sighs.

"Once, some girls asked me if I would go to a dance with them. They said, "If you go, if your Pa will let you, then our parents will let us to go, too."

We drink tea as Andrea muses.

"When I finally left for college," she says, "I came home *every* weekend. I mean *every* weekend. I didn't hang out or spend time with friends. Pa required me to come home and I didn't want him angry."

Izaak demanded that his twenty-year-old daughter come home. And she did.

"The last few years before he died, Pa did his own shopping, but I did his laundry. He dropped it off every Friday at 4:00 p.m. Seven dress shirts. Seven handkerchiefs. Seven undershirts. Seven briefs. Always the same. Then he'd come back on Monday morning to pick it up all washed, ironed and folded correctly."

I laugh listening to her. It's funny and sad and absurd.

"Once—only once—I couldn't stand the idea of him coming. I knew he'd come in an hour and I just left. I went out and did my own shopping. Pa was so mad. He called me up demanding, "Where were you? You weren't home!"

I shake my head.

"I've heard that voice in my ear, too," I tell Andrea. "You weren't the only one."

We talk late into the night, bonding, becoming more than friends. Two women, two sisters, with a shared history and family.

"He never once asked if he could come. Or if a day or time worked. He chose it and he came. That was Pa."

Andrea says she didn't start to know who she was until after Izaak died.

"After Pa died," she continues, "I began to think, 'Who am I?' 'Who do I want to be?' Before he died, I only thought, 'What does Pa want?'"

Intelligent Conversation, 2016

Johan returns from his Africa trip, and we get together with several old friends. Dutch people we knew in Zambia, or in Indonesia. We visit old classmates of Johan. Look up a couple of cousins. In general, the Dutch love a good debate and a good discussion. They're well-spoken, blunt, honest, and well-educated. It's one of the things I love about the Netherlands—the articulate, interesting, intelligent conversations. I've found this over the years in every area from debating soccer team successes to immigration, from political parties to asylum, to educational methodology. Dutch people are opinionated and well-schooled in American politics, from gun control to prisons. They are sometimes seen as impolite, curt, or rude, but I've come to think of them as straightforward and honest. They don't mince their words and are proud of their directness. Growing up hiding my own thoughts and feelings, I've come to appreciate this side of the Dutch personality. *Tell it like it is* could be their country's motto.

During this trip, however, I begin to notice that something doesn't add up. When friends or family ask what I'm writing about, I say euthanasia. As I begin to talk about my research, there's a subtle, slight turning of the head, or a wary look in an eye, or a scowl in an upraised eyebrow. I'm taken by surprise. I don't expect any resistance to the conversation.

One friend interrupts me, saying, "You're not Dutch. You don't understand."

A family member says, "We do everything by the law in the Netherlands. There are controls and strict guidelines."

Some people think I'm a whack-job. "You must be getting your information on some right-wing, offbeat blog. Those things are not true."

When I reply, "No, not really. I got it from Newsweek" or "BBC had an article . . ." or "Recently CNN said . . ." people shake their heads at me in disbelief or anger.

I don't mind disagreement. It's the straight-up *that's not true*, coming out of a Dutch friend's mouth that baffles me. This isn't the Dutch debate I've come to know and love.

The people I talk with don't want me questioning their thoughts. I expect people to ask me for my opinion, to ask what I think about this or that law, this or that interpretation. Usually, our conversations are bilateral. Back and forth. But not now. Not this subject. It's the first subject I've found my Dutch friends to be hypersensitive about. I wonder why. Why this sensitivity, this sidestep from debate?

This is what I hear:

> We follow the doctor's rules.
> It's not used much. It's for the very sick.
> Two doctors must agree.
> You don't understand. You don't live here.

This is what I don't hear:

> What are you learning? What do you think? Is
> euthanasia legal where you live? What do the American
> people think about it?

Something is off.

Operation Market Garden, September 1944

The front between the Allies and the Nazis now existed, more or less, along the Belgium-Dutch border. There were only two routes to Berlin: north through the Netherlands, or east, directly into Germany itself. Montgomery believed the Allies could push the Nazis back to Berlin and win the war by Christmas. He set up Operation Market Garden to do just that. The Allies would bypass the Siegfried Line, capture a series of bridges—liberating Dutch cities as they progressed—and secure the bridgehead over the Rhine.

On Sunday September 17, 1944—only three months after the D-Day landings in Normandy—the Allies launched Operation Market Garden. The fleet of over five thousand planes was so large that the first planes were over Dutch soil when the last ones were still taking off from their bases in England. Bombers led the way, 1,400 of them pounding German antiaircraft positions near drop zones. Two thousand troop-carrying planes followed, with nearly five hundred gliders in tow. The gliders carried guns, jeeps, trailers, and other equipment too heavy to be dropped by parachute.

While the airplanes dropped soldiers and equipment behind enemy lines and near bridgeheads, on the ground, troops of soldiers stretched back for fifty miles. Trucks, guns, bridging equipment, and assault boats moved along one road at an excruciating eight miles per hour. A road elevated above the low polder land it traversed, exposing the tanks like sitting ducks. A road running through some of the most heavily-wooded areas of the Netherlands. A road bumper-to-bumper with traffic and nowhere to turn around or hide. Barely wide enough to maneuver around the bombed-out tanks and trucks littering the road.

Highway 69. One road and a hundred miles to go.

By the end of the first day, the plan was already falling apart. Radios malfunctioned. Maps were less than accurate. Dense fog hampered landings. But still, bridge by bridge, the Allies advanced up to and toward the final bridge at Arnhem, only eleven miles away.

But Arnhem was cut off. Desperate Arnhem . . . the tip of the spear of Market Garden. They'd been told reinforcements would arrive within forty-eight hours, but after four days and no reinforcements in sight, the soldiers there were out of ammunition. Out of food, overrun by Nazis, the men hid in houses, in attics, in cracks in the walls. No relief columns came.

Two thousand five hundred British airborne troops eventually made it out of Arnhem. They left behind 1,500 dead and more than 6,500 prisoners.

In the end, the Allies had a sixty-mile-long finger of Allied troops sticking out into the Netherlands, going nowhere. The soldiers who fought on that narrow corridor road, Highway 69, called it Hell's Highway.

Of the 10,000 Allied forces who made it north of the Rhine, some 7,900 were killed, wounded, or taken prisoner. Allied casualties totaled more than 17,000 men. A military disaster.

What remained was a Netherlands shorn in two. The southern half of the Netherlands liberated. The northern half not. A Free Netherlands and an Occupied Netherlands.

And Izaak? Izaak was living only a few miles from the dividing line.

On the wrong side.

Line-Crossers, 1944

Jopie's older sister, Cor—a nurse by training—had been caring for the wounded since the bombardments of Rotterdam back in 1940. In 1944, she came home to visit along with another nurse. Izaak was visiting Jopie when they came.

Since the failure of Market Garden, the Biesbosch—just south of Dordrecht where Izaak lived—had become the front line between the German and the Allied troops.

The Biesbosch is formidable countryside containing thousands of acres of freshwater delta covered in rivers, streams, and marshland, filled with rush and willow, and patrolled by Nazi soldiers. Two routes across the Biesbosch had been established through the hard, careful work of twenty-one men. Those who attempted the trek, desperately fleeing from occupation in the hopes of freedom, were called line-crossers. Those the Germans captured were shot.

Cor told her family that evening that she was leaving. "We're going to try the Biesbosch," she said. Perhaps she was ready for adventure. Perhaps, it was the call of freedom pulsing in her young life. Perhaps, she felt she no longer had any options. For whichever reason, she had come home to say goodbye.

If they made it, they planned to travel through Belgium and on to England to join the resistance movement. Cor had always been lively and headstrong. So, that was that. Cor was leaving. And now it was Jopie's turn to bid an older sibling goodbye. To walk out the door. To hold up her hand and wave.

Jopie and Izaak both had siblings off to war.

During the next months, this desolate marshy land would be crossed hundreds of times by men navigating in small boats, risking their lives towing, rowing, silently sitting, alert for Nazi patrols. Waiting, listening, navigating the savage landscape and pitch-dark waters. These line-cross workers carried lifesaving insulin. They carried microfilm, downed airplane pilots, the Jews and the Dutch seeking freedom. Each trip a risk, an unknown. Each trip a cat and mouse game of stealth and evasion, hope and fear. Each trip a bravery of desperation.

Decades later, the five-thousand-acre Biesbosch National Park will be established as one of the largest national parks in the Netherlands. Still later, in 2015, renovations will turn the Biesbosch Museum Island into an architectural wonder, sporting pyramid-shaped-buildings completely covered in grass. A peaceful, idyllic countryside where lovers will come to stroll.

Back in 1944, none of that was known to Izaak and Jopie. They only knew the Biesbosch was out there, taunting freedom and swallowing lives . . . and Cor was headed into its waters.

Saltwater, October 1944

The fighting raged near the Netherlands, long and costly to the Allies. Long and costly to the Dutch, also. Hitler ordered the demolition of the Rotterdam and Amsterdam harbors, afraid they might fall into enemy hands.

Antwerp, in Belgium, was the main Allied port, the one used to supply advancing troops. The Germans might block the entire port of Antwerp by controlling a small area in the southwestern corner of the Netherlands, an area called Walcheren. The Allies needed their supplies. Plain and simple and costly.

Ten thousand tons of bombs were dropped on Walcheren, flooding 80 percent of it with salty seawater. At the seaside town of Westkapelle, 10 percent of the population perished in one day—October 3, 1944—the first day of the battle.

It took a month. When the Germans finally surrendered the estuary, there was little to celebrate. Dutch citizens who had survived were stranded in their villages, living on their roofs and in their attics. The dead not yet buried. Mines floated in the waters.

Liberation was liberation, but it was also a devastation that would take decades to recover from. Flora and fauna and human tragedy. Saltwater rubbed into raw wounds.

Hunger November 1944

Izaak was still living in Dordrecht, less than fifty miles from the fighting around Antwerp. As November turned into December, gas and electricity were shut off. Even the weather, colder than usual seemed to be against the Dutch. Disease increased; malnutrition flourished. By mid-winter, people began to starve.

Twenty thousand Dutch people died of starvation during what became known as The Hunger Winter. Community food kitchens handed out one bowl of soup per person per day—soup made of sugar beets, tulip bulbs, and weeds. People in line fainted from hunger, waiting for their bowl. For the rest of his life, Izaak would remember eating rotten potatoes, black and gummy. Swallowing the gluey mass, thankful for something, anything, in his stomach.

Later at the Nuremberg Trials, Seyss-Inquart would say, "I always had the food ration statistics of the concentration camps and prisons reported to me. The food rations were satisfactory. I believe that the Dutch in the concentration camps and prisons, at the end of 1944 and in 1945, received more than the Dutch in the western Netherlands."

Razzia, November 1944

On Sunday, August 14, Johan packs up to return to the United States. Andrea and I drop him off at Schiphol Airport, and an hour later my friend Michelle arrives. She's recently graduated with a degree in art and is here to study Dutch art. Andrea and I pick her up. The three of us have two weeks. It's Michelle's first time in the Netherlands and we have a full itinerary planned.

Andrea, Michelle, and I spend the next day at Culemborg. We walk the polder passing cows, swans, and egrets. Andrea points out funny things, the small white morning glories that are called *pis pots* by the Dutch. We walk by old German bunkers with memorial photos and historical information plaques. Twenty anti-tank poles are set at an angle in the earth. Black pointed metal, menacing and solid. Several large bunkers sit in the middle of a farmer's field, surrounded by mounds of mowed hay.

As we walk, I ask Andrea about what WWII stories she remembers.

"I guess the one we heard most frequently was about the razzias," she says. "Raids that were conducted by the German soldiers in that last winter. German soldiers hunting for something new, hunting for manpower."

During a razzia, both ends of a street were blocked by the German soldiers, while other soldiers went door to door searching for men and boys. The soldiers herded those captured onto trucks, transporting them directly to Nazi Germany, putting them to work in munitions factories and concentration camps.

Izaak's brother Piet lived in an upstairs apartment. No place for him to hide. Izaak lived with his parents, who had a ground level apartment with a crawlspace underneath. It resembled a small dirt root cellar. The access to the crawlspace hid beneath Izaak's parents' bed, underneath the rug and a layer of linoleum.

On an early morning in November, Piet slipped over to his parents' house. "There's rumors of a razzia coming to our street. Anytime now."

Piet and Izaak and their parents ran to the bedroom, moved the bed, moved the rug, and lifted the linoleum; the boys crept down. Their parents moved everything back into place and waited. After a long while they heard trucks rumble up. Soldiers tramped down the street, going house to house. Banging on the doors. Men shouting. Boys screaming. Mothers crying.

They heard the soldiers enter their neighbor's house—noise traveling through a shared wall—cupboards opening and banging shut, boots clomping up steps. Soldiers beating on the walls looking for hidden rooms. They heard the knock on their own front door. Father saying, "No. No one else here. It's just us." Boots entering the bedroom, stomping overhead.

Piet and Izaak hid all day in the dank darkness. There was no bathroom. Izaak crawled to the edge of the tiny space and found a corner of sand. They hid even after the tramping boots left their house and went farther down the street. Even as the noise died down. Even after hours of quiet.

That evening, Jopie snuck over. *Was Izaak safe?* She said she'd be back later with her sister. She had a plan. It was time for Izaak to leave. Time for him to hide.

The Blue Cotton Dress, 1944

There are facts the family repeats: Jopie came. Izaak wore a dress. Izaak said the Nazis would notice his legs weren't *girl* legs. When I ask for more details, there aren't any. I'm told the same few tidbits over and over again. Enough to tantalize, but not satisfy.

And so, I imagine.

I say the dress was blue. I say it belonged to Jopie's sister.

Jopie and her sister arrive at Izaak's home. His mother lets them in, whispering, "Quiet now," as she eases the door shut. Izaak stands before Jopie, his breathing shallow. They smile shyly as young people do. Jopie holds out a blue cotton dress.

"At least it is not pink floral," she says as Izaak takes the dress and feels the soft fabric slide over his palm.

"Put it on now. Quickly," his mother whispers.

Izaak removes his shirt, slides the dress over his undershirt. Removes his trousers. His socks. They stand and look at each other, Izaak and Jopie. Her courage, the smile she wears. Her pluck, the crinkle of her eyes when she speaks. "You look fine," she whispers.

"Go, go," his mother intones, but she holds his arm tightly, reluctant to let him go. "Go with God," she rasps. Her voice husky. "Be safe." He is her youngest son, her boy, her baby.

They slip through the door, out onto the dark street.

This wasn't Izaak's first time to hide—he'd hidden in one form or another since the beginning of the war. They all had. But it was his first great act of hiding, the leaving of home, sneaking off in the dark, a real fear of reprisal. This was real life. His life. And Jopie came. His Jopie. Twenty years old and sweet as the summer sky. Holding out a dress.

Someday they will look back at that blue cotton dress and marvel at their nerve. Sneaking off together. Just two friends, hands swinging, down a dark street in a dark time with nothing ahead but hope, and nothing behind except fear. And so, they moved, buoyed by a future they couldn't see, compelled by a past they couldn't contain. Izaak never forgot.

There were times, when I visited them, that I saw Izaak looking at Jopie. His eyes soft. His voice light. He was at his best with Jopie. Although I found his dismissiveness and authoritarian household difficult to swallow, although I found his overbearing treatment of Jopie sad to watch, there were times I could see that he genuinely cared.

I like to think Izaak's comfort in Jopie's presence started that night. That it started with the bravery of a vibrant young girl and a blue cotton dress soft as the skin on her wrist.

The Attic, 1945

When Izaak and Jopie slid out into the night, it was no treasure hunt, no teenaged version of Capture the Flag or Ghost in the Graveyard. The Nazis played for keeps.

Izaak and Jopie headed to Tollenstraat, the home of an older friend. They'd known Henk Goulouze from the Jubal Band days. Now he had a wife and two children. His in-laws were also living with him, to save on fuel.

What kind of man was Henk, already caring for six other people—including a toddler and a baby—that he was willing to bring another person into his home? Willing to shield and feed Izaak in those tension and hunger-filled days. Izaak could only stay a few days; still, it was a respite of sorts, an in-between location, until he and another young man, Dick Jongeneel, were told of a longer-term solution. Another hiding place opening up.

A few days later, Izaak again went under cover of darkness, out into the streets, out into the curfewed night. This time to the home of the Breemer family. The Breemers were staying elsewhere with their children, and their house stood empty. Mr. Breemer came over each night to help cover up the boys' existence. In case the neighbors noticed and were suspicious; he came and made some noise and was a presence in the house. He brought food.

During the day, Izaak and Dick had to remain absolutely quiet. No flushing of the toilet. No talking loud. The neighbors might hear. They might notice something off. The winter days were cold, and Dick and Izaak crawled into a double bed and covered themselves with a blanket by early evening. They passed their days making bookmarks and drawings. Jopie and Dick's girl tried to sell the things they made.

As the days turned into weeks, Mr. Breemer became nervous and said a better situation had to be found. The neighbors might start thinking it was odd, Mr. Breemer coming each night, but not living in the house and without his wife and children. He knew what would happen if he got turned in. Not only would he be arrested, his family would be taken, too. Each day, each evening, each visit, a ticking clock.

Mr. Breemer found Izaak and Dick a place in an upper apartment of a row house belonging to Mr. and Mrs. de Jong. De Jong was a railroad man, heavily built and strong. He liked to laugh. The de Jongs had a "citizen's garden" for extra food and an attic full of neatly split and stacked wood. The roof of the row house, up in the attic, was angled perfectly to fabricate a hiding place.

Liberation Museum, 2016

Andrea knows a man named Edwin who does volunteer work at The National Liberation Museum in Nijmegen. He agrees to give Michelle and me an insider's guide to the museum and the town. The museum has a mix of Dutch and English signs. We walk, year by year, through the war. Photographs in black and white, posters in bright colors, wooden-soled shoes, a hay box for keeping food warm. Edwin is astonishing. There isn't a question that stumps him.

So many of the things I've been reading about and thinking about are here. The weapons, the bombs, one of the canvas boats—so much larger than I expected—that crossed over near Nijmegen Bridge under heavy fire. It is both exhilarating and sad to be so near the pieces and reality of this war. Identity cards, heavy wool uniforms, dog tags, remnants of a large net made of steel rings, which had been suspended in the Waal River and found only recently. Unbelievable pictures of Hell's Highway.

After spending hours in the museum, we hop in a car and drive to town for lunch and a walk. I sit at the restaurant eating a fancy salad while looking at a billboard type photograph across the street. In the memorial photo, three soldiers from the US 82nd Airborne pose in front of the same house that this sign stands in front of now. They are two paratroopers and a glider pilot named Dana T. Mudd. The picture was taken in September 1944. Mudd has only a few days to live. He will die at Uden on September 21.

There are several of these large photographic memorials, words written beside them in Dutch, English, and German, telling the story behind the photo. Each photograph is set in the actual location where the picture was taken.

After lunch, we take a ride around town and the countryside. It isn't just the large photos that are a reminder of the war. The war is everywhere. We pass Parachutistenstraat—Parachutist Street—and memorial plaques set into church walls. We stop and read historical markers set into massive rocks. The plaques have pictures, information, and website addresses for more information.

A life-sized replica of a Waco glider sits in one field. It's a frame only, made of metal pipes and rods. You can walk up some steps and go in. When I go up, three young boys are kicking a soccer ball around inside.

Edwin talks about the Nijmegen Bridge Crossing and the failure of Operation Market Garden. "You should watch *A Bridge Too Far*," he says. "Quite accurate actually!"

He looks sad, but brightens suddenly saying, "And then there's Veritable!"

"Veritable?' I ask.

Edwin sighs. "Everyone knows about D-Day," he says. "Many people know about Market Garden. Why doesn't anyone know about Veritable?"

Imagine, February 1945

While Izaak hid in Dordrecht, fifty-seven miles away, the Allies planned their next assault: Operation Veritable, the final showdown of WWII in Europe.

Two hundred and fifty thousand troops served in Market Garden. Twice as many troops assembled for Veritable and gathered in Nijmegen for the final push into Germany.

Imagine all the preparation. The movement of thousands of troops and convoys through the cities and towns of eastern and southern Netherlands. The disruption to the local population of twenty thousand troops tramping here and thirty thousand trudging there. British accents, Canadian, American, Scottish, Welsh. Fields confiscated for hundreds of planes and tanks and thousands of troops to gather on. The food required. The gasoline. Tents set up to house the men. The bustle and activity of preparing for yet another battle.

Operation Veritable began February 8, 1945, with over four hundred RAF bombers dropping heavy loads, followed by a frontal infantry assault beginning with fifty thousand men and five hundred tanks.

Imagine the deafening roar: hundreds of airplanes taking off, smoke and bombing and concussive activity on land and in the air. All the Dutch men and boys, hiding in tiny attics, peeking out the windows, seeing planes by the hundreds, flying overhead like flocks of gray starlings in the early spring. Consider Izaak holding his breath, wondering once more, if the time for liberation had come. If this time, it might be true. If this time, the war might be over.

Imagine the rubbish left behind as the men battled their way across the Netherlands. Rations torn open, fire pits, toilet holes, rusted useless gear. Worn out radios, bloodied bandages, homes bombed into piles of charred hot bricks. The roads, the bridges, much the same.

Allied troops crossed over the Dutch German border, and the battle raged into and across Germany. The slow advance toward Berlin—against the last of the elite German troops, against a strengthened Siegfried Line, dense minefields, and a deliberately flooded Rhineland—came at a great cost of life. General Eisenhower later said, "It was some of the fiercest fighting of the whole war . . . a bitter slugging match in which the enemy had to be forced back yard by yard."

By the end of Veritable, the dead German soldiers numbered ninety thousand. The Allied troops lost 22,000 men. Many of the men had been fighting for two, three, and even four years, some for nearly five . . . only to fall in the final months, in February and March of 1945 . . . Victory in Europe Day only a heartbeat away.

This is the leftover litter of war. planes that fell burning from the sky, smoking in the fields; smoldering tanks blocking roads and belching black smoke into the spring-blue sky; helmets torn by shrapnel; and all the broken bodies of all the broken men, lying where they fell.

Veritable, February 1945

"Allied troops marched across the Rhine and into Germany," Edwin continues telling me. "Much of Germany conquered while parts of the Netherlands were still occupied."

I'm incredulous. It must show on my face. "Still occupied?" I ask.

"Oh. Yes." Edwin states. "Still under Nazi control. The Canadian troops were fighting their way across the northern Netherlands."

We hop back into Edwin's car. I assume we're going back to the museum, but after about ten minutes driving, he says, "Now, we're in Germany."

"What?" I ask. "We are?"

There's no border. Nijmegen lies just a few miles away from Germany. Ten minutes later, on our way back, he points out the old border crossing, only a small-roofed canopy remains. The rest of an old cement building lies crumbled in the grass.

Back at the museum, we're joined by Edwin's friend, another curator, for tea.

"Why do you work here," I ask him.

"I grew up hearing stories about the war," he answers. "My grandparents' house was right near Nijmegen Bridge. One day when they were out, a bomb hit their house. When they got home, only the door and door frame were left standing. Their clothes and sheets hung in the trees, blown there by the bomb. My grandmother couldn't believe it. Her clothes all over the trees, her house gone. She started to shake. My grandfather looked at the trees and the remains of the house. He looked over to my grandmother, and he said, 'Stop whining now; wipe off your feet, and let's go inside.'"

The Naked Remains, 2016

Andrea arranges for us to meet a local author who writes about death and dying. The author has spent three years interviewing people, asking them about deathbed experiences. She interviewed people in the medical profession—doctors, nurses, hospice workers. She interviewed people of faith—Buddhist Monks, Christian Clergy, Muslim Clerics. She talked to people who've been at loved one's deathbeds.

We sit at an outdoor café and drink tea, talking about death and dying, hospice and palliative care, Hindu and Christian values and concepts surrounding death.

I ask her, "In three years of interviewing people and talking about death, what's the most important thing you've learned?"

She thinks a long time. Sips her tea. Then softly says "You have to be naked."

"What do you mean?" I ask, confused, not quite understanding.

"To have a good death, you have to be willing to not hide yourself. To be vulnerable and open. Our suffering has a purpose; it helps us let go; it helps us soften and give ourselves away. Death humbles us."

We talk about her books and articles. The work she's doing. "Life is precious," she says. "Death is precious, too."

On the way back home, Andrea and I can't stop talking. She says she needed this meeting as much as I did. She's putting together the threads of her father's death, too.

I go up to my bedroom thinking long and hard about our conversations, falling asleep with the words of Job floating up through my memory: Naked I came from my mother's womb, and naked shall I return.

Vincent, 2016

Our two weeks brim with spectacular days. Michelle and I take a train to Utrecht and climb the Gothic-style Dom Church Tower built in the 1300s, take a boat tour of the canal, eat at a pannekoek house on the *gracht*. We travel to The Hague to tour the Mauritshuis Museum, standing face-to-face with Vermeer's famous *Girl with a Pearl Earring* and Fabritius's *Goldfinch*.

But of all the fabulous things I do on this trip, none of them compare to Thursday, August 18. Ever since Johan and I were married, some thirty-odd years ago, I've wanted to see the Van Gogh Museum in Amsterdam. It never worked out. Not until today.

Van Gogh Museum stands bold and contemporary before us. We enter through the newly remodeled entrance. The spectacular transparent glass structure leads us into a light-filled, four story building. The museum turns out to be not just a showcase of Van Gogh's art—with more than two hundred of his paintings and five hundred of his drawings—but the story of his life. The museum holds letters between Vincent and his brother Theo. His paints. An easel. A box of colorful yarn; he arranged and rearranged the yarn creating color combinations he'd later use in paintings.

We walk slowly, absorbing Vincent's life work and story. We go up and down the turquoise glass steps and peer over the glass ledges, taking in all four floors at once. The walls are mostly white. The lighting, perfection. The architecture alone takes my breath away.

The top floor of the museum shows Vincent's oldest artwork. The pictures are dark and muddled grays, browns, and greens. *The Weaver*, 1883. *The Potato Eaters*, 1885. Before he began painting with his bright colors. As we move down the floors, his works become brighter, livelier, more the Vincent that I know. *The Yellow House*, 1888. *Wheatfield with a Reaper*, 1889.

His work is so different from the art I have seen at the famous Rijksmuseum. I'm tired of those old Dutch masters, their dark and muted world, their white starched collars and stiffly held manners. The paintings there are masterful and precise, but they remind me too much of Izaak. Stiff and correct. Organized. Aligned.

Vincent surprises. Yellow upon yellow! A turquoise splash across a face. His wild work swirling and vibrant. His colors soar off the canvas in exuberance. The irises dance. He makes me laugh.

Michelle and I spend the whole day at the museum. We go up and down the stairs. Listen to the audio tour. Turn it off and sit and look. And look.

I see the paintings that I've long known only in books. *The Bedroom. Almond Blossom. Irises. Self-Portrait with Grey Felt Hat. The Pietá.* Some are much bigger than I expected. Others surprisingly tiny. Some are painted on cardboard; the only thing Vincent could afford. Painted in 1887 and 1888 and 1889, yet fresh and brilliant as if they are only a few years old, not decades, not a century.

We save this year's special exhibition, "On the Verge of Insanity: Van Gogh and His Illness," for last, walking through it just before the museum closes. Reading Vincent's sad letters. Feeling his despair.

How can it be that such a sad, complex, ill man created so much joy?

What is it that draws millions of people every year to this museum?

In 1888, Vincent wrote in a letter to his sister Willemien, "The uglier, older, meaner, iller, poorer I get, the more I wish to take my revenge by doing brilliant color, well arranged, resplendent."

There's something in these words that touch me. His tenacity, his nerve. His fight against established protocols and dictates. All my life, I've connected with Vincent's work. It buoys me. His yellow happy house, my lifeboat. His slant and tilted bedroom, my resting place. When I'm blue and drifting and drained, I'm lifted by his swirling stars. Vincent's joy-soaked work and pain-filled life, a lens that lifts me beyond myself.

The museum exit takes us past the gift shop. I don't buy anything. It all seems cheap. Or cheapening. Puzzles, pillows, potholders. Salt & pepper shakers. A set of Samsonite luggage. Fabric doggie coats covered with sunflowers. A keychain in the shape on an ear, with the lower lobe bitten off.

I want to remember the vibrant art. Not the trinkets. Not the reproductions.

There was only one Vincent. Some things cannot be reproduced.

I go to bed that evening wondering about Vincent's life and works. What if Vincent Van Gogh had walked into a Life End Clinic, at the age of eighteen, or twenty-four, or thirty-two, and said, "Let's just get it over with."

Vincent, a poor utterly depressed man, in love with an alcoholic prostitute. Argumentative, hospitalized multiple times, nomadic. He sold only one painting in his entire life.

Vincent. Hailed as the greatest Dutch painter after Rembrandt with more than 2,100 completed works. His *Irises* sold for $53.9 million. *Portrait of Dr. Cachet* for $82.5 million.

He has his own museum. But I know what would have happened if he'd walked into a Life End Clinic. He more than met the criteria. He exceeded it thoroughly: mentally ill, below the poverty line, unemployed, homeless, violent.

Imagine the world without Vincent Van Gogh's yellow upon yellow sunflowers and circular starry nights. No wild irises blooming blue and bright.

Imagine the world, with less.

Then, consider this possibility: death is not a remedy or a retail service or an answer. Death is a taking away.

The Coffin, 1945

Izaak would later write about his days in hiding.

> Dick and I threw two blankets onto the attic floor and slept next to each other. A thick wall of stacked wood separated our space from the rest of the attic. On the head-side of the "bed" we left a small hidden opening as an entrance to crawl through.
>
> Each night, we closed it off with wood. We switched sides, back and forth every other night, taking turns laying on the smaller side, up against the angled roof.
>
> A thin wall separated our attic from the neighbor's attic. We heard every sound next door. We heard airplanes overhead. We heard the low rumble of Hitler's V1 and V2 Rockets.

It was early 1945. Nazi Germany had occupied the Netherlands for nearly five years. Five years of German control, surveillance, and supervision over this tiny nation. Five years of kidnapping, coercing, and murdering.

How did Izaak and Dick spend those days?

Not much to eat. Certainly not much to do. The hours crawled by. The days. The weeks. They had a lot of time and not much else. They feared being found. Feared starving. Feared the sound of boots tramping down the street, stopping at their front door.

But even fear must become monotonous when you are young and vibrant and eager to live. Izaak and Dick had barely left their teens. Young manhood something they were just beginning to crawl into. Life in an attic, quiet, cold, scared, and hungry must have gnawed at their youthful hearts.

Did they pretend they were camping? Sleeping blankets thrown down on the hard ground. Perhaps, they silently drummed out rhythms and patterns of familiar songs they'd played together in their band days. Their fingers tapping softly on their thighs as they relaxed into the music. Perhaps, Izaak retold family stories, the stories he'd heard all his life about the glorious years in the Dutch East Indies, the years before he was born. Most likely he thought about his girlfriend, Jopie, wondering what the years ahead would bring. Wondering if there would be any years ahead. They needed to keep their minds busy, pushing the real question away: *What would happen if they were discovered?*

Years later, Izaak would say little of the actual time he spent hiding in that attic. But he did say this: "We often told a sort of joke to each other, trying to be funny. We said, 'What could go worse? We're already lying in our coffins.'"

Pa, 2016

I ask Andrea about their family trips to the Alps.

"Oh, I hated those trips," she says.

I'm incredulous. "What? Johan always talks so fondly about the Alps. He loved your family vacations."

"Ya, but we always went to the same place!" she responds. "The same village, the same cabin. Pa wanted to hike the same trails. Every summer the same. It was so boring."

I'm amazed. Her words have changed my idea of my husband's vacations. What I once thought of as ideal, now appears to be routine, regimented, and quite frankly, tedious. I cannot imagine taking the exact same vacation year after year after year.

I tell Andrea about my ironing debacle with Izaak. She laughs a little ruefully. "Oh, *yah*. That was Pa. When he got older, I did his ironing. I even ironed his handkerchiefs."

She asked him once, "Pa, why must I iron your handkerchiefs?"

And he replied, "*Zo is het.*" Literally: Because it is. A Dutch version of *because I said so.*

And that's Izaak to the letter.

Zo is het. Because I said so.

Fear, 1945

In the end, hiding was all that was left, Izaak, and you ran to it, as to safety. Ran to hiding like a refugee. Ran from fear and found a tenuous security. I think you never really left; that heap of wood, above the creaky steps, the dusky attic became your safety zone. The place you clung to. The wall you hid behind most of your life.

After the war, you clothed yourself in prosperity and digni-ty and marriage and fatherhood. The shell you presented to the world, accrued praise and prestige: a tower of virtue, strength, and decisiveness. But you never fully left that room, your young life too chipped, too hewn. You didn't know how to climb back down those stairs. How to open the door and go outside again, into the raging sun.

Perhaps, you thought no one would notice. After all, who would ever see beneath your three-piece suit, your black and stately cassock, your crumple-less exterior?

We would have loved you. But you only pushed us away with your all-consuming need for control. Always and forever to be in control. To be certain. To be sure. To be in charge.

Uncertainty must have felt like a dank crawlspace hiding be-neath thin linoleum, a musty wooden hidey-hole squeezed into the corner of an attic.

Oh, Izaak. You were so afraid of the unknown future, the possibility of terrors lurking ahead, that you forgot how to hold the present. The wonder of your everyday and oh-so-daily life. The wonder of your breath.

Jopie's Secret

Earlier, during our trip, Johan and I spend a night at Bert's house. On a whim, I ask him to tell me a story about Jopie.

"Did I ever tell you about when I had surgery?" Bert asks.

"I don't think so," I reply.

"Me neither," Johan says.

"My girlfriend and I were living together," Bert says. "At one point, I went in for surgery on my knee. After surgery, when I was recovering back in our apartment, there was a knock on our door. It was Mother. When I invited her in, she said, 'Pa strictly forbade me to come visit you. Absolutely, not allowed. But you are sick. I want to visit my son! How are you?'

"Mother was so sweet and kind," Bert said, "She was always there for me in a way Father never was. When she came, she brought me a present and said, 'We won't tell your father that I came. He does not need to know.'"

Bert looked over at Johan as he continued talking.

"Father took up so much space. There was little attention for Mother. But she was in the resistance, just like me. I never told Father about her visits. Not even after she died."

I tear up as Bert finishes his story.

Jopie in the resistance.

Jopie doing what *she* wanted.

Izaak died without ever hearing the story.

Jopie's secret kept.

The Mixed Verbs of War, February 16, 1945

We only have one letter written by Izaak during the war years. He wrote the letter to Jopie. On the top, the letter bears two dates and one word: 16 February 1941–16 February 1945 Hurrah!

It is 1945, the fourth anniversary of their first kiss, and Izaak is in hiding. The letter, written on both sides and folded in the middle, looks like a page taken out of a small school journal. Yellowed paper with blue ink lines. The letter itself, written in pencil. Over the years, the penciled words faded and smeared. After I took photographs of the letter and enhanced it to the max with brighten and contrast, Johan and I were able to decipher most of it.

Izaak writes in formal Dutch. The *you* in the form of *uw* and *uwe*, not *je* or *jij*. I don't understand this choice. They've been going out for four years and still Izaak refers to Jopie in formal language. Is he trying to be funny? Or perhaps this is merely a reflection of 1940s Netherlands. A time when men wore three-piece suits accompanied by ties and hats. A time when protocol and procedure and formality were revered.

He begins his letter.

Zeer geliefde schat. Very beloved treasure.

> On the evening before this important date in your life,
> I consider it my duty to write specifically and wish you
> the congratulations that belong to you considering our
> four years of existence, united in hugs and kisses. Also,
> I'm willing to be of service, am your servant, and am
> still under the pressure of hiding.

I read through the old Dutch words in these rich sentences and try to get a feel for Izaak. I'm frustrated by his word choices. *Duty. Existence. Servant.* It sounds like a military record.

I read through it again and pick out the many endearments sprinkled throughout.

Geliefde schat, innig geliefde, Meid, meisje: Beloved treasure, dearly beloved, girl, young girl. Sweet, tender words. A love letter.

> It's pleasing for me to be able to write to you on this day
> because many young men my age are suffering under
> the heel of the enemy. Therefore, my greatly beloved,
> rejoice that, although this is written by pencil, I'm able
> to send you a letter.

Suffering. Rejoicing. Writing. Sending.

The mixed verbs of war.

He doesn't use her name in the letter. Perhaps out of safety issues. The letter might fall into the wrong hands. Who was going to bring it to her? Would someone else find and read it?

He sends greetings from Dick, and he has news.

> There is a 99% chance that next Saturday I will be home.
> Although it would probably be better if I'd stay away, but
> then I'd have to live without any food.

He's coming back home! Not because he wants to, but because the people caring for him in his hiding place have run out of food. There's nothing more to give. Not even a scrap.

The sorry truth is that it's better for Izaak to face the Nazi razzias, the fear of being kidnapped and sent to Germany, than it is to face another week with nothing to eat. Starvation, at this point in the war, a surer death than the alternatives.

> Please don't tell anybody yet about my (nearly for sure) travel back home. It's possible, if there is imminent danger, that I might disappear again. Maybe you are surprised about this letter and that I'm coming home, so make sure that Jan keeps on writing until he is allowed to know that I am at home.

I think about the words he uses.

Do not tell. Imminent danger. Disappear again. Not allowed.

These words sound so familiar. How often I felt them over the years. Never spoken. But underneath. So much fear. So much disappearing. Do. Do not. Allowed. Not allowed. The constrictors he was forced to live within settled into his life so young and so deep; perhaps he never even knew.

> I want to remind you that it was today four years ago, that you had the chance to eat a whole roll of King Peppermint. Four years ago, girl. Where did the time go? We've had a lot to deal with, but I believe the worst times are behind us. Heh? Girl?
>
> I hope that we'll be spared for each other. So, girl, I'm going to end now quickly because the letter needs to be sent. Girl, love, and hugs from your very much in love, Iz.

They were young in a time when eating one roll of peppermints was a memorable happening. A whole roll! They were full of hope and thoughts of their future. Hoping to be spared in the last months of the war. Not knowing what the final days would bring.

At the bottom of the letter, there's a postscript. Crooked writing by the same hand, but a larger script than the previous, as if written in haste:

You know what you are getting, right?

Walking Tour 2016

Michelle wants to spend a day at the Rijksmuseum, but over the years I've been there dozens of times and don't want to see it again. I email a website that does WWII history walks through Amsterdam and sign up for a three-hour walking tour. I'm thrilled they still have an opening.

On Sunday, August 21, we head out to Amsterdam. When we arrive, it's not dripping rain; it's pouring. Michelle hops a tram and I run over to the corner by the Anne Frank Museum, the tour's rendezvous spot. My sneakers are soaked before the guide even shows up.

Ben de Jong—a retired professor—has led these walking tours for years. We stand together, chatting, wiping the rain out of our eyes, waiting for the other tour members. They don't show. We wait half an hour, and he asks if I still want to do the tour in this rain.

"Yes, absolutely," I say. "It's the only day I have left."

He agrees and we take off in the downpour, the two of us and our soggy umbrellas.

Professor de Jong must be used to rain; he's wearing water-proof clothing from head to toe, and when my cheap umbrella blows apart in the wind, he shares his large one with me.

As we walk, Professor de Jong stops on occasion and points out buildings and corners. He carries a waterproof three-ring binder with pictures from the war years. We walk by the old Jewish section of town and I realize how easy it must have been to form a razzia. Whole areas in this section of town are bordered by beautiful canals. Natural blockades. We pass areas where mass Jewish roundups were held. Professor de Jong talks nonstop. Stories and anecdotes spill out from his vast knowledge of history. He makes Amsterdam come alive.

Of all the things I see, what I'll remember most vividly in years to come are the Stolperstein set into the cobblestone streets and sidewalks of Amsterdam. The word itself means a stumbling stone, or stumbling block. German artist Gunter Demnig created the first Stolperstein in Berlin, in the 1990s. Square brass markers, each one only four by four inches, inscribed with a name and information about a person murdered by the Nazis. The stones are inlaid at the foot of the house where they had lived. Before. Before the Nazis came.

Upwards of 60,000 Stolperstein dot Europe, memorials for individuals killed under Nazi Germany: Jewish victims, Roma, homosexuals, Jehovah's Witnesses, the disabled. Each one bearing testimony to a person's life.

Hier Woonde
Joseph Bronkhorst
Geb. 1911
Gearresteerd 11-11-1942
Gedeporteerd 1942
Uit Westerbork
Vermoord 28-2-1943
Auschwitz

Translated into English the Stumbling Stone reads:

Here lived
Joseph Bronkhorst
Born 1911
Arrested 11-11-1942
Transported 1942
From Westerbork
Killed 2-28-1943
Auschwitz

Another Stumbling Stone next to it. Here lived Judith Bronkhorst-Trompetter. Born 1913. Judith carried away on the same day. Also, taken to Westerbork and on to Auschwitz. Killed two months before Joseph, on December 11, 1942.

I look across the canal at a line of tall Dutch row houses. A whole canal length of them. At my feet, are dozens and dozens of small brass memorials. A twenty-three-year-old man. A twenty-three-year-old woman. A one-year-old girl. They all bear the same last name.

Ages vary. Thirty-one, fifty, twenty-seven, sixty-three, twenty-two.

Names include Sara, Roosje, Karel, Max. Andries, Marianna, Elvira, Simon, Esther, Eliazer.

I walk for blocks reading the brass name plates. Walk beside the homes these people used to live in. Homes they were brutally taken from.

There are other people living in the houses now. Windows open, people coming and going, geraniums blooming in a pot, a cat beside a stoop.

Not so long ago, a very different world existed.

We end the tour with a stop at the Auschwitz Memorial, known as the Memorial of Broken Mirrors. Artist Jan Wolkers placed six large panels of shattered glass upon the ground and framed them in with metal. Today the blue-gray glass reflects the cloudy sky and the nearby trees. Today the broken glass panels are covered in rain. A few leaves have fallen on them, blown in on the wind.

My sneakers squish with water; my backpack's saturated and dripping. I'm damp to the bone and chilly-cold. But this memorial holds my attention.

It's so perfect. Lying shattered on the ground, reflecting a world that appears to be broken into pieces, as if even the sky can never be whole again, not after Auschwitz.

There's another plate of glass at the head of the memorial; this one is standing upright and has three words etched deeply into it with a bold block print.

Nooit Meer Auschwitz
Never Again Auschwitz

I've been taking pictures all day long. In these, the last of my photos, I'm reflected in the glass. I'm a part of the picture, too.

Each person who stands at the memorial becomes a part of it. *Never again, Auschwitz.*

I turn and thank my guide. He says, "I've been doing these tours for years and I've never seen the weather this bad."

I tell him no problem, "I'm so grateful for the opportunity."

It's been the most amazing three hours. I tip him generously, hand back his umbrella, pull up the hood on my rain jacket, and feel a hood full of cold water run chilly down my back.

Operation Manna, April 29, 1945

When the German defeat was thought to be inevitable, Henk and Izaak joined a group of twenty young men preparing to do the work of running errands when the Liberators arrived. They were fed confiscated food. A warm meal, once every day! Compared to the scraps he'd been existing on this was pure luxury.

And then, bread from heaven.

On April 29, 1945, the Royal Air Force Lancaster heavy bombers were on their way from England to the Netherlands. The planes, manned by British, Australian, and Canadian crewmembers, buzzed Holland's lowlands. Weaving between church steeples and windmills, the pilots flew so low they made eye contact with the Dutch citizens. The bellies of their planes fully loaded, not with bombs, but with food parcels. Codenamed Operation Manna after the story from the book of Exodus where God rained bread, in the form of manna, down on the hungry Israelites.

Wary Nazi soldiers followed the planes with anti-aircraft guns but didn't shoot. As the engines roared overhead, Dutch men, women, and children waved handkerchiefs and Dutch flags at the Allied pilots. The planes let loose their payload and boxes rained down, filled with chocolate bars, margarine, coffee, milk powder, salt, cheese, flour, and bread.

Two days later, May 1, the American B-17 Flying Fortress bombers joined the relief mission, codenaming themselves Operation Chowhound. As food fell from the skies, crews saw the gratitude of the Dutch people in messages such as the tulips arranged by one farmer spelling out, "Thank You Yanks!"

For ten days, Allied bombers flew back and forth across the North Sea carrying food to the starving Dutch. At the height of the relief effort, nine hundred bombers flew each day. In total, Allied aircraft transported more than 11,000 tons of food, saving thousands of Dutch lives.

Izaak well remembered those food boxes. He always said the best thing he ever tasted in his whole life was "the bread that dropped down from heaven." Whenever he talked about it, his countenance changed. His face softened and he'd smile in remembrance. I could almost feel him reach out and take a loaf in his hands and lift it up to his nose as he breathed in the clean, wholesome smell of fresh bread. As he held it out to his mother and his father with a sort of unbelieving rapture. As he cut the loaf and lifted a slice to his lips. As he watched his family eat. Simple, sweet, and absolute joy.

So, there he was. Twenty-one years old, out of the coffin, and into the world again. With food to be eaten. The Allies it seemed only days away from a final victory. What a spring it must have been. April and tulips and blue skies and the fresh breeze of freedom. It was the talk of the town. The talk of the whole country. The Allies were on the move, and Germany, finally and at long last, backed its way out of the Netherlands, turned tail, and ran home, where nothing much good awaited.

Liberation by the Inch, April–May 1945

Liberation of the Netherlands came in the step-by-step, steady advance of the Allied soldiers. Slowly, city-by-city, an inching forward that brought death, destruction, and violent fighting along with it. Destruction came from both the Allies trying to push the Germans out and from the Germans leaving chaos and havoc in their wake.

In April of 1945, several Canadian Infantry Divisions fought their way through Occupied Netherlands, liberating the city of Hengelo on April 5. In Zutphen, the Germans blocked roads with anti-tank obstacles and blew up bridges. Still the Canadians battled and won, freeing the town. On April 12, Westerbork—the transient concentration camp from which Anne Frank had been transported—was freed, along with the cities of Brummen and Deventer.

On April 13, Assen, Diepenveen, and Olst were liberated. In Apeldoorn, RAF Spitfire and Typhoon fighters attacked the German defenses. The city took days to liberate. By April 17, it was cleared.

The last battle fought on Dutch soil, Operation Canada, began April 23. The Canadians suffered over 250 casualties as they advanced through flooded terrain, minefields, and heavily fortified gun batteries.

And then, on the evening of May 4, Allied soldiers in the Netherlands and Dutch citizens cheered together as Premier Gerbrandy gave the much-anticipated Radio Oranje announcement: Germany had surrendered. All hostilities were to stop on May 5 at 8:00 a.m.

On Saturday May 5, the Germans negotiated the terms of German capitulation in the Netherlands at a hotel called De Wereld, The World. May 5 is often called Liberation Day, but the actual signing of the surrender took place on May 6 on a farm just outside of Wageningen.

Red, white, and blue posters in both Dutch and English lined the streets.

Welkom in Het Vrije Nederland!
Free Holland Welcomes the Soldiers of the Allies!

The war in Europe was over.

Casualties May 7, 1945

On May 7, 1945, thousands of Amsterdammers gathered on Dam Square to await the arrival of the liberators. The crowd of Dutch celebrants swelled into the thousands. The first of the Allied tanks arrived at 1:00 p.m. and were swarmed by crowds of people, the situation celebratory, but chaotic. German soldiers were still being routed from buildings and hiding places, and German vehicles were still fleeing the city.

At 3:00 p.m., shots rang out from the nearby Grote Club. People panicked, fled, hid behind lamp poles. A second round of shooting followed and continued for half an hour.

Approximately 120 people were wounded that day. Thirty lost their lives. These people had survived long enough to hear the happy news of liberation, run into the streets, party and dance and laugh. They had waved their flags. They had sung their national anthem. The war was over. But so was their time. One day. That's all they had. Just one day.

Those thirty people, casualties who technically died after liberation, would be followed by thousands of others. Those whose trauma, wounds, infections, or starvation-related illnesses caused their deaths in the months and years to come. And there were those who never recovered—even though they lived—that would forever remain casualties of the war.

As the weeks passed, Izaak began to put his life back together in an orderly manner. He insulated himself from uncertainty and question by developing a ready answer, a steady gaze, and an unwavering calendar. These responses became his art form, his tour de force. He perfected himself into a man in control of his schedule, his meals, his wardrobe, his life. A man in control of everything. Steadfast. Solid. Punctual. Dogmatic.

By the time I met him, he was a man who had all the answers.

Sitting behind the Geraniums

Andrea's English is better than my Dutch. But I still try to speak Dutch. We often switch languages back and forth while talking. Sometimes I find myself speaking Dutch poorly and she answers me in tentative English. And then we hit upon a better approach. She speaks Dutch; I speak English. It's much easier to hear a language than to speak it. Our arrangement works for the most part. But when we're not paying attention, there we go again. Me speaking Dutch. Andrea speaking English. We muddle along, laugh at each other, and switch back to our mother tongues.

While we are talking, Andrea uses a lovely Dutch idiom, *achter de geraniums zitten*. Translated literally, it means "sitting behind the geraniums." Since geraniums are flowers typically grown in window boxes, the elderly in the Netherlands often sit behind their big (and spotlessly clean) living room windows and look out at their world from behind the flowers.

For centuries, this Dutch expression described a normal part of life. Aging. Slowing down. An idiom conveying a sense of contentment and pleasure. The idea of aging and resting going hand in hand.

Today if you ask a Dutch person about the geranium saying he's most likely to reply, "*Ik ga zeker nog niet achter de geraniums zitten!*" I am certainly NOT going to sit behind the geraniums!

Somewhere in the past decade, sitting behind the geraniums has become unacceptable; it's become an idiom of contempt and scorn. If an octogenarian can no longer bike across Europe, can't cruise the Rhine, or run a marathon, somehow, his life is considered worth less or even worthless. Sitting at home is no longer enough. Enjoying the flowers, a waste. While I'm all for keeping fit and active, since when did *sitting* become a term of derision?

I never heard my grandmother's voice. She spent twenty years in a wheelchair, her right side crippled by a stroke while in her forties. She could barely walk. When I was young, she'd scribble little notes with her good left hand, and Mom would read them to me. We'd laugh and play our paper-worded game. I'd sit beside her, pencil in hand, pretending I knew how to make words on paper that my mother would be able to read. The squiggles of black pencil intrigued and captured me. I became a writer because of her. I remember Grandma's infectious smile. She taught me joy. She taught me laughter. She taught me not to be afraid.

In our frenzy to go and do and see and hectically experience everything, we've overlooked what a quiet breath feels like. In the fury to keep up with a spinning world, we've forgotten the gentle things. The things we have to sit quiet and still to notice.

The wrinkled smile of a grandfather.

The gentle touch of a papery hand.

The bright red of a geranium, new buds coming, blowing softy in a blue-sky breeze.

The Marshall Plan, June 1945

In the summer of 1945, the Netherlands welcomed Queen Wilhelmina and the Government-in-Exile back home; they found their country very changed. As a nation, the Netherlands had been on the frontline of the war for nearly nine months. One of the many goals of Germany in the last year of the war had been to reduce the Netherlands' independence, making it entirely dependent upon Germany. The damage to the infrastructure of the Netherlands was immense. Over five hundred bridges had been destroyed; only fifty-nine of the most important bridges remained useable. Of the railroad bridges, only twenty-six were intact. Mines floated in the rivers and canals. Mines covered much of the agricultural land, stray bombs lying in the grass like spring lambs. Anti-tank equipment blocked roads. Broken-down tanks littered the ditches. The massive concrete bunkers of the Atlantic Wall poisoned the landscape the entire length of the country.

There was so much to do. Clean the canals. Reinvigorate the flooded, salty land. Rebuild the bridges, the tunnels, the railroad lines. Rebuild the rail stations, the roads, the homes. Of the 25,000 homes in Arnhem, only 145 remained intact.

Nobody had the time, inclination, or energy to worry about getting rid of Nazi fortifications. And so, they stayed. And sunk. And moldered. How would you remove a ten-ton piece of concrete from your pasture anyway?

Food was in short supply and rationed. Life was chaotic. The Dutch harbors of Rotterdam and Amsterdam were completely ruined. "No country in Western Europe was harder hit than the Netherlands, ruined and robbed," Dutch historian E. H. Kossmann wrote.

Hundreds of thousands of Dutch citizens began to emigrate, primarily to Australia, Canada, and the United States. So many families torn apart, so varied the casualties of war.

The Wieringermeerpolder, flooded by the retreating Germans in April of 1945, was drained and slowly put back into agricultural production. And over the next years, the Dutch received approximately one billion dollars in aid from the Marshall Plan. It would take more than ten years before the devastations and deprivations of WWII began to fade. Still, the Netherlands found her footing. Found her way. Rebuilt.

It makes me wonder. If the landscape of a nation takes over ten years to move on, how long does it take a person? If the physical deprivations are overcome by outside help and money and support, how does an individual find these things and begin to repair himself internally?

Cor, 1946

In 1946, the war had been over for a year. One afternoon, a uniformed soldier, riding a big army motorbike, turned onto Jopie's street. Stopped in front of the ten Hoope family home and walked up to the front door.

The soldier knocked and waited. The door opened.

The soldier stood there smiling, such a familiar smile.

Cor! Jopie's sister Cor! Alive and well and home. She'd made it across the Biesbosch. Traveled to England. Enlisted in the Women's Help Corp and had been involved with bringing children to safe locations.

Cor stayed in the army for a few more months and then went back into nursing.

There was no news of Wes. Not yet.

An Offering 2016

While visiting Andrea, it comes as a complete surprise to me, that there are actually some things I miss about Izaak. I miss the sweet, sculpted pastries he always served with coffee, fluffy almond cream. I hardly eat sweets while in America, but I've come to expect the taste of them as a part of feeling at home in the Netherlands.

Andrea says, "Pa had such a sweet tooth. I never buy gebak."

On my third day in the Netherlands, feeling so hungry for what I remembered, I bike alone to Bakkerij & Banket and purchase four pastries. I bike home practically drooling and eat two of them at once: a *tompouce* with pastel pink frosting, which I lick from my fingers, and then a coffee-flavored wedge topped with a dark chocolate curl. As I eat, I marvel at my stupidity.

What I'd taken for everyday normal Dutch life, what I'd seen as just another custom, had really been a piece of Izaak, a look at who *he* was.

After thirty-three years of being married to Johan, it's often still a puzzle, this distinction between what is specific to the Dutch people as a whole and what is just the individual.

As I ate the last of the cake, I remembered how Izaak used to call my name.

"Yill," he used to say, holding out three dessert plates. "Yill, *neem een*." Take one.

"Yill, *Kies er een*."

Choose one.

I thought of it as requirement.

He handed it to me as an offering.

Love is Not a Victory, March 2016

It's hard to love. It's harder still to love someone you don't really like. There wasn't much in Izaak that I was drawn to naturally, not much I laughed at or enjoyed. I search for memoires of a time when we were together with joy and ease and come up empty-handed.

One day in a discussion—one of those ongoing Let's-talk-about-Pa-again discussions that follow Andrea and I like lost dogs—Andrea says, "He really loved you, you know."

I shake my head in disbelief.

"He talked about you and Johan all the time," she says. "He adored you both."

"Yeah, well. He never said it to our faces," I reply. "I can't remember one time he ever told me that."

"I don't think he knew how," she postulates. "I don't think he ever learned how to express love. I think his way of caring for people was to protect them. All his controlling was his way of protecting us."

To love a person and never tell them. To admire someone and criticize them freely. I just don't understand.

That night, I remember a day when Kristina was about five and Joren four. It must've been in that time between England and Indonesia.

We're at Izaak's house and he tells us to all come out to the shed. He has a surprise.

In the shed, on the wooden table, he's set out a row of candles. They are "glued" onto the table with their own wax, six or eight of them, tall and burning bright.

"*Komen*, Kristina en Joren," he says. "Let's blow out the candles!" He stoops over to blow but purses his lips to the right side of his mouth. Out comes all the sound of air, the candle flickers, but remains burning. The children laugh.

He says, "Oh, my!" and he blows again. This time pursing his lips to the left, and his air blows past the wick; the candle burns.

The children step up to the table, six inches from the flames.

"Blazen, nu!" Blow now! Izaak says.

Kristina blows and Joren blows and the candles all go out. Izaak claps his hands in delight.

"Ja! *Goed zo!*" Yes, well done!

He relights the candles. The children blow. He blows again, and misses.

This candle game delights them all. They are all laughing.

"Light them again, Opa!" they shout. And he does. The match sizzles, the candles light, the cheeks puff out and blow.

I'm so surprised. I wonder how long their game will last. They blow until they are dizzy, and all the breath has gone out of them, and the candles are only melted nubs. There's wax everywhere. Smiles everywhere. Even Opa looks tired from the joy.

I'm reminded of Leonard Cohen's "Hallelujah."

I see a part of that hallelujah when I think of Izaak. Yes, he was cold, and yes, he was broken.

But still, he loved us.

Hot Pink Lilies, 2016

What was your mother?
Your mother was like a vine in a vineyard planted by the water
Fruitful and full of branches
By reason of abundant water. Ezekiel 19

After eight weeks in Europe, the night before my flight back to the States, Kristina calls me at 1:00 a.m. "Oma is in trouble," she says. "I think she needs to go to the hospital. Her bowels are all stopped up. Hospice won't let me make any decisions for her since you are her power of medical attorney." Kristina can't get ahold of my sister, so she is caught in the middle of all these questions and medical decisions on her own.

I talk with hospice staff, nursing staff, and my mom. Mom desperately wants to go to the hospital and is in a lot of pain. She's been blocked up for three days. I do paperwork over the phone by voice, and she's allowed to go by ambulance to the hospital.

I call Kristina back every few hours. My sister arrives to help out.

I know enough about blocked bowels and my mother's heart to realize she isn't a candidate for abdominal surgery. I know enough to know it doesn't sound good at all.

I fly out the next morning, bleary from interrupted sleep and arrive home at 9:00 p.m., jet-lagged and exhausted. Johan picks me up and we bring my suitcase home, then we go to the hospital. Mom welcomes me back, weak but coherent, talking, happy. She asks about my trip. She falls asleep every ten minutes, and finally we leave her to get some rest.

The next morning, I go to the hospital. Mom's been given some medicine to move her bowels, but it hasn't had any affect. We wait to see a doctor, while I watch Mom's blood pressure slowly fall. We wait all morning and into the noon hour. In the early afternoon something happens. Mom's blood pressure falls to dangerously low levels. She becomes groggy. Her stomach swells even more. She responds slower to our questions.

We hear buzzing, and a team of nurses and doctors rushes into her room. They want answers right now!

"Her blood pressure is nearly too low to sustain life," they say.

They want to run invasive tests, do exams, take her to ICU, prep her for possible surgery.

"She needs emergency surgery," they insist.

My sister and I look at each other. She nods at me and I—the nurse in the family and mother's designated medical care person—say, "No. She didn't want extensive medical intervention. She has acute congestive heart failure, three leaking heart valves, and is eighty-six years old. She wouldn't survive surgery."

One of the doctors scowls, looking annoyed. He's clearly rushed into the room in ICU mode. The other doctor looks me in the eye and slowly nods his head.

"I agree with you," he says. "She wouldn't live through any of these procedures." He asks if Mom had talked about her death and what her wishes are.

"She filled in that Five Wishes end of life booklet," I say. "She didn't want to be resuscitated. Regular, good medical care, yes. Interventions, no. She asked that there wouldn't be any invasive medical procedures done."

The staff leaves and the room suddenly goes quiet. One of the nurses stays and is so kind. I ask her, "Do we have to move Mom out? Does she have to leave?" I'm confused by what to expect.

"Oh, no," the nurse says, "She can stay here. We'll just change the focus of her care to comfort only."

I place my hand on Mom's stomach and whisper, "They can't fix it, Mom. The problem is too large. They can't fix your stomach anymore." She doesn't respond, but still I think she might hear me, and I want her to know what's going on.

The nurse takes out Mom's nasogastric tube, takes off her stained gown, and puts a fresh one on her. We straighten Mom's pillows, wet her lips with a sponge, hold her hand, brush her hair. When she starts moaning, the nurse gives her a small dose of morphine. She quiets.

Mom's grandchildren are scattered around America, but the nearest ones—Kristina, Anneke, and Ben—are all at her bedside. They've been here off and on for two days. It is an amazement to watch them as the hours pass.

As Mom fades in and out of consciousness, they hold her hand and tell her about favorite memories they have of her. Her lakeside antique shop. Playing with the hats that filled her closet in round, cardboard hat boxes. Going out for donuts. They sponge her dry lips with a moist cloth, then gently apply lip balm. This bond between grandchild and grandmother tears my heart. It is a sacred offering to watch.

We turn her favorite hymns on and take turns reading Psalms, talk to her about all the ways she's blessed us.

My sister and brother and I decide to take turns sitting with Mom. I need to go home and sleep. I volunteer to come back later and do the night hours.

Kristina bends over and kisses Oma goodbye, whispering, "You can go now, Oma. When you are ready. It's okay. I love you."

Johan, Kristina, and I walk out of her room together.

It's only a ten-minute drive home. I can barely think straight for lack of sleep and the time change.

Johan says he's so impressed with our children. "They seemed to know exactly what to do for Oma," he says. "I'm glad they were there."

I walk down to my bedroom, open the covers, and crawl in. The phone rings. It's my sister.

"Mom's gone."

We meet back in the hospital room and sit by her bed for a while. We say our goodbyes and lay out clothes for the mortuary to use.

After my siblings leave, I take the long-stemmed hot pink lilies—the ones I'd purchased for Mom just the night before—out of their vase and lay them on her chest. I cross her hands over them, like she's holding a bouquet.

She always loved that shade of pink.

I turn and walk out of the room.

I've been back in the States for eighteen hours.

Part 9: WHAT REMAINS, 2017—

Izaak Kandel at the first Dakajam Camp, Meppel, The Netherlands. 1950.

The Things My Mother Knew

My mother was a storyteller. After she dies, her stories come—frequent, bright, and unrequested—into my thoughts. I'll be falling asleep, or walking down a street, and suddenly I'm overwhelmed with her presence or a memory of her words.

A few weeks after she dies, I go out to get groceries. As I reach for a jar of olives, a story comes vividly to mind, one of her favorites to tell.

When she was a young married woman, my mother placed first place in the Mrs. North Dakota pageant, but the judges disqualified her when her husband refused to attend the ceremonies. She lamented his refusal the rest of her life.

I've heard the story often before, especially when Mom was annoyed with my dad.

The story always ends in Mom's favor, as she proudly recounts: "I was the only contestant who knew the proper etiquette for eating a large green olive. The other women just left theirs lying on their plates. They didn't dare eat them!"

Do not use your fingers.

Do not spit the pit.

Hold the olive down with your knife and stab it with your fork. Place it in your mouth.

The pit should come out the same way it went in.

Place one hand in front of your mouth to hide this activity. Gently push the pit of the olive onto a fork. Use your tongue to guide it.

Place the pit on the rim of your plate.

Oh, the things my mother knew.

Treasure Found, 2016

Two months after Mom dies, a second grandchild—a little girl—enters our lives. She's a calm baby, as perfect as they come, chubby, soft, and quiet. We travel north to visit our grandchildren as often as we can. Johan's enamored and can't stop smiling when he's with them. He's the type of grandpa who's on his knees playing and wrestling, hugging, and teasing. I don't know that I've ever seen him quite so happy. He loves being Opa.

Kristina finds a bargain house—on the market after being repossessed by the bank and standing empty for a year—and buys it. She spends six months pulling carpets, scrubbing, and painting. When the house finally sparkles, Kristina moves in. Anneke decides to join her and moves in, too. They call it The Sisterhood. I love their enthusiasm, painting, decorating, joy. I'm happy they're such good friends.

I've kissed my girls goodnight for decades.

Good night. Sleep tight. Don't let the bedbugs bite.

And now their room is an empty cavern.

There was a time when life was sweet and simple. School days, ABC and 123. Innocent days of first readers and chalkboard pictures, Calvert School boxes, pencils, and penmanship. Dr. Seuss and Dick Bruna days, all primary, thick black lines and sunshine happiness.

There was a time, and I loved it.

The day after they move out, Johan heads to work and so does Ben. I wander my empty house. So silent. The day stretches long and quiet before me. I drift from room to room as if waiting. I'm so unsettled, so restless. I clean the girls' old room. Then, tearing up the dingy carpet, I find beautiful wood flooring underneath. This leads to weeks of sanding, bleaching, and oil rubbing till the old oak glows. I paint the walls fresh white and spring green, then hang sheer curtains.

At first, I think I'll make it into a guest room. On reflection, I'd rather have my own space, a writing room. No more writing on the old desk in the basement. I empty the large closet and put up shelves, floor to ceiling, wall to wall. Plenty of room to organize the mountains of letters, journals, publications, photographs, and cassettes I've stored in boxes all over the house. Never enough space it seemed. Never enough until now.

While sorting through old homeschool papers, I come across a box and find Izaak's old family history inside. The one he wrote so long ago for Kristina.

Thumbing through the pages, I see the thirty or so pages that Johan translated and I typed. Pages about Izaak's childhood and WWII. But there's more. I find a thick stack of additional pages. Izaak's life after the war. The years he married, had children, and pastored.

I can't believe it. More pages? I'd been sure we'd translated them all, but here they are, in black and white. We surely read them to Kristina as they arrived but didn't find the time or have the inclination to translate them and type them up.

That night, I show the papers to Johan and ask if he'll translate them. I'm both curious and hesitant. Hopeful and jaded. I doubt these pages will contain much more than his other writing did. Facts and figures. Numbers and data. But then again. These pages cover the years from 1945 to 1986. Izaak's wedding, the birth of his three children, Johan's growing up years. What will he say about his children finding spouses, getting married?

I'm curious now. I wonder if he'll write anything to Kristina about meeting me. What will he write about the day Kristina was born? Where was he when he heard the news? What did he think of that day when he became Opa?

When I Think of Them, 2017

Johan and I have lost all four of our parents now. In a way, we are orphans. We are the next elderly. Our parents have gone on before us. But still, I think of them.

When I think of my dad, I'm sad. I miss him. I miss his laughter, his quiet kindness. It's easy to remember his face, his lanky frame, the confidence he portrayed, the nonchalant way he strode through life. Sometimes, I see him in my sons.

When I think of my mother, I'm more muddled—her life strung and tangled throughout my life in complicated knots.

How fast she walked; I could never keep up with her, not until she turned seventy and slowed. How much she needed, wanted, demanded out of life. Vibrant to the point of tears, both hers and mine. Happy! How my mother could laugh. Weeping. How she handed me her tears to hold, and I dried them with my own.

I dreamt of her last night. She walked down a long hall at some unknown university, arm in arm with two girls. She walked in the middle. They were all three dressed in white and laughing with each other the way young women do. When she passed by, I waved and she waved back. I heard her tell the girls, "That's my daughter." They walked on by, jubilantly happy, so young; she'd found her best friends at last. The ones she always wanted.

Jopie is a blur in my mind. A hazy, friendly, sweet mirage. A veil. When I step closer to peer at her, she shrinks into the fog of language and Alzheimer's and countries that lay continents apart. I only see her shroud. I'm sorry that I never really knew her. I wish I had. I liked her very much.

When I think of Izaak, I can't help but think of euthanasia. I don't know how to separate the two. There are times, when I read a good book with an unsatisfying ending and throw the book up against the wall, a bad ending leaves me both unsettled and irritated. Thinking of Izaak, I have a similar reaction. Unsettled and irritated. Most often when I think of Izaak, I'm just tired. I'm tired of my dislike. Tired of our decades-long aversions. Tired of my anger.

The Cautious Man, 1945–1950

Months after my mother has passed, as I'm getting used to life without parents, Johan begins translating the last of Izaak's papers. I thought the information would bring clarity. It's brought facts and numbers, dates and happenings, but not clarity. Not really.

After the war ended, Izaak waited six years before he married Jopie. He said he'd get more education. He said he'd save up for their marriage. He said there wasn't any place to live. He said they should wait and be better prepared. Izaak said *not yet* in 1946, and '47, and '48. He said *not yet* in '49 and in '50.

Jopie led the children's gymnastic club DIO at this time. She took evening courses at the Language and Administration Institute, learning typing and stenography. Later, she worked in an office that did political investigations, locating people who'd collaborated with the enemy during the war, bringing them to justice. While she worked, she saved diligently, putting away money for her *uitzet*, her trousseau.

From the spring of 1946 until the spring of 1947, Izaak worked in Dordrecht in the financial division of social services and prepared for the WIKA Youth Leader exam. In 1948, when he passed the exam, he moved to the Horst for four years of study. In June of 1951, he earned a diploma as a WIKA Evangelist so he could do work with youth groups in churches.

During those four years, Izaak only returned to Dordt a few times, but once every month, Jopie came to visit him. Izaak wrote, "It was a big commitment for Jopie. We postponed our wedding for four years so I could go to school. She never complained about it. Not one word."

When Izaak wrote his life story to Kristina, he included ten full pages of information about his four years of school at The Horst. He wrote about the married couples in his class, his teachers, the quality of leadership. He wrote about the chapel, the singing, the evening prayers. He told her about lectures he attended on techniques to stimulate conversations, methods of teaching catechism, and the number of times he spoke to groups in Utrecht, in Sluis, in Vlaardingen. He wrote about the camping trips he went on, a guest lecture from the Minister of Education, a guest lecture from the Minister of Social Public Affairs.

He wrote in blinding detail about the Tuesday afternoon he went to the Palace Soestdijk and talked with Mrs. Avis, secretary to the Queen, about the upcoming Christmas Celebration for the Royal Family. How he was asked to plan the whole event. The afternoon of the great event, Izaak was introduced to Her Majesty Queen Juliana, who thanked him for the lovely day. He spoke with Prince Bernhardt. Izaak included the smallest of details in his writing: the traditional chocolate milk they drank, the raisin buns they served, the book the Queen signed and presented to him, which he still had in his possession forty years later.

When Johan finishes translating these pages about Izaak's schooling, I'm relieved. Finally, the schooling is over! I'm looking forward to what's next. Wedding and family. I wonder what he'll say about Jopie on her wedding day.

Wedding, 1951

Tonight, Johan's going to translate the next pages of Izaak's story. The wedding day pages! I'm so curious what Izaak will write about. Johan gets out the papers and I sit at the computer to type. All of my expectations dry up in the first sentence: "When it was time to get married, all of Jopie's savings went into furniture and other things we needed to start our household."

There's not a word about their wedding. Nothing about preparations, celebrations, food or guests. Not one word about his bride, what she wore, her flowers. He doesn't even write the date. Izaak doesn't write to Kristina anything about her grand-mother, about the day Jopie had been planning for five years.

The first uninspiring sentence is followed by an equally distant one.

> On top of that, we had to borrow 1,500 guilders, without interest from church funds. It was a lot of money. But although our salary that first year was only 5,400 guilders, she managed the household in such a way that after one year all of the money was repaid. *Geweldig!*

Geweldig translates as *incredible*. His words are, indeed, incredible to me.

Izaak's story continues with this third sentence: "This was especially well done because on 7 August, 1952, our first son was born and we did need our monthly pay desperately."

Izaak has married. He's become a father. He has a son. Yet the page marches on, methodical and empty. He writes eleven pages concerning his work results, colleagues, and goals. But only the three following sentences about anything familial.

It was also important to our needs to do a better job in washing. After using a wringer for several years, we bought out first centrifuge. About the time our second son was born, we had some extra money enough to buy a washing machine.

I want to scream. Izaak's writing to Kristina and he doesn't even write out his son's beautiful full name. Nothing about his birth, his first breath. Nothing on how Jopie did. How did they choose Johan's name? Did he have much hair? How much did he weigh?

"Is that all he writes?" I ask Johan. As if maybe he's skipped a few pages.

"Yup. That's it," he replies.

I shrug my shoulders. Just another letter from Izaak. Nothing new. Just his money to the cent, the centrifuge, the washing machine. Unbelievable.

I ask Andrea for stories about that time. She says, "Pa always told me that money was very tight. I remember this strange little story Ma told me. She said Pa bought a new suit, but he wouldn't wear it. It hung in his closet for over a year before he got it out and finally put it on."

I haven't got a clue what that story means. It's just so odd, it sticks in my mind.

I get out my copy of Jopie and Izaak's wedding photo. Izaak dapper in a black suit with tails, a wide striped tie, flower in his lapel, and a top hat in hand. A top hat! Jopie wears a long white dress with veil floating over her shoulders and flat white slippers like a dancer. The flower bouquet she holds trails down in front of her almost reaching to the ground.

They're posed on a carpeted step, either at the courthouse or the church, I can't tell. The sun is shining. Little girls all dressed in matching white dresses line the narrow steep steps top to bottom on both sides. The girls wear enormous white bows set atop their plaited hair, and a silky ribbon graces each waist. They all wear white shoes and bobby socks. I've been told they're girls Jopie taught. Her gymnastic girls. They look to be six or seven years old. I count twenty-two of them in the photo: eleven on each side of the step.

The wedding is well planned and expensive. The clothes and flowers, the little girls all in white. It could be a picture from a magazine. A lot of planning went into that day. Yet this one photo is the only record of it. Izaak silent about any of the details.

I know Jopie birthed all three of her children at home. But there are so few particulars. Was Johan a happy baby? What were his first words? Did he and his brother enjoy playing together? What did they think of their new baby sister? Did Jopie like being a mother? Did Izaak like being a father?

I long for some sort of connection to Izaak's stories, some humanity, and I'm sorely disappointed. I have a thousand questions and his spreadsheet tallies of job contracts and guilders saved and washing machines purchased doesn't answer one of them.

How He Saw Himself

How does a man remember his own life?

I try to imagine myself being the same age as Izaak when he wrote his life story and mailed it to Kristina, back when we lived in Indonesia. I pretend I have an eight-year-old granddaughter.

"Tell me about your childhood," she asks. "Tell me about Africa and Indonesia!"

I write to her about horses and prairie grass between my toes. I write about the slap of horses' hooves on pavement and the thud of them on grass. I write about the color blue—the blue of North Dakota skies, the blue of her grandfather Johan's eyes.

There are so many things I want her to know about. The sound of Johan's accent, how hard I fell when I met him, and how he caught and held me. I write the story of her grandfather, the young man I knew. I introduce them to each other. I write about her Auntie Kristina's birth in Kalabo Village, and the day Joren was born, all wiggle and restless, with sparkling blue eyes that never wanted to sleep. I tell her how he (my son, her daddy) toddled relentlessly after his big sister, about the elephant he rode in Indonesia, the helicopter rides, the lionfish he found.

I write about the movie scripts her daddy wrote and how he tore our house apart in Red Lake Falls, making movie sets.

I might tell her a little about how I loved words and wrote books, but not about the Excel financial sheets, the literary publications, the work with renowned editors, the Goodreads' stars, the Amazon ratings. The nuts and bolts of twenty years of writing have a different audience.

When I think about Izaak and what he wrote to Kristina, I'm baffled by his stagnant, proficient writing. How he continued page after page to write about his professional decisions and choices, his board meetings and executive conclusions.

How little he noticed his wife. How seldom he mentioned his children.

How much he focused upon his achievements and himself.

A Man with Two Faces

In the letters he wrote, Izaak mostly comes across as an accommodating man.

Accommodating: obliging, helpful, considerate, adaptable, inclusive. Agreeable, pleasant, unselfish, friendly. To accommodate is to make room, to receive, to board, to welcome, to shelter. To accommodate is to adjust, adapt, attune, yield.

The accommodating person is gracious, affable, deferential, good-natured, solicitous.

The accommodating man. Secure in his work, his degrees, and his profession, Izaak thrived.

Andrea once told me that when she was young, she used to watch Pa. "I'd peek into his room and he'd be standing in front of his mirror, preening like a girl," she said. "He used hair products before men did that. He had that side to him. He was always concerned about the impression he made."

So, while Jopie ironed his white shirt to perfection and brushed his black velvet cassock till spotless, he gelled his hair. Then, every Sunday morning, he climbed the stairs of the pulpit and did something quite spectacular. He both shone and hid. Under the glare of the public light, he hid behind the wooden-walled pulpit. A hundred eyes watched his every hand gesture and every nod and crinkle of a smile. Yet, not one of his parishioners saw Izaak, the man—as they sucked simultaneously on their white peppermint sweets—hidden in the glow of the church light. They saw their professional, amiable, solicitous, personable, pastor.

But work became a hiding and Izaak learned early to pick up a professional mask (What doctor or clergy doesn't do this? What nurse or teacher?) and tied it securely in place. He veiled himself with a cassock, inside the church; he played his role well.

Then home he went to a wife who had her own dreams, and children he wasn't exactly sure of. Sons with ideas. A daughter growing up. He hadn't studied to be a husband, to be a father. The eyes that looked at him were full of needs and questions. And so, he did what came naturally. He hid in the certitude and the decisiveness of the rules he imposed.

The opposite of accommodating: obstinate. Averse, biased, narrow. Dour and testy. Contrary and crusty. The obstinate person is sober, uptight, strict, and strait-laced. The obstinate person is fractious. This is the man that I knew. Saw most often. A proper man who knew what and when and where and why. A man who knew what was best and good and right. A man who had all the answers and none of the questions.

How can a man carry two such contradictory personalities within one beating life?

It is difficult to put the two men together. Will the real Izaak Kandel please stand up?

How tired you must have been managing that life of yours, Izaak. Watching your parishioner's adoring eyes. Watching your Jopie grow silent and weary. Watching your children balk and move away. You hid from them all, but in reality, you were hiding from yourself.

Destroyed Diversity

The headquarters for Hitler's T4 Euthanasia Program no longer exists, though some of the old buildings where the killings took place still stand. If you want, you can travel to Grafeneck Euthanasia Center in Germany; it's a historic building, a grand castle, the final home of 10,654 disabled and sick people, killed in Hitler's T4 Program by lethal injection or gas.

Or you might go to the actual location of the old T4 headquarters. The nondescript original building was torn down but, years after, became a historic landmark. Today, a sculpture stands there, on that square in front of the Berlin Philharmonic. On the right day, you might hear a Mozart sonata wafting over the square as you stand contemplating the sculpture, two vast, curved, walls of steel. A plaque set in the pavement nearby reads simply, "In Honor to the Forgotten Victims."

Walk over to the onsite open-air exhibition, next to the plaque, as you listen to the music. Walk by the sign near the entrance that proclaims, "Destroyed Diversity." Walk by the photographs and consider how one man's choices and one nation's acquiescence changed and shaped reality.

Walk by the photos and grab onto this one fact. There was a time, not so very long ago, when a nation believed, really believed that their actions were not only justified, but good.

Pave the Way

There's one fact that I return to again and again: The Nazi Euthanasia Program predated the Jewish Holocaust by several years. Predated. I don't know why this realization startles me over and over. In my mind, WWII begins and ends with the Holocaust. But then, I come back to this. To T4. To the elimination of diseased German children. Not Jews. Not yet.

The cleansings of the Germanic population began with the infirm. The unstable. The severely disabled. It began with the genetically compromised. The Germans killing their own *insane, retarded, dependent, incurable*. The Nazi Euthanasia Program did not target Jewish people. The Jewish solution would come later, a logical progression, a change of emphasis, a different bowl of soup.

Add in a pinch of propaganda and a little hatred.

Let it stew.

The Nazi Euthanasia Program began with the compromised. The newborn. Those without a voice. The weak ones. The flawed ones. The it's-too-bad, so-sad, sorry-for-your-loss ones. Better for the nation. Better for the economy. Better for the next generation. Believe us. Better all around. The doctors acted out of caring and compassion. Those patients didn't have much of a future anyway. Let's just end their suffering.

This was the beginning. A precursor to pave the way.

A forerunner to indicate the approach of another.

Ruach

I circle around the idea of death and life and divine purpose or lack thereof. I circle into an unfathomable spiral. Reading and writing about euthanasia and life and death and all the various controversies and arguments surrounding it is driving me crazy. I can't stop my mind and all its bleating questions.

What *is* life?

One day, I stumble across this. The Jewish people call *life* the *ruach* of God.

Ruach, a noun, interestingly in the feminine form, has a Greek counterpart: pneuma. Call it what you will: divine energy, existence, lifeforce, wind. Spirit, blast, breath, mind, strength. Whatever you call it, this thing, this life is a mystery.

Izaak had this ruach at his first breath when his mother, weary, held him in her arms, her third son, her fourth and last child. He took a breath. He mewed or cried and stretched his arms. He opened his tiny fists. He turned pink and blinked his dark baby eyes. He lived, and his parents named him Izaak, from the Hebrew, meaning *laughter*. He was their baby. Their last born. The one who brought them joy, made them laugh.

To whom does this ruach belong? Are we really autonomous? We, who breathe and cry long before we have an understanding of *self*? We, who were held in our mother's arms, squalling, here, present without our own knowledge, assent, or agreement. This gift of air within us. This mystery. Unfathomable to the decades, the centuries, and the millennia.

Who are we to think life belongs to anyone?

Who are we to say, *it is wholly mine*?

The Doctored-Dead, Nuremberg Trials 1945 and 1946

A vast amount of information concerning WWII was collected at the Nuremberg Trials. Some of the most compelling words came from the men charged with murder, tortures, and other atrocities committed in the name of medical science. Those who, headed up the T4 Program.

Dr. Valentin Faltlhauser, director of a T4 medical clinic responsible for the death of thousands of children between December 1941 and April 1945, said of his decisions: "The decisive motive was compassion."

Pediatrician Ernst Wentzler said, "I had the feeling that my activity was something positive, and that I had made a small contribution to human progress."

Hugh Gallagher's fascinating book, *By Trust Betrayed: Patients, Physicians, and the License to Kill in the Third Reich*, spends over three hundred pages investigating what prompted German physicians—some of the most highly educated and respected medical men world-wide in their professions, scientific research, and knowledge—to embrace killing their patients.

The book ends with Dr. Karl Brandt's final statement at the Nuremburg Trials, in its entirety. Brandt—Hitler's personal physician, as well as the chief physician and co-director of the T4 Euthanasia Program— said,

> I assented to euthanasia. I fully realize the problem; it is as old as mankind, but it is not a crime against man or against humanity. It is pity for the incurable, literally. Here I cannot believe like a clergyman or think as a jurist. I am a doctor and I see the law of nature as being the law of reason. In my heart, there is love of mankind, and so it is in my conscience. That is why I am a doctor!
> . . . I am fully conscious that when I said "Yes" to euthanasia I did so with the deepest conviction, just as it is my conviction today, that it was right. Death can mean deliverance. Death is life—just as much as birth. It was never meant to be murder."

Pity for the incurable. For love of mankind. Death is deliverance. It was right.

By the end of the war, over 200,000 children and young adults had been systematically killed within the parameters of the T4 Nazi Euthanasia Program. Children, many of whose only crime was that they were born deaf. Or blind. Or with a physical disability. Clubfoot, shall we say? Or the residual effects of polio. Take your pick. The list is quite extensive.

These children constituted something new. You might call them the doctored-dead.

Saint

Mother Teresa spent her life caring for the destitute and the dying. Awarded the Nobel Peace Prize in 1979, as an elderly woman, she ranked first in Gallup's List of Most Widely Admired People of the 20th Century.

What did Teresa do to merit this adoration? She comforted the dying, giving people a place to rest, a cot or mat, some clean clothes. A place to die with dignity and care. A drink of water. It wasn't much, yet it was everything.

I wonder about her work, a lifetime spent in heat and squalor and poverty.

What if? What if instead of food and water, a little soap and a washcloth, an ordinary cot to rest on, and a ramshackle room to die in . . . what if instead of this, she'd offered the dying superior comforts? A room with flowers on the table, Mozart playing overhead, and modern reclining beds to rest in — how gezellig! — and then (out of mercy) simply euthanized them.

The deaths would have been quicker. Certainly, more comfortable. Undeniably efficient.

If she'd done this, what would the world think about her now? Would she be so widely admired? For all that we say of euthanasia, of its mercy or kindness, there's something else that we're not seeing.

Ah, Mother. If you were a saint, we haven't grasped your lesson.

What Remains, 2017

Today over three hundred fortifications or parts of fortifications remain hunkered down in the everyday landscape of the Netherlands, remnants and reminders of WWII. They include a large variety of shapes and purposes: forts, casemates, military depots, security batteries. Tank bunkers, telephone bunkers, whole bunker complexes. Antiaircraft placements, gunpowder warehouses. Anti-tank ditches, anti-tank walls. *Trobruks* are seen here and there, smaller bunkers with rounded openings on top for machine guns or flame throwers.

These fortifications are leftovers from various Nazi projects including the Atlantic Wall, the Grebbe Line, and the Maas Line. Most of these buildings are massive cement block-like creations, tilted over the years, sunken, desolate hulks. Gray and rain-washed and dreary. Solid and visible, they dot the landscape of the Netherlands.

More concerning than these bunkers are the remnants and remains of bombs. Explosives make themselves known. How could they not?

Think of the Germans bombing the Netherlands.

Think of the Allies bombing the Germans on their way through and out of the Netherlands.

Think of the Netherlands, a country approximately the size of Maryland, with bombs falling, falling, falling from the sky. Hundreds of thousands of tons. Not all of them exploded.

In August of 2012, builders digging around Terminal C at Schiphol Airport, Amsterdam, uncovered a large unexploded WWII bomb. The terminal was closed; flights were cancelled. A bomb disposal expert was called in to detonate the bomb. It was thought to have been dropped by the RAF or the American air force when Schiphol acted as a military airfield for the German Luftwaffe.

In April of 2014, five WWII aircraft bombs, were found in the dunes at Bloemendaal. All five explosives were detonated by an Explosive Ordinance Disposal Unit.

Thirty WWII bombs were found in the Rijsenhout area near Schiphol Airport in January of 2017. Explosive experts detonated the larger bombs, two per day, in special ditches. The smaller ones were dismantled on site.

And then there are the bodies. Still being found. Even after seventy-plus years.

A soldier fell at Ginkelse Hei on September 18, 1944, one of

2,300 British Paratroopers. His body was found by a Dutch man using a metal detector, sixty-eight years later, in 2012. Two hand grenades lay nearby.

In 2014, the remains of Canadian soldier Private Albert Laubenstein were recovered and identified. He'd been killed seventy years earlier, on January 26, 1945, at the Battle of Kapelsche Veer, along with 234 other Canadian soldiers.

All of these remains. Seen. Unseen. Hiding. Waiting to be found. Yet, all of this is physical. A bunker. A tank. A bomb. A body.

What of the nonphysical? What of the spiritual debris, the emotional wreckage, the mental casings? What of these, the leftover carnage, floating near the surface?

Heroes, 1994

Once upon a time, in a land far away, Kristina asked her Opa Kandel a question.

"Opa, were you a hero?"

Izaak shook his head and replied.

"None of us were heroes. We just wanted to survive."

I think about those words. Something in them won't let me go. They feel like both Izaak's greatest accomplishment and his greatest failure.

We just wanted to survive.

I would that he had wanted more.

It's unutterably sad to me, that in the end, the only way Izaak knew how to survive was to take his own life.

Time Will Tell 2017

As I study euthanasia chronologically in the Netherlands, a whole host of new opportunities, thoughts, and experiences begin to present themselves. One of the newest concepts is *voltooid leven*—a completed life. If a person is satisfied with his or her life—has lived a good one and is ready to stop living—then so be it. People need to have the freedom to say *Enough. I have had enough life. My life has been completed.*

A person doesn't need to be facing any particular medical difficulty to request voltooid leven euthanasia. Some Dutch are now throwing parties the day before they choose to die. They invite friends and family, reminisce, drink some wine, look at old photos, say goodbye. People taking up this option say they want to enjoy their life to the last. They want a *good goodbye.* After all, life is complete. Let's celebrate. Hasn't it been good! Balloons anyone?

Some couples in the Netherlands are choosing to die together in a form of couples' euthanasia. If you don't want to live alone, without your spouse, it's your right to die with him or her. Otherwise your suffering would fall into the category of *unbearable.* You can choose to go out together. Accompany one another on your journey.

There's also growing social pressure to choose euthanasia. If you have cancer or a terminal illness, it's considered a selfless choice. You'll save your family the pain of caring for you. You'll be able to pass on more of your inheritance. You won't waste medical community resources, time, and money.

The Dutch NVVE—Right to Die Society—is currently pushing to consider the so-called end-of-life pill. Originally called the Drion pill or suicide pill, the NVVE now refer to it as the last-will-pill and believe it should be available to all people over the age of seventy-five.

This type of euthanasia may or may not be legalized. Time will tell.

Imagine. There are no constraints. No papers to sign. You don't need a doctor's order. You don't need medical permission. It's your right. Free for the taking.

Reach out. Your fingers lightly grasp the tiny oblong pill.

Perhaps it comes with a label: *When you're ready for the end, this capsule is here to help.*

There will most likely be a warning: *Keep out of reach of children.*

Instructions: *Store in a dark cool location.*
Disclaimer: *We take no responsibility for any or all damages caused. Use of this medication is entirely up to your own discretion and is therefore entirely your own responsibility.*
The small white pill burns in your palm. Disconcertingly heavy.
Once you have felt the heaviness of it, you can't stop thinking about it. It weights you down, focuses your thinking, draws you toward itself with a strange and magnetic pull.
There's no getting away from it.
Where will you store such power?

Rubicon

Among the many controversial ideas within the euthanasia debate, the most controversial by far, is the word *unrequested*. It is the word people hang their hats upon, the Rubicon which separates euthanasia death from murder.

In R. Cohen-Almagor's book, *Euthanasia in the Netherlands: The Policy and Practice of Mercy Killing*, there is an entire chapter, "Worrisome Data," in which he states the following: "Some of the most worrisome data in the two Dutch studies are concerned with hastening of death without explicit request of patients. There were 1,000 cases without explicit and persistent request in 1990."

One doctor stated, "I am quite liberal about termination of life when people are suffering, even if they are incompetent . . . compassion is the primary consideration for euthanasia."

Anarticle in *The Journal of Medical Ethics* states, "[There is] some concern expressed about the 1,000 cases of unrequested termination of life . . . the request of the patient is not in practice the basis on which physicians decide to perform euthanasia, but rather they base such decisions on the condition of the patient."

They base their decision upon the condition, not upon the request. Compassion is the primary consideration.

The Nazis didn't accept certain conditions: the deaf, the homosexual, the schizophrenic, those with genetic diseases. These people were murdered. There's no question about it.

But there is a question that remains.

What are the conditions *we* do not accept?

Who are *our* unworthy, *our* burdensome?

Who are *our* useless eaters?

Who are *our* embarrassments?

Those with Alzheimer's, the ancient elderly, the unconscious, the nonverbal severely handicapped? The imperfect newborn?

Unrequested. Such a little word to bear a world of implications.

This is what I am *not* saying. I am not saying that euthanasia under Nazi Germany and euthanasia today are the same thing. They are not the same in any way.

What I am saying is this. There are parallels. And they are chilling.

Carapace, 2017

As I think about my parents' deaths, I remember their hospice and palliative care nurses with great respect. I wonder how Izaak might have flourished under such care if he had allowed his natural time to come. I wonder what he might have learned, how he might have softened.

The word *palliative* comes from the medieval Latin *palliativus*, meaning *under cloak*. A covering. A protection. A shield. There's a hint of the covert within the word. A concealing.

In today's vocabulary, palliative refers to medical care that alleviates symptoms or problems without addressing underlying causes. Palliative care shields the body from itself, covers, protects the dying from their own frame.

I think about this word. About the ways we shield and cover ourselves. I think about the words *naked* and *vulnerable*, which lead me to crustaceans, the lobsters and crabs and shrimp who carry their skeletons externally.

In order to grow, crustaceans must molt, shed those external hard shells, those carapaces, or they die, trapped within their own outer skeleton. This process of molting is a place of great vulner-ability for the creature, a dangerous place with little protection.

When a grasshopper molts, it leaves a perfect replica of itself behind, the exuviate. A shell so delicate you can see through it. A transparent likeness.

I think of Izaak. Trapped within his own skin, trapped within the protections and shells he built around himself. His inability to shed control. Without the shed, there's no growth. Without vulnerability, the rigidity of our protective shell becomes a death sentence. Shed the outer skin. Or die.

The process of dying is our last molt. Death our final carapace.

We want everything so quick, so orderly, so efficient. Sterile and controlled. The very thing we are afraid of is that which sets us free. We must stand naked before it and vulnerable. We must be humble. We must let it have its way.

Even nature teaches so.

Activate, 2017

When I think of the natural process of dying and what it might have to teach us, my anger flares. I'm angry at the laws in the Netherlands, the doctors, the system. I'm angry at Izaak. I go to bed and wake up day after day with my anger, until one morning I'm fully sick of it. I want to vomit. I want the hatred and gall out of my life.

Friends tell me, "You just need to forgive Izaak," but forgive-ness has me stymied. Friends declare, "Just say the words, 'I for-give you.' It's easy. Just say it."

I say the words, "I forgive you." At first, they stick in my throat, but I repeat them anyway. Force them out. Say them over and over. The Bible teaches, "Forgive seven times seven." I try it out, but it's a numerical endgame that doesn't make any sense to me.

Repetition doesn't change my feelings.

Maybe forgiving a person who is dead has other barriers. It's not like I can sit down and talk to him face to face. I wonder if you can forgive someone who hasn't asked for forgiveness. Maybe that's the problem. He didn't see the need for it, understand the hurt of it.

What is forgiveness anyway? I've heard the word all my life, but don't have a clue.

I get out a dictionary, my safe haven.

> Forgive (v.)
>
> > The old English *forgiefan*, means to *give, grant, allow; remit (a debt), pardon (an offense)*. Or to *give up*, in the sense of to give up desire or power to punish.

The root word of forgive comes from the Latin *perdonare, to give completely, to give without reservation*. In modern English, forgive has taken on the meaning *to renounce anger at*.

Give up . . . *the desire to punish*.

Pardon . . . *an offense*.

Renounce . . . *your anger at*.

Remit. Grant. Give. Allow. These are the active verbs of forgiveness that I am not ready to activate.

Falling Out, 2017

Maybe it's more than forgiveness that I'm searching for. Forgiveness isn't mine to grant or hold back. Who am I to do that? Perhaps what I am searching for is mercy. I'm looking for reprieve, for both Izaak and for myself. Searching for grace. Maybe it's like falling in love, but in an opposite way. Not a falling into, but a falling out of.

Out of your tight hold, your obsessive thinking, your dislike of Izaak.

Out of your need to point a finger.

How you love holding onto your anger.

How you like the way it feels, this hearty indignation.

Come. Fall out of that behavior.

Overlook what you have so long remembered to remember.

Come and tilt. Tilt into compassion. And if you tilt far enough, perhaps you will fall.

Come. Let go. And fall.

Of All the Days

One evening at supper, Johan blurts out, "I'm still angry about that one day."

"Not sure what you're talking about," I say.

"Remember when Bert called and said if I wanted to see Pa again, I'd better come home right away?" he asks.

"Yes," I answer, throwing my memory back to that time, the rushed decision, rearranging his grad schoolwork, the long flight.

"Bert knew when he called me that Pa wasn't dying. He knew. Andrea knew. And nobody said anything to me. They just let me fly home the whole-time thinking Pa was dying." He shakes his head. "They were just doing what Pa told them to do."

I look at my husband. His father has been dead for over ten years and it still wounds him.

"That's the day that sticks in my mind," he says. "Pa meeting me at the door with that look in his eye. Like he'd won or something. Like he'd pulled one over on me."

"Bert regrets it, too," I remind Johan. "He asks questions himself, 'Why didn't I say no to Pa? Why didn't I tell him to make that phone call himself?'"

"I know," Johan replies. "I don't blame them."

Of all the days, of all the things we've seen and heard and lived, that's the day that still gets to Johan. The day his brother regrets, too.

"Your dad deceived you," I say gently. "He manipulated you."

"Yes," Johan says. "Yes, he did."

I feel both relieved and sad to watch Johan come to this knowledge. To begin to see his father as something more than the saintly, perfect man he's loved so desperately for so long.

Untying, 2017

Maybe this forgiveness, this compassion and grace is like muddy silt piling up along a canal. Fine particles drifting downward, sediment depositing on the bottom, filling it up, imperceptible until, finally, the canal clogs. Maybe this is a truer reality. Mercy drifts slowly down, and over a vast space of time, a change occurs.

I want this. I want to be clogged with kindness, to make bold statements—*I'm not angry anymore; I forgive you*—but these words are falsities, words I wish for, but don't own. The words I'm discovering are softer, slower found, more tentative.

I'm sorry for your pain, Izaak.

I'm sorry for the walls, the distance.

I'm sorry you were so afraid and felt such a need to have control.

I'm sorry for the years and years of misunderstandings.

And this much is true. I am sorry.

I'm sorry for Izaak. I'm sorry for Johan. I'm sorry for me.

As I try on these new soft words, this mellow almost-forgiveness, this almost-caring, I continue to read and study. I still throw books across the room in anger and frustration. Forgiveness is all so ethereal. So otherworldly. So high-in-the-sky, pie-in-the-sky, let's all sing hallelujah.

Then, a metaphor comes to me that I can finally grasp: Tying knots, untying knots.

Untying from the past.

I've spent much of my life tying knots around my relationship with Izaak. And, to put it simply, it's time to untie. It's time to bend down and untie our knotted history in all its complexity.

I want to bend over and untie the rope. I want to watch my relationship with Izaak drift away, out into its own history. An abandonment. A leaving. A wave of the hand, bye-bye, birdie, bye-bye.

If this is what I understand, and what I want, can you tell me please, why is it so hard? This unforgiving spirit sticks to me, like dirt beneath my fingernails that doesn't quite scrub away.

The Hardest Work We Do, 2017

I may not understand what forgiveness is, but I know what it isn't.

Forgiveness is not agreement.

Forgiveness is not endorsement.

Forgiveness is not reconciliation. It doesn't mean trust.

Forgiveness isn't weakness.

Forgiveness isn't about changing the past.

Forgiveness may be many things, but most of all, forgiveness isn't easy. American novelist and nonfiction writer Anne Lamott says, "Forgiveness is the hardest work we do."

My resentment has stewed these thirty years; I'm well aware of the shape and smell of it. Anger sticks fast to my life, like tomato sauce burnt to a black crisp on the bottom of a pan.

Get out the Brillo pad— the razor blade— the Comet.

Forgiveness is scraping the black away, flake by flake, rinsing it down the drain of my memory. Forgiveness is a weary shaky muscle, tired of rubbing and scrubbing, looking for the glimmer of copper underneath the hardened black.

Forgiveness feels incessant.

Forgiveness realizes how stupid you were in the first place; the pan left on the stove, unattended. Scrub on.

Forgiveness is drudgery. Forgiveness feels backwards. Sounds cliché. Sets my teeth on edge, rubs me raw. Scrub on.

Forgiveness is unnatural, not at all intuitive. Forgiveness hurts. Forgiveness is the hardest work we do.

Scrub on.

Contranyms, 2017

Perhaps to understand my antipathy towards Izaak, I need to look closer at the contradictions within which he lived his life. So many opposites. So many incongruities. In English, there's a category of words called contranyms. They're spelled alike but have opposite meanings.

Clip: to bind together or to snip apart.

Contranyms are also called Janus words, Janus being the Roman god depicted with a beard and two faces. He could see forward and backward without turning his head. Izaak and Janus, caught between two worlds, peace and war, earth and heaven. January, the first month of the year, a time to look back, a time to look forward. Regrets and resolutions.

Izaak lived caught between the past and the future, fear and hope, anger and love. I think he lived much of his life with one foot in the war of his youth and one foot in the prosperity of his adulthood.

Bolt: to secure or to flee.

Perhaps it was these very contradictions which wore him out. Janus, the god of beginnings and endings, the god of entrances and exits, the doorkeeper of heaven.

How do you navigate a world that presents you with such opposites?

Cleave: to adhere strongly or to separate.

How do you live in freedom when you're caught in a trap?

Left: to remain or to depart.

How do you find a way to breathe when you are already in your coffin?

Wear: to endure or to deteriorate.

Forgive Yourself, 2017

I never wanted a pastor-perfect, *clean-father* for my father-in-law. I wanted someone who was humane and honest, a person both flawed and brave. I wanted what he wasn't. I wanted *real*.

Forgive him that. Forgive yourself, too.

Forgive yourself your petty meanness.

Your self-righteous indignation.

Your silent scorn.

Forgive yourself, your clinging anger and unrelenting grudge.

Realize this.

He never lived up to what you wanted; you're not the standard.

Forgive your bitter longing for relationship, no kinder than his self-protection.

He wore you out.

Forgive yourself for wearing out. For giving up. For despising another human being.

A Lion in His Underwear

There's an old Dutch saying: Let the lion not stand in his underwear. Dutch people chant it at soccer matches: *Laat de Leuwe Niet in Zijn Hempje Staan.*

Don't let the lion stand in his underwear. It sounds perfectly bizarre, but it's a great image. The lion represents the Netherlands—the Royal House of Orange—and is seen on her crest.

Don't get caught with your pants down.

Don't humiliate our country!

In other words, Go Holland! *Hup, Holland, Hup!*

Long after Izaak died, Johan was going through some of our wedding day slides and found two pictures of his father. Johan converted them to digital format and sent them to me. When I opened the file, I was flabbergasted. In the photos, Izaak is in his underwear!

He stands in white boxer shorts and a white, sleeveless undershirt. He's putting on a white dress shirt. Jopie stands beside him dressed in a long black dress with a floral rose pattern. It is scoop-necked and long-sleeved. They both are laughing.

In the second picture, Izaak stands in front of a white porcelain sink, still in his white boxers. A laundry basket sits near his feet. He faces the mirror.

I have no idea who took these photos. Most likely Johan or Andrea. It is the morning of my wedding. These are the *getting ready photos.*

There are no getting ready photos of Jopie. None of Johan, my groom, standing in his briefs, either. But there is this. Izaak standing in his underwear, smiling at a camera. I don't know

324   Part 9: WHAT REMAINS, 2017–

what to think of the photo, this Dominee, this lion, standing partially unclad.

Johan gets a big laugh out of the photos. But something in them unnerves me. I can't put my finger on it. Izaak looks jovial. Both he and Jopie are laughing. And then it hits me. How seldom I saw him laugh—he whose name *Izaak* means *he who brings laughter, he who laughs.*

How seldom he looked at ease, looked like a real person. Took off his mask. It moves me to see these two pictures and makes me sad. I wish he could have smiled more, laughed more. I wish there'd been more joy.

Ironically, the one time he let his pants down, and stood in his underwear, was one of those rare times that he didn't let himself down. A smile. A laugh. It was all I really wanted.

Button, Button, 2018

A long-ago memory returns to me, late one evening in the fall of 2018.

In the memory, Izaak's playing with Kristina and Joren. They're young, and we're sitting around in Izaak's front room in the Netherlands.

It's a chilly, damp day, and the kids are restless.

"Want to play, Button, Button, Who's got the button?" I ask.

Izaak finds a large red button and calls the kids over.

I see Kristina and Joren pry his hands open, one after the other.

Izaak shakes his head no. The button isn't in his hands. They reach their tiny hands into one of his suit pockets and there it is!

I remember them throwing back their heads in childish laughter, the excitement of finding the button too magical to keep inside.

They play again. This time the button is in Izaak's hand.

They tap his hand. "Here, Opa. It's in here. Open up."

Izaak opens his fingers and they spy the bright red button in his palm. After giggles and smiles all around, they hide their eyes. Play again.

They are such little things, the moments that make our lives good.

Count, 2018

We were meant to matter or, as American philosopher Dallas Willard writes, "We were built to count."

Izaak wanted significance. He wanted to do good. He counted seconds, hours, days, months, years. He counted out routines and rituals. He laid out his life on the solid grid of a daily planner. He died in control, choosing the day and time, tapping his watch, but he didn't understand that it was he, himself, his very being that counted most.

The Easiest Death

Dying is hard work. Much of Western culture doesn't prepare us for it. Culture emphasizes education, appearance, finance, status, profession, accomplishment. These values carry us through the first thirty or forty years of life, but then begin to fall short. We're left with an incomplete or shallow view of self. We're so much more than our education or profession. So much more than our bank account or how we dress.

We can't escape the wrinkles, the graying hair, the sagging chin. Culture offers Botox and facelifts, hair dye and anti-aging serums. We hardly know how to consider our own aging, our failing bodies, let alone our dying.

At birth, we leave eternity and enter earth's gravity with the holy still clinging to us. As the English Romantic poet William Woodsworth wrote:

> Trailing clouds of glory do we come
> From God, who is our home:
> Heaven lies about us in our infancy!

From these beginnings, our egos start to form and build our sense of self. We find our toes, our voices, our will. As we grow, our thinking minds take charge and we leave that exuberant childish wonder in the dust.

Somewhere in midlife, our journey shifts and instead of building ego, we begin to let go of it, find a truer life. In her seminal book, *The Grace in Dying*, Kathleen Singh refers to this change in our journey, this coming back to the sacred or the real, as The Path of Return. Singh, who has spent her life working with the dying, talks about the "nearing-death experience," which jars people out of their ego-bound self.

Singh writes, "The act of dying can bring us home." Home to our heart, our center, our best self. Dying brings us back to where we began. Back to the organic reality of our being. *Trailing clouds of glory, we come.* Shouldn't we return the same way, with something of awe or wonder or the sacred lingering behind us? Something of mystery. Something of glory.

This moment will come for each of us. This moment, this time over which we have no control. Like a baby in a womb, warm and wet and cramped grows ready for the birth canal, the wild hard push into a bright new world, so our spirit forms through life in the womb of this world. Then, the birth canal again, when the dying process comes hard and wild and once more contracts and hardens, shoving us willing or not into a new unknown. This second birth, which we call death, shrouded in gauze and mystery. The dying process itself fearful and unrelenting. A mother must let her body do its job, its work of separation. And work it is.

Because Izaak wouldn't face the *process* of dying, the *work* of dying—needing to control it, shorten it, be in charge of it—he didn't experience the freedom that comes with a stripping of the ego. Without the letting go, there's no movement, no softening, no mercy. There's only the tragedy of dying. Medically swift. Scientifically efficient.

I imagine Izaak making a different choice, facing the humiliation of his weakening body, the slow intimate process of failing and failure. I imagine him letting others care for him; his heart softening as his body relaxes, releasing the burdens he's carried throughout his life. Gone the pastoral image, the pride. Gone the need to impress. The need to be in control.

How hard, this letting go.

I like to think of Izaak, sitting behind the geraniums, taking a deep slow breath. Smiling as he remembers his own grandfather. How he loved Opa Schuller. A man gentled by advanced age, a kind man who taught him how to pray.

It's only my imagination. Who knows? Who's to say what might have been. The recurring question remains. *What if?*

I'm reading *When Breath Becomes Air*, by the late Dr. Paul Kalanithi. The book has touched me more deeply than any book I've ever read. Facing advanced lung cancer—as a thirty-six-year-old neurosurgeon—Kalanithi writes about his life, his experiences walking his patients through their own processes of dying, and finally, about his own approaching death.

"After so many years of living with death," Kalanithi writes, "I'd come to understand that the easiest death wasn't necessarily the best."

This sentence slays me, says it all.

The easiest death isn't necessarily the best.

Amen. And amen.

Come Again, 2019

Spring arrives. I bike and hike and garden. I revel in the tulips and daffodils. The spherical purple allium.

One sunny morning, I sit in the doctor's office with my youngest son, Ben. Recently employed fulltime with benefits, he's in for a general checkup. The physicians assistant sits at her desk, face to the computer screen, filling in the required paperwork. She begins with complaints, pain, symptoms and quickly moves on to allergies, surgeries, and family history.

Grandparents? They've all died.

Mother's mother, cause of death? Congestive Heart Failure.

Mother's father, cause of death? Complications due to hemo-chromatosis.

Father's mother? Alzheimer's Disease.

Father's father? Ben looks at me. I look at him. We don't know what to say. It's so strange, but I'm stopped cold and can't find a suitable answer. I'm totally unprepared for this question that drags me back into the past. How did I not see it coming?

"Um, well," I mumble. "Euthanasia."

The PA turns her head abruptly to look me in the eyes. Her eyebrows knit together, and she has that "come again?" look on her face.

I nod at her and repeat, "Euthanasia," then add, "It's legal in the Netherlands." I try to soften the word.

"Wow," she replies. She can't contain her questions.

"How old was he?"

"What was he sick with?"

"Is it common?"

Despite the fact that I'm obviously struggling to articulate a simple answer, the PA presses on. She's clearly looking for dialogue.

"Why did he choose it?"

"He was afraid of becoming dependent and afraid of losing control. He was a man filled with fears."

"Well, that's a first," she says. "I haven't heard this one before."

I understand. It *is* new for her and she'll go home and tell her significant other, "You'll never guess what I heard today," and they'll discuss the issue, while being HIPAA compliant and pro-fessional. This new issue for them, which is very not new for me. It rises up to the surface of my life, unasked for, unwanted and unexpected.

I think about that office visit and once again see her surprise, her curiosity, her eyebrows knitting together in puzzlement, "Come again?"

And there it is. Euthanasia, an issue that in one form or another, will always come again. Like it or not, euthanasia will always be a part of my life.

Camp, 2019

I thought my journey and writing were over. My healing done. But recently, I've had this new feeling, a premonition, that it's not finished yet. I can't explain it even to myself. There's just this gut instinct that I have something else to learn, or unlearn, or open myself up to. Something still waits in the wings. I'm missing one last piece. I have thought of forgiveness as the *answer*. What else is there? What am I missing?

I skype Johan's sister, and we talk.

"I'm finding that forgiveness—or mercy or whatever you call it—isn't enough," I tell Andrea. "It doesn't feel like I'm at the end of my search. I'm reaching for something. A generosity of spirit? I don't know. I'm not sure."

Andrea nods over the Skype miles. She says, "It's so strange how we are continuously on this same journey together."

"Love seems too much to ask," I say. "But I feel a need to see Izaak at his best, to know that we do share a common humanity."

"I'm beginning to learn the same thing, Jill," Andrea says. "And something really weird happened. Listen to this!"

She proceeds to tell me about a phone call she got just this past week. A woman called searching for some information. Seventy years ago, three men began a camp in the Netherlands specifically for children who had been through WWII.

The woman emailed Andrea an old newspaper article with a photo of a man named Izaak Kandel. Did Andrea know the person in the picture? The Kandel name is a bit unusual in the Netherlands. Was he, perhaps, Andrea's father or a relative?

Andrea said she looked at the photo; it was her father.

The woman gushed over fond memories from camp and spoke to Andrea about how excited the children had been! How very grateful so many parents were for the camp. Their children hadn't known much except war for most of their young lives.

In the black and white photo, a young Izaak stands in a light shirt and dark pants. His sleeves are rolled above the elbows, his collar unbuttoned. He's casual and also definitely in control. His hands are clasped together, and he looks rather self-satisfied.

Nine young girls stand behind and beside Izaak, all wearing summer dresses. Three of the girls tilt their chins toward the ground, but their eyes stare up at the photographer. Their faces are serious and thin. Perhaps they are uncomfortable with cameras. The girls look unsure, hesitant. There's not a smile in the bunch.

The newspaper caption says, "*De heer Kandel legt de bedoeling van een spel uit.*" Mr. Kandel is explaining the rules of a game.

The woman who called Andrea was helping to plan the upcoming seventy-year celebration of the camp. It still exists! She'll email Andrea more information and will appreciate anything Andrea can find about her father and the camp.

Andrea marveled at the call. "I don't know this man who started a camp and played games with children," she says to me. I feel the same.

After she hangs up, I can only wonder. I wonder about this journey Andrea and I are on to forgive, to, I don't know, redeem Izaak's life? I wondered who that Izaak was, just after the war, in the first flush of manhood, the first flush of spring and summer and freedom? With all the world alight with possibility and hope.

This new information amazes me. Izaak worked with two other men and dreamed of helping children. They not only dreamed; they organized, planned, built, and made a camp into a reality.

Children came to their camp. Children who were babies when the war began. They'd never had the freedom to walk the seashore or stay out after dark. The only streets they'd known had German soldiers holding guns. And then a miracle: the war was over. And then another miracle: a camp! The first they'd ever been to. The Dutch called these children *bleekneusjes*, white nos-es. Children who hadn't had enough to eat, were rail thin, and had barely seen the sun. Many of them were sent to England after the war, to go to camps with good food and games and medical care. To gain strength and health. Izaak began his own camp, too. In the Netherlands.

I don't know this Izaak. It's hard for me to visualize him so generative, so positive, so hopeful. But there it is in black and white, a newspaper article and a photo. There's Izaak, sleeves rolled up, collar unbuttoned, standing in front of a circus tent. A man who founded and ran a children's camp more than seventy years ago. And never told us a word about it.

Dakajam, 2019

Izaak called the camp he founded Dakajam. It's an abbreviation of the Dutch words Dagkampen Jeugdactie Meppel. Literally, Day Camp Youth Action Meppel.

Meppel is the city Johan was born in. I've walked its streets and heard some of the old stories, but I didn't have a clue that this camp existed. Still exists. They have a Twitter account and a Face-book page. The photos are full of smiling children, smiling adults, and all kinds of activities from hiking, to path building, to build-ing castles in huge sandpits. There are bonfires and face paint-ing, a falconer showing off his birds of prey, treks in the woods and kids wading in streams. A rope obstacle course through the woods. Soccer games.

The Dakajam Facebook page says, "Since 1950, children from the area of Meppel can go to camp during the last two weeks of summer vacation."

There's one newspaper article on their Facebook page. An old black and white photo showing a group of twenty-one girls hud-dled together, sitting on the ground beside a young woman, their camp counselor. The article says eighty children came the first day of the three-day camp. They were divided into two groups of girls, de Margrieten en de Tulpen (the Margarites and the Tulips) and two groups of boys, de Herten en de Tijgers (the Deer and the Tigers). They played soccer and *trefbal*. They had sandwiches for lunch. The weather was perfect. The day went by too fast. But there were still two days to go. At the end of the day, the article continues, "Mr. I. Kandel, who is in charge of the general management of these day camps, was able to safely deliver the children back."

A second three-day camp was scheduled for the following week. The article ends, "The organizers received great honor from their work. The camp was met with much satisfaction."

I open YouTube and watch footage of the opening day of camp 2018. The buses arriving, the children noisy and energetic. Last year, five hundred youth attended Dakajam Camp.

I've disliked Izaak for so long, it almost seems like a part of my identity. This animosity defined me for decades. Yet, I find something in myself feeling happy for him. Happy to see a work that he began celebrated. I want to share this common humanity with him. To see him as human, both frail and strong, with foibles, faults, quirks, and grace.

I'm finding Dakajam Camp a place of reconciliation. A place to see Izaak in a new light, a better light. I look at the videos again and again. Remembering the Dutch landscape and the lilt of the Dutch language. I marvel at the surefootedness of the young soccer players, the energetic enthusiasm of youth. I watch a child break into a heartfelt smile, and I feel my heart breaking open, too.

Smile for Smile

As Andrea and I correspond over Dakajam and our thoughts on Izaak, she sends me a couple of old photos, taken when her son was young. He's playing with Izaak.

Her son sits on Izaak's lap inside a small red car. Izaak smiles broadly and holds the steering wheel. His grandson reaches out his hand, honks the horn.

In another picture, Izaak's propped up on a couch with his sweater pulled up revealing a white shirt and tie. His grandson stands beside him sporting a green surgical cap and white lab coat. He holds a red plastic stethoscope on Izaak's chest, and they look into each other's eyes.

I can almost hear their conversation.

"How am I doing, doc? Am I going to make it?"

"Yes. You will live. Here. Just take this tablet."

I open Andrea's final picture, a collage made up of several photos, and actually startle when I see it. Izaak playing with his grandson. Shirtless.

The indoor pool temperature must be warm to hot; Izaak's face is red. His slightly sunken chest, his smallish potbelly, his arms, all so pale I doubt they've seen the light of day for decades. I'm used to Izaak's red and freckled face, his dimpled chin and Roman nose. But I'm surprised to see his alabaster skin. He looks so vulnerable. So bare.

Izaak wading in a swimming pool next to a large yellow toy. A floating ball with a mouth and eyes. Izaak aiming the mouth of the toy at the back of his grandson and squirting him with a jet of warm water. A smile on his face.

Izaak sitting in the shallow end of the pool. His grandson holding a red plastic watering can tipping over Izaak's head, watering his bald forehead. Izaak shuts his eyes and grins.

Izaak wearing blue-striped pajama pants, sitting on a chair. His grandson rubbing Izaak's face with a shaving brush lathered in white soap. Izaak's face white with foam.

Vacation days and smiles, water and swimsuits, a boy and his grandfather enacting gezellig morning rituals.

Looking at the photos, I'm thankful Izaak had grandchildren in the Netherlands who lived in close proximity. Grandchildren he could be more relaxed with. Grandchildren who were a more normal part of his everyday life and culture and language. Not foreign. Not come and go and mostly saying goodbye. Just kids. Just kids with their granddad.

I wonder what our relationship would have been like had I been Dutch. Had I known this Izaak, comfortable in his own skin. Easy with his grandchildren. No language barriers, no cultural gaffes, no geographical oceans between us. I think how differently things might have been.

But might is a large word, too big for this world, and too big for me.

We might have found a better way. We might not have. Who's to say? It does no good to imply. He was who he was. And I was who I was. Still, I'm thankful for the photos, for a glimpse into a part of Izaak's life that caught me by surprise. A part of him where grins and honking horns and waterspouts existed. A part of him open and exposed to joy. Returning smile for smile.

The Gift of Years

When I think about Izaak these days—which isn't often—I see how much a part I played those long years ago, in all our ins and outs, our rifts and rivalries. I see my own smallness.

I'm learning to value mercy and to extend grace to both Izaak and myself. I'll never understand the decision he made. I'll never agree with it. But the heart of the story doesn't require me to agree or disagree. It wasn't my decision. What remains lingers fleeting as a shadow, constant as breath.

As I grow into my sixties, I'm drawn toward understanding more about the aging process. I walk for hours listening to podcasts on getting old, on aging well. Mentors—mostly online or virtual—talk and write about becoming sage, embracing age, learning to be wise and to retain curiosity. Izaak didn't have half of the resources that I possess. Authors such as Joan Chittister and her splendid *The Gift of Years*, teaching about the satisfaction that comes with age. Showing me a way to enter this time of my life. Guiding me.

"Every stage of life is interesting," Chittister says, "if we will only allow ourselves to explore it. There is no perfect, no ultimate, no crowning stage of life. Whatever we are now, that is it." Her words give me hope. Age isn't a problem. Age isn't a disease. To age is to live.

I've known pain and sorrow, hunger and fear. I've known the Kalahari sands, the grasp of a newborn's hand around my finger, the whisper of my father's last words. I've known love and ridiculous joy. But I haven't known old age. Not yet. Funny, being old is new for me.

My life isn't over and old age has its own lessons to impart. Wisdom to bestow. I'm learning to hold each day as a revelation, a wonderful unfolding, a surprise package. I'm learning to live in the present. To hear the siren-like call of a Northern Cardinal signaling its mate. To notice the brilliance of a red chenille plant hanging from the birch in my backyard. I hear the rustle of wings, a Ruby-throated Hummingbird settling onto a branch, warming itself in the bright and morning sun.

This *present*, being *here*, the *now* of it all, astonishes me.

The fact that Izaak threw away his elderly years, gave up the opportunity to live them out, will always remain, in my mind, a great failure. But I've had my failures, too. Pride. Impatience. Envy. The older I get, the less I'm certain of, but I'm easily astonished these days. Purely being alive can move me to tears.

Age isn't granted with any particular rhyme or reason, not granted to everyone, given out stingily or generously or not at all. Age is a privilege. I am a privileged person. To throw this away would be unthinkable, the greatest of sacrilege.

Epilogue: Hand in Hand

Jill and Johan Kandel standing near the Andaman Sea in southern Thailand.
December 2019.

Johan and I have been married now for nearly forty years. We've lived in the United States for three times as long as we lived and worked overseas. When we first moved back to North Dakota, I was both grateful and embarrassed, grabbing onto Johan's goodness as he embraced my culture, found a job, and agreed to settle here. I wasn't prepared for the deep and daily guilt I felt, navigating our newly lopsided life. One set of grandparents just hours away. The other grandparents—4,000 miles distant—steadily becoming a blur, photos in an album, an envelope with an exotic Dutch stamp containing a weekly letter.

We are a hit and miss, fly in fly out, shilly-shallying part of our Dutch family. We attend one wedding; miss the next. Graduations, funerals, births. All those building blocks of society, of family, we miss out on most of them. And vice versa. They miss out, too.

Somedays it feels not so much like we've built a family, but that we've torn one apart. One ocean. Two sides. A transatlantic cable laid across the floor of the ocean relaying messages, but not lives.

People still ask Johan where he's from. I'm often surprised when they ask. To me he's just Johan. Then I remember, oh, yeah, he's got an accent. I keep forgetting. I don't notice it anymore. The thing that first drew me to him, that lovely accent, no longer exists in my mind.

Once, a few months ago, I was tuning the radio and came across a Dutch voice. It took me a moment to realize it was Johan speaking on a local agricultural show.

Wow, I thought. *He's got an accent!*

I don't understand the dynamics or the science behind it, but when I hear Johan's voice on the radio, I hear his accent, pronounced and heavy, and then he comes home and he's just Johan, the man I've been married to for nearly forty years. His voice is his voice. Not Dutch. Not American. Just him.

Once a year, Johan and another professor take some of their master's and PhD agricultural students to a distant country: Vietnam, Kenya, Zimbabwe, Nepal, Chile. Johan says no one should graduate with an advanced degree in agriculture without visiting farms and learning about research, crops, and harvesting in a far-flung part of the world.

Last year Johan and his students traveled to Thailand. It's the first trip I've ever accompanied them on. While they toured farms, research stations, and joined in university lectures, I attended a Thai cooking school and spent days wandering through ancient temples and fanciful floating markets. After the students finished their study tour and returned to the United States, Johan and I flew to the southern tip of Thailand.

Living in the middle of the United States, we both long for the waves and water, the taste of salt upon our lips as we swim. We spent two weeks hiking, biking, kayaking, and beaching.

One night, we took a longboat trip, and far out from the shore we jumped into the black ocean. Thousands of tiny bioluminescent plankton drifted just below the surface. When we moved our arms or legs, the plankton sparkled in water all around us. Tiny spots of light flickered on and off, a fingertip away. Like swimming among the stars.

We returned to twenty-below and blizzards, winter wonderland and a cozy woodstove. I cooked Khao Soi—a hot curry noodle dish famous in northern Thailand—and served it to our kids. Johan and I talked too much and showed too many pictures.

Typical tourists returning home with a bounty of exuberance. There's an amazement in those words. Returning home. I realize then, that it's true. Johan and I have somehow, against all odds, over the miles and over the years, created a place of our own, a place to call home.

This international cross-continental family we're creating is a beautiful disarray. A glorious tangle of humanity. We're a blend of American and Dutch, Zambian and Indonesian. But after all is said and done, we're just humans. Each of us nothing more and nothing less than a holy mess.

As winter unfurls into bitter cold, the days grow short and the darkness lengthens. I return in my mind again and again to Thailand, to that last warm swim off the coast of Krabi, in the Andaman Sea.

Once upon a time, a herd of elephants tramped slowly past my tent and I felt their weighted footfalls vibrate in the sand. Once upon a time, I felt the language of Indonesia glide silken off my tongue. And once, I swam among the stars, with a blue-eyed boy beside me. We swam, hand in hand, lighting up the sea.

Acknowledgments

There are many people who made this book possible. Thank you to Dr. Suzzanne Kelley and the wonderful staff at NDSU Press who believed in my writing and brought this book to publication. I am indebted to my editors Kyle and Kiri for their fine work.

I'm grateful to Dr. Lauren Winner and Leslie Leyland Fields for their expertise, which was instrumental in this book's origins. Special acknowledgment owed to the editors and staff at *The Missouri Review*, who first published my essay "Paying the Piper," which appears here in slightly different form.

Exuberant thanks to the funny, dedicated, wise women whose writer's club I'm delighted and grateful to be a part of: Paula Lovgren, Karin Almjeld, Denise Lajimodiere, Melanie Iverson, Kirsten Shockley, Stephanie Manesis, and Sarah Coomber. I love you all.

I am indebted to my sister-in-law, Andrea, who walked alongside me in living out much of this story, read through my manuscript, and offered insights and critiques on all things Dutch. Thank you to my brother-in-law, Bert, for letting me add his stories about Jopie's life. To the rest of my wonderful Dutch family, thank you for teaching me not only about Dutch culture, but inviting me into your lives.

Immeasurable thanks to my lovely children, their spouses, and my grandchildren, Kristina, Joren & Jill, Jory and Willow, Benjamin, Anneke & Randall: you all bring me joy. And finally, all my love to my husband, who introduced me to the Netherlands, took me around the globe, and whose kindness, love, and faithfulness are my rock in this ever-changing world.

Discussion Questions for
The Clean Daughter:
A Cross-Continental Memoir

1. Jill Kandel writes about her relationship with Izaak as half open and half closed, much like a Dutch door. What was open and what was closed?

2. Izaak feared losing control more than he feared his own death. How was his death a lost opportunity?

3. One of the author's favorite quotes in the book comes from *When Breath Becomes Air* by the late Dr. Paul Kalanithi. "The easiest death isn't necessarily the best." Do you agree or disagree, and why?

4. Kandel received a letter from Izaak after his death and never opened it. Over the years and chaos of raising four children, the letter was lost. Why didn't she open it? Should she have? Would you have? What do you think Izaak would have written in the letter?

5. The daughter-in-law relationship is one of the central topics of this book. Where did Kandel succeed? Where did she fail? What does it mean to be an in-law?

6. Did reading this book influence or change your thinking about death and dying? Does the *process* of dying, in and of itself, hold any value?

7. What have you learned about the immigrant, cross-continental life? Has reading *The Clean Daughter* made you see people from other cultures differently?

About the Author

Jill Kandel began writing at the age of forty. She writes to fill in the gaps and questions formed over forty years of cross-cultural marriage and a decade working abroad while living on four of this earth's continents.

Kandel currently lives with her husband in the Fargo/Moorhead community, a few blocks away from the Red River, which joins North Dakota and Minnesota. Watching wild turkeys strut down her street each morning makes her laugh. Spotting a red fox with pups loping silently by lifts her heart and gives her joy.

Kandel's essays have been published in *The Missouri Review*, *Gettysburg Review*, *River Teeth*, *Pinch*, *Image*, and *Brevity*. Her work has been anthologized in *Best Spiritual Writing 2012* (Penguin Books) and in *Becoming: What Makes a Woman* (University of Nebraska Press, 2012). Her first book, *So Many Africas: Six Years in a Zambian Village* (Autumn House Press, 2015), won both the Autumn House Nonfiction Prize and the Sarton Women's Literary Award.

Kandel blogs about writing and her recovery from brain injury. To read her blog, order signed books directly, or watch her evocative book trailers, visit www.jillkandel.com.

About the Press

North Dakota State University Press (NDSU Press) exists to stimulate and coordinate interdisciplinary regional scholarship. These regions include the Red River Valley, the state of North Dakota, the plains of North America (comprising both the Great Plains of the United States and the prairies of Canada), and comparable regions of other continents. We publish peer reviewed regional scholarship shaped by national and international events and comparative studies.

Neither topic nor discipline limits the scope of NDSU Press publications. We consider manuscripts in any field of learning. We define our scope, however, by a regional focus in accord with the press's mission. Generally, works published by NDSU Press address regional life directly, as the subject of study. Such works contribute to scholarly knowledge of region (that is, discovery of new knowledge) or to public consciousness of region (that is, dissemination of information or interpretation of regional experience). Where regions abroad are treated, either for comparison or because of ties to those North American regions of primary concern to the press, the linkages are made plain. For nearly three-quarters of a century, NDSU Press has published substantial trade books, but the line of publications is not limited to that genre. We also publish textbooks (at any level), reference books, anthologies, reprints, papers, proceedings, and monographs. The press also considers works of poetry or fiction, provided they are established regional classics or they promise to assume landmark or reference status for the region. We select biographical or autobiographical works carefully for their prospective contribution to regional knowledge and culture. All publications, in whatever genre, are of such quality and substance as to embellish the imprint of NDSU Press.

Our name changed to North Dakota State University Press in January 2016. Prior to that, and since 1950, we published as the North Dakota Institute for Regional Studies Press. We continue to operate under the umbrella of the North Dakota Institute for Regional Studies, located at North Dakota State University.